T0369065

SHORT
SHORT STORIES
AND
BRIEFS

DOROTHY ALEASE PHILLIPS

abbott press

Abbott Press books may be ordered through booksellers or by contacting:

Abbott Press
1663 Liberty Drive
Bloomington, IN 47403
www.abbottpress.com
Phone: 1 (866) 697-5310

Taken from the King James Bible.

ISBN: 978-1-4582-2175-9 (sc)
ISBN: 978-1-4582-2174-2 (e)

Library of Congress Control Number: 2018906553

Print information available on the last page.

Abbott Press rev. date: 7/16/2018

DEDICATED

TO MY

SEVEN GRANDCHILDREN

AND

FOURTEEN GREAT GRANDCHILDREN

Because of my age, I know I will not have the joy of spending much time with these beloved children, I leave with them my love for the Lord and my delight in writing. I'm sorry I cannot journal many wonderful stories about events in their lives. I want them to know that in advance I have undergirded them with prayer. I've asked the Lord to draw each one to Himself and to give guidance to a long, happy life. MAY ALL 21 BE HIGHLY FAVORED & BLESSED.

ACKNOWLEDGEMENTS

TO VERY SPECIAL FRIENDS:

MASHICA ROBINSON, my faithful assistant in all phases of collecting, organizing, and finalizing copy

BETTY HILL, a dear friend who read my stories and noted typos and often gave helpful comments

SANDRA NAIL who offered technical assistance, and to

A HOST OF ENCOURAGERS

CONTENTS

ESSAYS

BITS OF POETRY

WRITINGS FOR OTHERS

MEMORIAL TRIBUTES

SHORT NOVELETTE

PREFACE

WHY DID GOD NOT
ANSWER MY PRAYER?

I am ashamed to admit that for a long time, inwardly, I was troubled that God had not answered a prayer I had prayed for years. I never voiced my disappointment, but silently I wondered why this prayer was not answered. I knew scriptures like John 15:7 – *"If ye abide in me and my words abide in you, ye shall ask what ye will, and it shall be done unto to you"* or Psalms 37:4 - *"Delight thyself also in the Lord; and he shall* **give thee** *the desires of thine heart."*

I claimed such verses and waited, but the answer never came. That is, I thought the answer never came; but I was wrong. God was true to his Word. He did answer my prayer.

Let me share with you this prayer that formed in my heart when I was a teen. Shortly after I came to a saving knowledge of Christ at 17, I learned that I loved to write. I began by writing skits or plays for our church. I loved the way I could put words together to get across Christian thoughts and emotions. I was delighted that messages on paper could be read over and over. Seeking to know God's will for my life at that time, I felt I had found an avenue of service.

When I went to college in the mid 1900's, however, few schools in America had journalism or creative writing courses. Hardly any offered writing majors. I earned a Master's degree, majoring in Secondary Education and minoring in English. I took every course that offered writing opportunities. In my college notebooks, I scribbled in shorthand (so that no one would know what I was asking) *Dear Lord, please let me write.* Years later, while going through college books, I was surprised to see how many times I had penned that same request.

Immediately after graduation, I did write. I had the opportunity to write and illustrate Sunday school literature and teen articles, but these ventures ceased when I became so very busy as a high school teacher, minister's wife, and mother of three children.

My greatest classroom joy came when I accepted a job in a large high school to teach eleventh-grade English and Journalism I and II. My journalism students and I learned together, raking in many national awards.

Over the years, I wrote poetry, essays, plays, short stories, and even books and tucked them away. I never pushed to see my writings in print. I did not consider myself a writer. I was a typical English teacher who liked to write.

I attended writers' conferences and came away inspired; yet I was not a true writer. To me, God had not answered my prayers.

BUT I WAS WRONG. Over the years, God had answered that simple prayer I had prayed over and over – "Dear Lord, please let me write." I now know He did let me write. I have written stories about my parents, my husband, my three children, grandchildren, students, and friends. I have written accounts of births, marriages, and achievements. In my husband's churches, I have written church newspapers and local newspaper releases.

In addition, I have had the opportunity to write biographies and obituaries of deceased loved ones.

I have written poems, essays, short stories, newspaper stories, and books – some published; most unpublished.

God, in his wisdom and care, knew that, as a "people person," I would not have been happy daily writing in seclusion. In truth, I now know how much I would, with my personality traits, have missed working with students, fellowshipping with church friends, and spending time with my children and grandchildren.

True, I have not written anything to make the New York's Best Sellers list, but that is not what I asked. I simply prayed, "Dear Lord, please let me write," and He did. I now say, "Thank you, dear Lord for answering my prayer."

In "SHORT SHORT STORIES and BRIEFS," I share with you a few of the short stories, articles, poetry, and journal entries I have been blessed to write. Many, though insignificant, have captured a memory, prompted a smile, or caused a tear. All, I trust, have honored the Lord.

SHORT
STORIES

A CRY FOR HELP

Teresa Thurman quietly slipped through the front door onto the porch where she lingered, adjusting her eyes to the sudden darkness. Inky black, she thought. Much like the ominous darkness in Moses' day – a darkness so thick that one could almost feel it. She hated nights like this, especially when she had to travel long stretches of road alone. She glanced at the one-bulb fixture beside the door and felt thankful for even a faint glimmer of light.

She heard the door squeak behind her and turned to see the fragile figure of Mr. Humphrey, the dear soul she had spent the last three hours trying to comfort. Ella, Mr. Humphrey's beloved wife of 58 years, had finally surrendered to death after a courageous, but often painful, five-month battle with cancer. Teresa, as a Hospice nurse, had bravely waged the battle with her, giving love both to Ella and to her grieving mate.

She had received the final call at eleven-thirty that evening. Mr. Humphrey's pathetic wail relayed the message even before he spoke a word. Teresa had slumped down upon the padded sofa and pressed her free hand over her mouth to stifle her own sobs. In the few months of this assignment she had learned to adore this aged couple – a sweet couple whose three children lived hundreds of miles away. Oh, they were honorable children who had begged their parents to move near one of them, but the older Humphreys had chosen to spend their last years at the old home place. The one son and the two daughters called daily to check on their parents and to visit as often as possible. Kevin was a Syracuse University professor; Diane, a teacher in Tennessee; and Megan, a stay-at-home mom in Alabama. The past several months had necessitated constant phone calls, texting, and hurried trips back and forth.

Now, standing on his porch, shivering, Mr. Humphrey zipped up his jacket as he adjusted his eyes and edged toward Teresa. "I want to thank you again, Nurse, for all that you did for my Ella."

His voice broke. Teresa stepped to his side and patting his arm said, "It was a great joy to be near your wife….and to you, too, Mr. Humphrey. You two have been so very precious to me. I think, maybe, I adopted you as my parents away from home."

Noting the chilled vapor that accompanied her speaking, the elderly man said. "Oh, my dear, you're freezing out here. Let me walk you to your car."

She had started to protest, not that she didn't want help, but mainly because she didn't trust her frail friend on the snow-crusted ground. Before she could speak, however, the door opened and Kevin stepped out. "Hi, Dad," he said. "I was looking for you."

"Good," Mr. Humphrey said. "You're just in time to see Teresa to her car."

"That I will be glad to do, but first, I must get you back into the house. It is far too cold for you to be out here."

~ ~ ~

Teresa eased out onto the road, once again shivering as she assessed the darkness engulfing everything, everything except the faint center line showing beneath the blurred gleam of her headlights.

"Oh, well," she said aloud. "Just twenty minutes and I'll be back in civilization where, at least, there will be street lights." It was then that she noticed the shadowy form of a pickup truck parked on her side of the road." "Oh my," she thought, "I surely would hate to have car trouble on this deserted roadway. Poor soul."

She had barely passed the truck when she glanced into her rearview mirror, alarmed at seeing the truck lights come on. Instinctively, she increased her speed, remembering that two women in the surrounding vicinity had recently been found dead on roadsides. She had willed herself not to think of this disturbing media news when she had set out for the Humphrey's home. Usually, her husband accompanied her when she had to make middle-of-the-night calls. But on this Friday, he was 100 miles away, hoping to lead his football team to a state championship.

It had been almost midnight when she had crept into her car, locked her doors, and bowed her head to pray, asking for divine protection. She knew she had to go. The Humphreys needed her.

Now, with someone tailing her on what locals called "Sinister Stretch," she began to pray aloud. In seconds, her fears where intensified as she noted the truck advancing at an unsafe speed. Even though she accelerated quickly, she could not escape the sudden jolt, the sickening thud as the truck rammed into her rear bumper.

Reeling from the impact, Teresa reached up and jabbed the On-Star button.

A voice said, "Good evening, Mrs. Thurman. Can we assist you with directions?"

"No. No," Teresa cried. "I'm a Hospice nurse and I'm all alone! Someone is trying to run me off the road. Please get me help! Please!" she screamed as the truck careened against her side.

Having heard the crash, the man spoke. "All right, Mrs. Thurman. I have someone here who is going to contact the police. We have you pinpointed and we'll send help from two directions. Just try to keep your car on the road. Mrs. Thurman, is there any other traffic on the road?"

Her teeth chattering, Teresa found it difficult to talk. "No, no, no. The road is deserted and there are no houses on either side for several miles."

"Then get into the middle of the road. You will see any approaching cars and can move if you have to. Try to stay calm, Mrs. Thurman. Help is on the way."

A deafening bang broke the conversation.

"Mrs. Thurman, are you still there? Are you all right?"

"Yes," she whispered and then she started praying aloud again, "Lord, the missionary who came to our church told us about their house being surrounded by vicious savages. All night the missionary family expected an attack, but it didn't come. The natives told later that they would have attacked if it had not been for the men in white who were sitting on top of the house. But there were no men in white!"

Then Teresa sobbed aloud. "Father, let that man see someone in my car. Send me someone to sit in my car."

"Ohhhh," she cried. "He's speeding toward me and blowing his horn! What is he doing? Oh, I think he's passing me! Yes. Yes, he ran off the side and passed me. He's still speeding away from me."

"Good," the voice said with a sound of relief. "Now, listen carefully. Slow your speed down. There are police cars heading

5

your way from both directions. Here is what we want you to do. We see a church a mile away on your right. Are you familiar with that church?"

"Yes." Her voice trembled, "I've seen that church before. It sits off the road a bit."

"Does it have a good driveway and parking lot?"

"Yes, I think so."

"Good. Now unless you see the truck stopped anywhere, we want you to pull up into the church driveway and turn around. Go into the church parking lot only far enough to turn around. Do you understand?"

"Yes."

"We want you to come out from the church and turn left. Go back the way you came. Two police cars will meet you soon. Can you do that?"

"Yes. Yes. I can do that. I see the church now. It's awfully dark but the churchyard is lighted, and I do not see the truck anywhere."

"Good. Now, pull into the lot and turn around quickly."

"I'm turning now and I'll have to drive up a little to make a turn."

She had swung to make the turn when she screamed. From behind the church, the truck rolled out and headed down the driveway.

"He was behind the church. He's coming out after me."

"Turn left, Mrs. Thurman, and go as fast as you can go safely."

She did as she was told, but then she shouted, "Oh, Sir. He came out, but he turned right! He's going the opposite direction!"

"That's fine. He'll have a welcoming committee waiting for

him. You keep going. Your police escort is only five miles away. You're safe, little lady. You can relax now."

Teresa did not cry until she was seated in the police car headed for home. She glanced at gray headed Officer Beaman and barely whispered, "Sir, do you mind if I cry?"

The officer reached over, patted her hand, and said, "No, my dear young lady. Cry if you want to. A good cry might make you feel better."

No other words were spoken until the officer pulled into the Thurman's driveway. He turned off the motor and sat quietly for a few moments. Teresa stopped sniffling and wiped her face with a tissue.

"We're home, Mrs. Thurman. Now, I would like to go in with you. I need to ask you a few questions." Not waiting for an answer, he opened his door and walked around the car to Teresa's side. She stepped out and faltered, causing the office to reach for her elbow to give her support. Together they entered the backdoor.

"Please go with me through the house," Teresa said.

"Of course," the officer said.

Following her, he watched as she rushed from one room to the other, turning on lamps and overhead lights. When the house was ablaze, she sighed and headed downstairs.

"I wish I could offer you some coffee," she said, "but we don't drink coffee. Could I get you a glass of milk and some cookies?"

"That would be fine," Officer Beaman said, taking a seat.

They sat at the kitchen table as he asked questions and took notes.

~ ~ ~

Twenty-five miles away, Captain Eckman and Officer Carns turned on their flashing lights and the siren. A dirty pickup eased over to the shoulder. Cautiously, the officers approached the vehicle. Captain Eckman motioned for the window to be lowered, relieved to see the driver put crossed, shaking hands upon the steering wheel.

Uh oh. This guy knows the ropes. He's been stopped before. At least he's not wielding a weapon.

"Sir," the officer said, shining a light into the car, "may I see your driver's license?"

It was only when the driver turned to hand him his license that the captain exclaimed, "Grimey Joe, is that you?" He glanced at the license. "Excuse me, Mr. Garfield. I did not know your last name. I've only heard you called by Grimey Joe."

"Yeah, it's me, Grimey Joe, Officer," he mumbled, squinting in the light.

"Would you mind stepping out and placing your hands on the car, Mr. Garfield?"

Both officers stared in amazement as the driver emerged, wearing clunky, chained necklaces and bracelets over his customary dirty clothes. A braided bead band covered his forehead, making his hair bush out on top and around his ears, and accenting his bulging eyes.

"Lock your car, Mr. Garfield. We need to take you in for questioning."

Mr. Garfield did not protest.

At the courthouse, the two officers busied themselves with papers, giving the suspect leeway to squirm, wipe sweat from his flushed face, cross and uncross his arms and legs, and mutter unintelligible rants.

They had barely begun their questioning when wild-eyed Grimey Joe blurted out, "Ya see, at first, I didn't see nobody in the car with that woman. They must have been sleeping. First, one sat up beside her in the front seat, and then two arose in the back! Yeah! Big, big guys! Now, I'm crazy, but I ain't stupid. I ain't never chased no woman with a man in the car. I ain't never" . . . He stopped in mid-sentence.

Captain Eckman stood and propped a foot on the wooden chair. Keeping his mouth closed, he gave a wide-stretched grin and lifted his eyebrows in his typical "Gotcha" fashion.

He turned to Officer Carns and said, "Go call the other officers. Tell them we got our man. Oh, yes, and call Officer Beaman. See if you can find out anything about those men who were in Mrs. Thurman's car."

Later, Carns walked into the Captain's office. "Captain," he said, "Officer Beaman says there were no men in Mrs. Thurman's car. He's absolutely sure."

"I thought that was what the On-Star gentleman said. He stated Mrs. Thurman was alone. Now, how do you suppose Mr. Garfield saw three men?"

"I don't know, but I'm glad he did. Otherwise, we would probably have had another unsolved murder on our books."

"The On-Star people have a recording of everything that went on in Mrs. Thurman's car. Maybe, we'll know the real story when we get that disc," the Captain said, pocketing his notebook. "Yet, this may be another case that will remain a mystery. The kind, you know, we can't explain."

HEARTBREAK OPERATION

I arose at 5:00, shampooed, showered, and sipped diluted coffee while drying my hair. I applied a little makeup, brushed my hair the customary 20 strokes, pulled on a rubber band, and fashioned a bun at the back of my head. As a surgeon, I knew my surgical cap had to fit.

It was 6:00 I wanted to arrive at the hospital before 23-year-old Sarah Morton was put to sleep. I really thought of her as "Little Sarah," for I had known and loved her since she was born to Dave and Donna Morton, our next-door neighbors.

When our only daughter arrived a week after Sarah was born, we jokingly told her parents, "We're going to have to give our girl a biblical name, so that, from the beginning, she and Sarah will have something in common."

They had much in common, except for looks. Sarah had jet black hair and olive skin. Our Hannah was blonde with fair complexion. But the two loved each other. They entered kindergarten together and stayed best friends in high school. Both chose to attend the University of North Carolina for undergraduate and graduate studies, with Sarah majoring in journalism; and Hannah in foreign languages. Graduation, however, brought a sad separation Sarah came back home to become the feature editor of her dad's newspaper and Hannah went over a thousand miles away to use her foreign language skills.

All these thoughts plagued my mind as I sped to the hospital. In the parking lot, I turned off the motor, put my head down on the steering wheel, and cried, "Oh, dear Father, I don't understand why one so young, so pure, so sweet should have a tumor, a tumor so very large and threatening. I don't know why I must be the one to operate. I don't understand but, Father, I know you are Sovereign and can control this situation. Help me, please. Help me."

Before entering the hospital, I dried my face and carefully wiped away damp eye liner. I took the elevator to the second floor and peered into the holding room, but Sarah was not there. I donned my cap and shoe covers and stood looking out the window as I waited.

When Sarah was wheeled into the room, I slipped by her side and whispered, "Good morning, sleepy head."

She opened droopy eyes and smiled at me. I could tell the small amount of analgesia was working; Sarah was completely relaxed. "Mama Sheeeeen," she slurred, calling me by the name she had always used, "do a gooooood job now. I've been praying for yoooou."

Even though I was acclaimed one of the most qualified neurosurgeons in the area, at that moment I wanted to leave the room. I felt completely inadequate. How I wished my colleague, Dr. Zoe Goldstein, were still on staff. I could trust him to take over if I faltered; but, regretfully, he was now teaching in a medical school out West. Why, oh why, had the Mortons insisted that I perform this operation? Didn't they know the dangers? Didn't they know how difficult it would be for me?

Earlier, when I had tried to protest, Dave Morton had said, "Kelly, we know how you ranked in your medical class, and we

11

know your superb track record for the past 25 years. Mary and I are confident you can do more for Sarah than anyone else. You see, you have an added incentive no other doctor would have. You love our child as your own."

I did love Sarah as my own, and that was the problem. The X-rays had shown a huge tumor, at least the size of a golf ball, resting on the auditory nerve beneath her skull. Couldn't her parents understand the inherent dangers of brain surgery? Even if the tumor were benign, removing it could damage vital nerves in proximity. I pressed my hands against my stomach to alleviate pain.

I glanced at the wall clock. I knew I must have prayer with Sarah, for they would come for her in minutes. The surgery was scheduled for seven o'clock. When I told Sarah I wanted to pray with her, she smiled and closed her eyes. I held her hand and once again talked with the Lord. When I said, "Amen," I opened my eyes to see an orderly standing close by with bowed head.

They wheeled Sarah into the operating room. Even though they were behind closed doors, I could visualize their placing small pads on Sarah's body and hooking her up to the monitor. Mentally, I could see the anesthetist carefully putting her under. I knew that in a few minutes the circulating nurse would come to the door to tell me the patient was ready. Then I would begin my scrubbing ritual. I was known for being meticulous with the scrub before surgery. I was aware that the nurses behind my back had nicknamed me "Dr. Kelly Sheen, the Super Clean." That did not bother me. I continued to ignore the minimum requirement. Carefully, I scrubbed my fingernails, my hands, and my arms up to my elbows. I concentrated on the rinsing process, tilting my arms upward under the water so that the rinse dripped downward, never to my hands.

Holding the upward-hand position, I went to the operating room where a nurse handed me a sterile towel, then helped with a gown and gloves. For the first time, I noted the large brown eyes of the circulating nurse and realized that I had not worked with her before. For a moment, this fact disturbed me. I had specifically requested certain team members for this operation, and usually my requests were honored. Soothingly, however, Scripture played upon my mind: "I will keep him in perfect peace, whose mind is stayed on Thee." Inwardly, I surrendered my skill to a Higher Power and walked steadfastly to the head of the operating table.

Dr. Michael Swartz stood across from me. I hesitated, looking around the table at the anesthetist, the second assistant, and the scrub nurse. I recognized these eyes. These were the people I had requested.

Sterilized sponges – four packs of ten, forty in all – had been counted. Sponges and instruments were recorded. Everything was ready. Dr. Swartz moved to Sarah's right side. His scheduled procedure was to cut through the skull an arc behind the ear and to remove the bone so that, in follow-up, I could reach the tumor.

Before he called for his first instrument, however, I felt compelled to speak. "I do not know exactly why, but I feel an urgency to pray before we start this operation. Does anyone object?" I noted unanimous consent and bowed my head. Briefly, I asked the Lord for wisdom, for absolute peace, and for protection. The operation began.

After Dr. Swartz had skillfully performed his procedure, I bent closely to gaze at the huge mass behind Sarah's ear. It did not appear to be malignant, for which I was immediately thankful. Even if it were not malignant, however, it would certainly be deadly if it continued to grow.

I was thankful for my long, slim fingers as I sliced and pulled away the growth, section by section. This outward part was not extremely difficult. I knew the real pressure would come once I reached the side of the tumor that either rested upon the brain or had become attached. I prayed that it was not attached.

The operation had been underway for over four hours when an orderly entered the room to bring blood from the blood bank. After the circulating nurse had taken his delivery, the orderly remained, attempting to whisper something. A gigantic man with a booming voice, he tried to whisper, but his whispering attempt was a farce. His gruff tones rose and fell, allowing a few distinct words – terrorists . . . the Twin Towers . . . both collapsed . . .all gone. I held my surgical instrument up and moved back from the table, petrified. I stared across the table into Dr. Swartz's kind, but sad, eyes. "Do you want me to finish?" he asked softly.

At first, I felt faint. Dr. Swartz rounded the table to stand by my side, even as a nurse supported my back at the waist. These were my friends. These people knew. They knew that my only daughter Hannah, as an interpreter, had an office on the 80th floor of the Trade Center, Building One.

I looked down at Sarah's open skull. I knew that the most delicate part of the operation was beginning. I remembered how professors had always stressed, "The patient must be your prime consideration. You must never, never let any other thought rob you of your undivided attention to that person. You must control your thoughts at all times."

I wondered why these early training memories returned so vividly. I had done twenty-five similar operations and never had these medical instructions flashed before me. Blinking back tears, suddenly, I felt a peace, a super-natural undergirding as though someone were praying for me. I glanced at my colleagues. "I'm all right." I said. "I'll finish." The scrub nurse handed me the needed instrument, and I began. What joy flooded my heart when I discovered that the huge mass had not metastasized. It was merely pressing against the brain. Carefully, I placed the last segment upon a tray and examined the operated territory. I felt confident that I had been able to get all the tumor, but I called for Dr. Swartz to check.

When he agreed with my assessment, he said to me, "I'll take over now. You go sit on that stool," he said pointing. I knew that another procedure was necessary, but I, also, knew Dr. Swartz was competent. He had performed this part of the operation many, many times.

I felt the circulating nurse escorting me across the room. Once I had been lowered upon the seat, the horror of the news overwhelmed me. I choked back an urge to weep. No matter how I grieved, I could not distract from the operation. I closed my eyes and, mercifully, felt a warm darkness rush downward.

I awoke, lying upon a gurney in the hallway just outside the operating room door. The circulation nurse whispered to me, "I'm so very, very sorry, Dr. Sheen. I didn't know you had a daughter in New York. Forgive me for letting you hear such horrible news."

I could not answer but tried to smile forgiveness.

The phone rang and the circulating nurse stepped inside the door to answer. In seconds, she returned, pale and shaky. "It's for you, Dr. Sheen," she said, handing me the phone.

Barely holding the receiver to my ear, I whispered, "Hello," dreading the news I might hear.

A frantic voice cried, "Mom, Mom, I'm all right! I'm all right! I had gone across the street to a coffee shop to sit and pray for Sarah ....and for you, Mom."

Rejoicing, I interrupted her to whisper to the nurse, "It's Hannah! It's Hannah! She's safe!"

"Mom," Hannah sobbed. "I'm safe; but, Mom, it's horrible here! Thank the Lord, I'm safe; but it's so, so horrible! Everyone is still screaming. Oh, Mom, they were jumping! They were jumping to their deaths! Bodies were...oh, Mom, Mom. All my friends!" She moaned. I held the phone against my heart and cried with my child. I wanted to be there with her, to hold her in my arms.

Slowly, her sobbing ebbed into an eerie whimper. I waited.

"Mom," she asked in a choked whisper, "How is Sarah? Is Sarah all right?"

"Yes, dear. She is going to be fine. She...."

"Mom, I'm coming home. I'm coming home now."

I was crying. Hannah was crying. The nurse was crying. The orderly was crying.

"Oh, Hannah, dear, do come home," I said. "Your daddy and I want you to come home. Come back to North Carolina. Come home to stay." And although I knew she needed no incentive, I added, "Sarah will be so very happy. She'll be waiting for you. You and Sarah can be together again."

"All of us together again ... yes, yes," she whispered. "I'm coming home. I'm coming home."

COLONEL BEAMAN'S REMINDER

As a military leader, I, Colonel Bruce Beaman, had always felt in complete control of practically all situations. I considered myself to be adequate for dire emergencies and difficult challenges. I had been thoroughly trained to draw from my mental resources to cope with even the most severe circumstances. In my position, I felt sure of myself and my ability to size up a situation and make right decisions that would remedy problems. In truth, I was known for decisiveness. Yes, I was a respected military leader who had led men into battle with undaunted steadfastness. I had a chest full of medals as proof; and yet, for the past two hours, I had been drastically destitute. I had been seized by a fear I had never faced.

Stumbling through the thickets, I searched for a clearing. There, I fell on my knees and prayed, "Oh, dear Lord, please give me a sign. Please help. You know, I need your help." Salty tears burned the scratches on my face. I was desperate. I don't know how long my praying continued; but when I opened my eyes, I spied a strangely broken branch, a mere broken branch amid bramble, stubble, and briar bushes, a broken branch; but, wonder of wonders, a broken branch adorned with a tiny fragment of red cloth, the red I had commented upon earlier in the morning as I had held my four-year-old grandson in my arms.

The day had started so beautifully. My wife Catherine; our daughter Cissy, and her husband, Tom; and our only grandchild little Jody had crowded into the meager space left in our stuffed van and headed for the mountains. We were in route to our favorite hiking spot. For several days I had talked with Jody about the adventures we would encounter, telling him about the squirrels, chipmunks, deer, and the streams with huge fish. I had bought him some hiking boots. Catherine and I discussed how foolish it was to buy expensive boots for feet that were growing so rapidly; but then, we reasoned we could save the boots for a later child. Cissy and Tom were hoping for another baby. If the natural did not happen, they were considering adopting.

We all slept under one roof the night before we left. Catherine and I were always thrilled to have our family in our home. After all was quiet, we paused in the hallway before going to bed. Catherine looked up at me and whispered, "Isn't it wonderful to have our family together tonight?" I nodded but didn't speak.

There was no need for an alarm clock to wake us. A joyful Jody bounded upon our bed at daylight, pleading, "Papah, Papah, it's time! Get up! We gotta go."

"Okay, big boy, okay; but first, come snuggle between Mom and me." I held the covers up and, with a leap, he wiggled into bed.

I laughed aloud when Jody exclaimed, "Papah, your breath smells like poopoo."

"I'm sorry, Jody," I said, being careful to turn my head away. "I'll go brush my teeth. You may lie here with Mom for a few minutes." I went to the bathroom, chuckling, and left him snuggling with his grandmother.

Soon, everyone was up. No one wanted to eat. All agreed:

it would be fun to stop at McDonald's for breakfast. And so, the wonderful day had begun.

We reached our favorite hiking location and were elated to see that the parking spot we liked best was not being occupied. As we unloaded our gear, we nodded or spoke to camping groups eating at nearby tables. Happy conversations and bursts of laughter surrounded us. Jody made friends with another little boy in the adjacent site. They played together while the rest of us set up camp. We thought we would eat a noon snack before we started our hike. No one was hungry, though, because of our McDonald stuffing; and so, we four adults sat and talked while Jody played nearby.

It was a somber little Jody who joined us much later, climbed upon his grandmother's lap, and said sadly, "Billy's gotta go."

"That's all right, Jody. It's time for you to eat something anyhow," I said. "We have to go on our hike, you know," I added, pretending to punch him in the stomach. He jumped back and gave his famous karate kick which nicked my shin. I feigned pain.

The women busied themselves, laying out the meal they had packed. There was fried chicken, potato salad, sliced tomatoes, chips and several specialties -- brownies, peanut brittle, and iced cupcakes. We thought we were not hungry, that is, until we started filling our plastic plates.

After lunch, when Cissy and Tom wanted to go down to the stream, Catherine and I insisted that they leave the cleanup to us. "Go ahead, Cissy," I said. "Mom and I will take care of Jody." I pointed to Jody who was busy in the clearing, trying to find a good walking stick.

In delight, soon Jody held up a stick slightly longer than his body. "Papah, I found one. Look, it is just the right size!" I grinned and gave him a thumb's up sign. I lingered to look at him, standing with his little legs apart and holding a stick that towered two feet above his head. He had made a good selection and looked just like a miniature mountain man, except for the blue Duke baseball cap turned backward on his head.

Sitting down to change to my heavy, hiking shoes, I called to him. "Jody, come. Put your boots on." Before I could tie my high tops, there he was standing by my side holding his boots, impatiently waiting for me to put them on for him.

As I held him on my lap and tied his laces, I said, "Boy, Jody, that's a pretty red shirt you're wearing. Do you think your mom could buy one just like that for me?" He giggled and said, "Papah, grown men don't wear little boys' shirts."

He leaped from my lap, stomped around to show off his boots, then, grabbed up his stick, and raced across the clearing, yelling, "Hurry, Papah! Hurry."

It took only three or four trips to the van to clear things away. Catherine washed the table top and called to me to put the bagged trash into the park's container. I smiled as Cissy and Tom came up the path, reveling in how clear the water was.

"We could actually see the fish swimming around," Cissy said; and then she asked, "Where's Jody?"

I turned around, expecting to see Jody where he had stood only moments before, but he was gone. "He was here seconds ago," I explained as I started across the clearing that led to the hiking path. "Jody," I yelled. "Where are you?"

When he did not answer, all of us began calling. Jody did not answer.

Then the horrifying hunt began. At length, Catherine was stationed by the van in case Jody returned. Cissy, Tom, and I took separate routes to begin the frenzied search down three different paths. We promised to return to the table in 15 minutes to report, confident that we would find him quickly.

That confidence was obliterated when we three returned at the assigned time with the sad news: Jody could not be found.

Our fears were intensified, knowing how urgent it was for us to find Jody before darkness came. In the mountains, it would be cold once the sun went down, and our Jody was wearing a short-sleeve shirt and light-weight pants. Trying not to panic, we searched and prayed.

And so, after tearful hours of leaving the beaten paths and scrambling through bushes and briars, I had found the broken branch with a scrap of Jody's red shirt.

I pulled up sprawling bush limbs and looked behind rugged, gigantic stones. I tried desperately to search every inch of ground for the slightest sign to show that Jody had gone a certain way. I prayed as I stumbled forward. Suddenly, I stopped, for my foot almost slipped on a slope, a slope that fell 20 to 25 feet downward. I drew back and heaved a sigh of relief.

"Is this another branch, Lord?" I asked aloud as though the Lord was walking by my side. I waited a moment. A quietness in my heart urged me to edge forward for a view below. How can I describe the joy, the grateful, exhilarating joy of gazing into the cavernous, gaping hole and seeing Jody seated on a grassy mound, grinning up at me?

"I knew you would come, Papah; so I've been waiting. Can you come get me now? I'm getting hungry."

"Yes, Son, Yes, Son," I said, seeking to control my voice. "I'll get you. You just sit still. I'll be right there."

It took several minutes for me to find a safe way to descend the treacherous slope. I noted the few jagged rocks that jotted out and places to latch onto but there were bare places with only struggling bushes, and long drops. Grasping any boulder, limb, or bush available, I started downward. I talked constantly as I inched down the slippery embankment, trying to calm a child who, for some strange reason, seemed to need no calming.

Perhaps it was only a short ordeal, but the descent seemed tediously slow. My heart raced. When my feet touched the grassy bottom, I took a deep breath, said thank you to the Lord, and stumbled across the mound to where Jody was standing, nonchalantly stuffing his toy men into his pockets.

With tears running down my face, I fell to my knees and clutched him in my arms, hugging him so tightly that he protested, "Papah, you'll squeeze me to death."

"I'm sorry," I said releasing him. "I had difficulty finding you. Come on, Son. Ride Papah's back." He leaped up and threw his arms around my neck, giggling as though we were in our living room, romping around.

"Giddy up, Papah," he shouted and prodded me with his little boots. I started the challenging climb up the jagged incline with Jody's arms around my neck

"I love you, Papah," he said, and then began telling me an awesome thing, something that I'll always cherish and ponder.

"Papah, when I was falling, I felt some strong arms under me. I thought you were holding me; but when I looked, you were not there. When I was put down, I heard a voice say, 'Don't be afraid, Jody. Your grandfather will come for you.' And so, I took my little men out of my pockets and played. I knew you would come, Papah."

When, at length, we crested the top of the embankment, I stooped to break off the broken branch with the red patch of cloth. I tucked it carefully within my jacket. Today that branch with its fragment of red cloth sits in a silver vase in my study as an ever reminder that there is a Supreme Being who watches over us and answers prayer, sometime with broken branches and bits of cloth.

THE ESCAPE

Since Raul Torres was the last person to squeeze through the narrow opening into the dreaded tunnel, he was responsible for tugging the thatched covering in place. Sweating, he meticulously pulled branches and stubble in place, frightened that the least movement or sound might attract attention.

At length, when he felt he had concealed the opening as well as he could, he turned from the faint light that trickled through the bramble and immediately became engulfed in murky, smothering darkness. With his lanky frame doubled over, he hesitated a few seconds, trying to control a sudden surge of panic.

"Get hold of yourself, Raul Torres." he chided. "Think of the women and children who have fled this way. Think of Christina and little Reuben." Tortured by the mental picture of his precious wife and little son being rushed into the tunnel, he groaned. Hot tears burned his scratched cheeks as he began inching his way through the inky blackness, ever mindful that he must always keep his right hand on the wall. He could almost hear the Old Timer's raspy voice barking out commands to every group: "Keep yer hand on the right wall at all times. If you ever git away from that wall, yer a goner fer sure."

Raul put his left hand over his nose and mouth as though he could close out the dank, musty odor that seemed to permeate his skin, his hair, his clothing. Strangely, he thought of old man Hinson's cellar. One time, Mr. Hinson had sent him down into the cellar to get some burlap bags. He remembered gagging as he crept down the crude wooden steps into a room with red clay walls, dirt floors, no windows, and no ventilation. The stench of rotting apples, spoiled tomatoes, and damp earth made him sick. Once he had given the bags to Mr. Hinson, he had gone behind the barn to vomit.

The only sounds in the underground tunnel had been Raul's breathing and the occasional scurrying of something small across his feet. He thought of Christina and little Reuben. Was Christina carrying him on her left hip or had fatigue forced her to have him walk by her side, holding on to her skirt as children had been instructed to do?

Moments later, or was it hours, he stopped, aware of a gurgling he had not heard before. No one had warned him about water. Could there be drop-off places? He wished he had brought a long stick to poke ahead. Gil, his childhood friend who was born blind, had used a white cane to guide him all over their small town, always without assistance. A sudden gush of icy water splashed across his legs, and then the gurgling was gone.

"I hate this blasted darkness," he shouted. Startled by his own voice, he stopped and waited to see if there would be any response. Only a deadly silence. Thick darkness, he thought. His Sunday school teacher once taught about one of God's plagues upon the Egyptians - a darkness that was so dark that it was thick. Often at night he had lain awake, wondering about a thick darkness. Now, he knew a thick darkness – a darkness he felt he could cut with a knife.

A jutting rock scraped the skin from his elbow and lower arm. He stopped to wipe away warm blood and to check the jagged rock. "Oh, dear Lord," he whispered, knowing that some shorter person would have hit this stone head-on.

Slowly he moved forward, letting his bruised fingers crawl over the rough wall. He stumbled backward a step when his hand passed from the usual rough sandpaper surface onto stones of slimy goo – a heavy goo that squished between his fingers. Though sickly repulsed by this unknown substance, he knew he could not take his hand from the wall. In time, however, as he forced his hand through the detestable scum, he realized that, though revolting, the slime coating his fingers was soothing.

Raul trudged ahead, again wondering how long he had been in this tomb. The tunnel, seemingly straight, now made a sharp turn to the right. Raul was thankful his hand had been upon the wall. The ground became stony. Moving more slowly, he gradually became aware of a putrid, stifling odor - the odor of rotting flesh. Horrified, he stopped. Did someone get lost at that right turn, or would he trip over some poor person who did not make it? What if it were a child? He sought to change the thought by reasoning that surely the dead thing was one of those eerie creatures that had scurried across his feet.

If he could not get past this dead thing, he wondered how long he would have to endure this stench. His uncle had said the olfactory nerves were delicate and would become fatigued after a period and would no longer register. He hoped his uncle was right.

Although he groped in darkness, Raul kept his eyes wide open, ever hoping for the speck of light at the end of the tunnel. The Old Timer had said, "It'll be just a little speck, but it'll git bigger and bigger, and you'd better blink a whole lot or the light will blind ya."

The light at the end of the tunnel? Raul remembered once his father and mother had struggled to keep from losing their meager piece of land. He recalled their sleepless nights and tears, but one day his father came in, held his mother in his arms and said, "Honey, I now see light at the end of the tunnel." They had laughed and cried. Raul had been too young to understand what his father meant. Now, he knew. His father was seeing a way out.

It was happening just as the Old Timer had predicted. At first, Raul blinked and squinted to be sure. The speck. The wonderful, glowing speck!

He cried, "Thank you, dear Lord. I see light at the end of the tunnel."

In fewer than ten, frantic minutes, Raul struggled through the bramble-covered opening and out into clear air. On his knees, he inhaled and inhaled and inhaled until his lungs felt as though they would burst.

He bent over and kissed the soil over and over.

"That you, Lord. Thank you," he cried. 'Thank you for letting me make it!"

~ ~ ~

**N O T E: TWO alternate endings follow:
C H O O S E THE ENDING you LIKE.**

2nd. **Ending:** In fewer than ten, frantic minutes, Raul struggled through the bramble-covered opening and out into clear air. On his knees, he inhaled and inhaled and inhaled until his lungs felt as though they would burst.

He bent over and kissed the Arizona soil over and over.

"America! America! America at last!" he cried.

THE END

3nd. Ending: In fewer than ten, frantic minutes, Raul struggled through the bramble-covered opening and out into the clear air. On his knees, he inhaled and inhaled and inhaled until his lungs felt as though they would burst.

He had dropped his head to his chest and closed his eyes, for only a few moments, when he heard the footsteps of someone running toward him. Like a frightened animal, he sprang to his feet, prepared to fight. He would fight or die. He had come too far to lose his freedom.

"Stop, friend," he heard a panting, small, black woman cry as she rushed toward him with outstretched arms. Recognizing the little black woman whose pictures he had seen posted on wanted circulars, he wrapped his arms around her.

"Harriet Tubman. Harriet Tubman," he whispered reverently, "Thank you. Thank you. Thank you."

Stretching upward, she cupped his face in her hands and kissed his forehead.

Before he could ask about his wife and son, the renowned Underground Railroad Conductor asked, "Are you Raul Cooper?" To his fearful, breathless nod, she added, "Your wife and son are fine. They're in the Safeway House up yonder road, waiting for you. God bless you, Son."

THE END

FALL FOLLY

Franklin Forbes parked the car in his favorite overlook spot and rested his arms on the steering wheel, relishing the panoramic spread of glowing reds, vibrant yellows, and tawny oranges.

"Look, Harriet," he said quietly. "Isn't it wonderful?" He heard her sigh and turned to look down upon her delicate form. He loved the blue woolen dress she was wearing and admired the way her hair had been tied back with a matching blue ribbon.

"You know, Harriet, you are as beautiful today as you were the day I brought you here for a special purpose forty-nine years ago." He thought she smiled. "Wait and I'll come to let you out. It's time for our annual walk in the leaves." He patted her folded hands and slipped from the car. He breathed deeply as he walked around to the passenger side. Today was as perfect as any autumn day he had ever seen.

With his help, Harriet stepped down gingerly from the car and giggled, almost girlishly, as she felt the bed of leaves crunch under her feet. Franklin took her hand, once again noting how perfectly her tiny, soft fingers fitted within his big, boney fingers.

They started down a familiar path magically festooned with an array of multi-shaped leaves with variegated colors. Franklin could sense Harriet's excitement.

"Harriet," Franklin said as he cupped her face in his hands, "I brought you here to propose a long time ago, remember?" Her pale blue eyes gazed at him and a faint smile flitted across her face but quickly disappeared. Using his pet name for her, he whispered, "We have had many wonderful years together, Muffin."

He put his arm around her and guided her down the rustic pathway. "God has been so very good to us over the years. We have brought up four wonderful children and now we have those five, unbelievable grandchildren!"

He stopped, trying to quell the grief in his heart as he assessed her blank stare. All these loved ones, whom she had served so very unselfishly, were no longer a part of her memory. Alzheimer's had slowly robbed his precious, little Harriet of almost all cherished memories.

He drew her close to himself. "Harriet, I love you and will always love you. Now for the fiftieth time, he re-enacted his original proposal, determined that nothing could ever alter this anniversary ritual.

He knelt and softly asked again, "Harriet Lynn Hunter, the love of my life, will you marry me?"

She touched his cheeks; and before the momentary, flickering light disappeared from her eyes, whispered, "Yes, yes, yes."

DOES GOD KNOW?

Ashley Blackstone sank deeper into the plush sofa that bunched around her as though attempting to swallow her petite frame. Staring blankly from one area to another, she wadded a tissue and bent, almost mechanically, to slip it into the ornate, brass waste basket at her feet. Reaching for the Kleenex box, she forced her eyelids open to peer at three men, all wearing dark suits, white shirts, and muted ties, bustling about, setting up equipment that would monitor telephone calls. Wearily, she watched their slow-motioned movement before she turned her head to study her husband pacing the massive foyer.

Denton Blackstone was not aware that he was being watched. His mind raced. He hated his thoughts - this magnificent, glorified foyer with its marble floor, the winding staircase that circled above his head, the pure gold chandelier with its hundred crystals, velvet covered, hand-carved benches, a six-foot sculpture in the corner. He could attach a dollar sign to each item. He was a rich man. A very rich man. This mere hallway could have built three houses for ordinary families. But then, the Blackstones were no ordinary family. Listed in the upper ten percent of wealthy Americans, they towered above almost everyone he knew. At this moment, however, he despised wealth.

"Oh, dear Lord," he muttered. "If we didn't have all this,"

he said gesturing wildly, "we'd have our little Amy safe in the arms of her family.

He stopped pacing. "I just said, 'Oh, dear Lord.' I said that. I said, 'Oh, dear Lord.' I thought Ashley had freed me from that kind of wording years ago." He glanced to see if anyone had heard. A guard stood at the front door with his back turned. He did not move.

In an alcove, across from the foyer, he saw Ashley, huddled against the cushions, eyes closed, trying to find a way to crunch into fetal position. He wondered if she could ever bring herself to call upon a Higher Power. She was the adamant one. She was the one who had insisted that their children would never be subjected to religious superstitions. She had cast aside every vestige of faith the semester they attended Professor Mark Anton's psychology class. In her home, she had withstood the pleas and tears of believing parents and grandparents. In spite of their reasoning, she had aligned herself with Atheists of America.

Denton clasped his hands behind him and began walking again. He was remembering some little happening that had troubled Ashley. She couldn't understand why four-year-old Amy, who had been so very carefully sheltered from churchy influences, looked up one day and asked, "Mommy, does God know we don't believe in him?"

The doorbell rang. A dark-suited man stepped from behind a column and took his place near the guard who opened the front door. An outside guard explained, "This is the minister of Hamilton Lutheran church. He would like to speak with the parents if that is possible."

Two of the men inside whispered to each other for a moment and then nodded consent.

Dressed in a black suit and black shirt with a rounded white collar, a tall man, with graying temples and kind blue eyes, stepped quietly inside the door. After shaking hands with the agents, he was led to Denton Blackstone.

"Mr. Blackstone. This is Dr. John Hartley, the minister of Hamilton Lutheran Church. He has asked to speak with you and your wife."

Denton extended his hand. Strange, but for a brief moment, that handshake brought comfort.

"Mr. Denton, the hearts of my congregation go out to you. We want you to know that we are praying for you and your family and would like to see if there is anything we can do."

Denton mouthed, "Thank you," glancing across at his wife who now sat up straight.

"May I speak with your wife?" the minister said. "As a matter of fact, if you don't mind, I'd like to have prayer with the two of you."

Denton took a quick breath. "My wife isn't doing well at all, Sir. I'm not sure she is up to seeing anyone. We'll see."

He started toward Ashley; and without permission, the minister followed, certain that with their little girl missing, prayer would be the one thing that any parents would welcome.

After Denton Blackstone introduced him, the minister stooped to look into Ashley's eyes as he spoke, "My dear Mrs. Blackstone," he said softly, "My heart and the hearts of my parishioners are with you at this time. We are praying around the clock for you and your little girl." He straightened slightly, really wishing he could back away. The cold, icy stare he had received conveyed a message he had never before encountered.

The petite woman stiffened herself and said loudly, "Get away from me! How dare you speak of prayer. This is proof: there is no God. If there were a God, he would have taken care of my little Amy. Where was He? I ask you, 'Where was He?' I hate the thought of God."

Mr. Blackstone knelt by his wife and pulled her into his arms. "Shhh. Shhh," he whispered. "Honey, Dr. Hartley is here to show he cares."

Mrs. Blackstone sank into her husband's arms and sobbed loudly while Mr. Blackstone looked up at the minister and mouthed, "I'm sorry."

Two dark-suited men touched Dr. Hartley's arms and said quietly, "Perhaps it would be better if you left, Sir," even as they steered him toward the door.

~ ~ ~

That evening, as the minister sat at the kitchen table telling his wife what had happened, he added, "Honey, they didn't have to escort me out. I wanted to be out of that lady's presence as quickly as possible. I cannot explain it, but I felt a piercing coldness in her icy stare; and her rant against God chilled my body. In all my ministry, I've never encountered anyone like her."

"Poor thing," his wife said. "What in her life could have made her hate God?"

~ ~ ~

The story of the missing four-year-old Amy Blackstone dominated media news for the next few days, and then a week, and then two weeks. Daily, the Blackstone Manor was filled with local police officers as well as FBI agents. In addition, Denton Blackstone had hired the best- known detectives locally and nationally. The Blackstones' two older children – eight-year old Vincent and six-year-old Rodney - were surrounded by bodyguards day and night.

So far, no one had communicated for a ransom. So far, there were no leads. The nursemaid who had been with Amy since birth was cleared; every hired person in the Manor had undergone stringent questioning. All told the same story:

The three children had eaten breakfast together that fatal morning. They had laughed, especially at little Amy's story about a dream she had the night before. It seems that in her dream. she went to heaven. She said she loved everything. The colors were "bright, bright, bright and everyone was happy." She said she talked with Jesus and told him she wanted to come there someday, but she didn't want to come without her mother.

"Mommy doesn't want to come here," she told Jesus, "but I was wondering, could I tie her up and bring her? I believe she would like it if she could see it."

Her eight-year-old brother said, "Shhh, Amy. You'd better not let Mommy hear you talking like that. But quietly now, Amy, what did Jesus say when you asked him that?'

Amy got down from her chair and went to her brother's chair to whisper in his ear. He snickered as she slipped to Rodney's side to whisper the same answer to him.

It was then that the school teacher came and encouraged the three of them to go brush their teeth and report to the classroom.

That was the last time anyone saw Amy.

Denton, Jr. and Rodney had been sitting at their desks for several minutes when the teacher looked up to ask, "Where is Amy?"

The boys looked at each other and shrugged their shoulders. "I don't know," Junior said. "She went to her room to brush her teeth and get her books."

"Was Mrs. Whitfield with her?" the teacher asked.

"I don't think so. I haven't seen Mrs. Whitfield this morning. Sometimes she lets Amy come to breakfast alone, now that she's four years old."

The teacher reached for her cell phone. The boys watched as she made two or three calls. As she dialed again, the door opened and the family's deputy entered and began questioning the children who, for the first time, were learning Amy had disappeared. They were told that everyone in the household had searched the manor and yards.

Deputy Smith questioned the boys, "Did Amy have any secret hiding place? Did she ever slip away like this before?"

"No, Sir. Besides, Mr. Smith, Amy loves school. She wouldn't miss coming to class."

"Have any of you seen Mrs. Whitfield this morning?"

"No, Sir. She didn't come to the dining room this morning?"

"Has she ever done that before?

Rodney had started to answer when the door flew open and Mrs. Whitfield ran into the room, red-faced and crying. She hurried to the deputy. "Oh, Sir, I'm so sorry I had to leave this morning. I got a call just before breakfast that my father had had a heart attack and was being rushed to the hospital. I just wasn't thinking straight. I knew that all the staff was here to care for the children. I just had to get my mother to take her to my dad."

Denton, Jr. interrupted, "Sir, may Rodney and I go look for Amy? We'll look in all her best hide-and-seek places."

The deputy thought for a second and said, "That may be a good idea, Junior, but you must have one of the staff members with you two at all times. Understood?"

"Yes, Sir." He looked at the teacher. "Could she go with us?"

"Absolutely."

And, thus the hectic search began. For an eternal two

weeks, the search extended from every closet and air space in the manor to servants' quarters, outer buildings, garages, and nearby communities.

Day by day, Ashley grew weaker. She refused to eat. The only nourishment she accepted was high protein drinks that her husband mixed for her.

"Thank you, Honey, for drinking this," Denton had said. "We need you to be strong for the boys and for little Amy when she comes home."

These words had brought another muted wailing that gradually ebbed into a whimper. Denton had slumped to the floor and placed his head on her lap. Not one other sound could be heard.

It was late in the afternoon when Ashley rumpled Denton's hair and said, "Denton, Denton, wake up. I need to ask you something. Do you remember the minister that came here the first day? Do you know where he is? I want to see him."

"Ashley, dear, I'm not so sure he will want to come back. After all, you did tell him you hated the very thought of God. Do you remember?"

"Yes, that is what I'm remembering; but for some reason, I want to see him."

Two dark-suited men had moved close as soon as Mrs. Blackstone had started talking. Denton turned to them and said, "Can you check on the clergyman who came here the first day and find out how we may contact him?"

"Surely," one man replied and left to consult an FBI agent at the front door.

~ ~ ~

Dr. John Hartley entered the Blackstone Manor, far from

the ease he usually felt when he called on his church people. He followed the FBI agent who had interrogated him outside, walking carefully across the marble floor, trying to make no noise. When he stood before Ashley Blackstone, sitting with her chin on her chest and her lids closed, he remained silent. The agent cleared his throat twice before Ashley opened her eyes. Seeing the minister's white, turned-around collar, she used her two hands to push herself forward. A slight smiled struggled across her face as she said, "Dr. John Hartley, I presume?"

Surprised by her opening words, Dr. Hartley stepped forward and said, "Yes, Mrs. Blackstone. I'm the pastor of Hamilton Lutheran Church."

"It's strange I've lived in this city all my life and I've never heard of your church. How is that?"

"That's easy to explain, Mrs. Blackstone. My church is in a small town, sixty miles from here."

"Sixty miles from here, but you came to see us almost immediately when our little girl was reported missing. How did that happen?"

Someone pushed up a chair in front of Ashley and the minister took a seat, now looking into light blue eyes that no longer flashed anger. He said, "You ask me why I came 60 miles to see you. I must tell you I have asked myself the same question many times. The answer that has come to me is always the same: God led me to do so. I was having breakfast in my kitchen, watching local news, and saddened by your loss when it seemed an inward compulsion urged me to come to you. I must confess, I questioned the Lord about that. I reasoned you must have your own pastor, and I would be intruding. I reasoned a lot of things, but the compulsion only grew until I knew I had to come."

"Yes, you came, and I was such an awful person. I wanted

you to come today so that I could say I'm sorry. Please forgive me."

The minister reached over and touched Ashley's folded hands. "Oh, my dear, of course I forgive you. Your sorrow was so very great at that time. Surely, you don't need to make an apology."

"Thank you, Sir, but I've done a lot of soul searching these past two weeks. I may have told you then that I hated you. I said that because at that time I hated all ministers; but I must tell you if there is anyone I should hate, it should by Dr. Markel Anton. I took three courses under the renowned Dr. Markel Anton. I thought he was the most brilliant man I had ever met. He hallowed his intellect, his Mensa status, and his accolades, but he hated what he called 'the ignorant belief of God.' He began each of those three courses I took by throwing a Bible in the trash can. I was young and impressionable. I idolized this super-brilliant man. Little by little, I let him strip me of all spiritual beliefs I had ever had. I grieved my family by my new atheistic views. When I married Denton, he had a nominal Christian background but I hacked away at every slight belief he had, and I made it absolutely clear that our children would never, ever be taught anything about God."

Dr. Hartley sat quietly, never moving his eyes from those of the speaker. He was understanding every word she said. He, too, had been a student under the renowned Dr. Markel Anton and had fought inward battles. In his mind, he now questioned whether he should tell her the sad thing that had happened to the professor.

The telephone rang. By instinct, Ashley grabbed the receiver even as three agents lifted phones and motioned for silence.

"Hello. Mrs. Blackstone speaking," Ashley said as she had been directed to do.

"Ashley, oh, Ashley!" All listeners heard the sobbing of an elderly person. "Oh, Honey, this is Great Grand. Oh, Ashley, please forgive me. I've done an awful thing. I've caused you to suffer, but I didn't mean to do that."

"Grand, what are you saying? What have you done?"

"Ashley, oh, Ashley, I have little Amy. She's with me! I took her because I didn't want her to have to give up Jesus. She told me on the phone that she wanted to love Jesus but you wouldn't let her. I'm so very sorry, but I didn't want her to have to give up what she knew was right in her heart."

Ashley surprised her great grandmother by crying out, "Oh thank you, Great Grand, thank you"; and from the other three phones could be heard comments like "She's all right!" "The great grandmother has her," and a loud "Praise the Lord!"

~ ~ ~

It took 45 minutes for agents in nearby Kilmer to bring 93-year-old Great Grand and little Amy to the Blackstone Manor where they were greeted with hugs and tears from family members, to doting staff personnel, and to the most stoic federal agents.

"Grand," Ashley finally asked, "how did you keep Amy hidden with all the media attention and with everyone searching for her?"

"Oh, that wasn't very difficult. Every day I pulled her hair up under some cute little hat, and she always wore sun glasses. When in public, we loved on each other so much that no one would have ever expected anything."

"Grand, how did you keep her happy? She has never been away from us before, and it's taken a full staff to keep her going."

"That was a challenge. I took her to the Flagtown Zoo every day and we spent hours in the park. I admit I was tuckered out at night."

"Did she ever ask to come home?"

"Yes, sometimes she would say, 'I want to see my mommy,' but I would tell her that she would soon be going home, and that would satisfy her. Ashley, I knew what I did was wrong, but I couldn't get up enough nerve to return her. Deep down I was very scared. I'm 93 years old and I was afraid I would be sent to prison. At my age, I didn't think I could survive prison. That's why I kept her so long. I'm so very sorry. Please forgive me."

Everyone listened in on their conversations while pretending to be doing something nearby. Amy flitted from one person to the other, seemingly unaware that anything unusual had happened.

Because of a pressing commitment, Dr. John Hartley left the scene reluctantly, promising the Blackstones that he would bring his wife with him on his next visit. Outside, he felt the urge to jump up and click his heels together as he had done in high school. He wanted to whoop and holler as he tried to walk in a steadfast manner to his car. Once inside, he shouted, "Hallelujah! Praise the Lord!" and "Father, two of your children have come home."

As he drove away, he thought, "Who knows? Someday I may tell Ashley the sad fact that poor Dr. Markel Anton committed suicide." He had this information, only because the older Anton family attended his church and had chosen to keep their tragic loss hidden.

~ ~ ~

The second night that Amy was at home, Ashley called her little girl to say, "Amy, before I tuck you in bed, would you like to come and kneel by my chair? I want to teach you a prayer Great Grand taught my mother, and my mother taught me?

Clad in her pajamas, Amy knelt at her mother's knees, folded her hands, and closed her eyes.

Tears rolled down Ashley's cheeks as she began, encouraging Amy to repeat her words:

> "Now I lay me down to sleep;
> I pray the Lord my soul to keep.
> If I should die before I wake,
> I pray the Lord my soul to take.
> God bless Mother and Daddy
> And, God, bless Junior and Rodney
> And, God, make me a good little girl."

Ashley was about to say, "Amen," but Amy stopped her. "May I add something?" she asked.

"Of course, Dear. Great Grand says we always may tell the Lord anything that's in our hearts." *How did I ever forget that?* she thought. For the first time, she was remembering how she, as a child, prayed for pets, dolls, and even doctor's visits. She listened as Amy prayed a strange prayer.

Her little girl whispered, "Dear Jesus, you can keep that golden cord I asked for. I was planning on tying it around Mommy to bring her to you. Now, I won't need to do that. I think my mommy wants to come to heaven, too. Thank you and thank you and thank you. Amen"

The End

REMEMBERING

Marshall Killgore sat by his wife's bed, staring down at her as though he had not seen her before. Strange the thoughts that come in a time of sorrow. He was remembering insignificant things, like the way Louellen liked the soft light from the bedroom lamp or enjoyed hearing birds sing. Now, as she lay rigid upon her bed, the softness played upon her face and closed eyes. Marshall reached over and touched her hair, admiring the way the graying black strands grew down in a peak in the center of her forehead, making her small, oval face look like a heart. He noted her dark brows and thick eyelashes. He knew her closed lids covered big brown eyes, eyes that always seemed sad. Yet, he remembered they were not sad the first time he saw her.

He and his father had walked up the long walkway to the Hathaway Manor and found Louellen Hathaway frolicking with her collie dog. She let her pet chase her, tugging at her clothes while she giggled. His father had cleared his throat to get her attention.

"Down, Champ," Megan had said to the dog as she brushed back her long, black hair and straightened her rumpled skirt.

Still breathless after her romp with the playful collie, she hurried toward them smiling and said, "Oh, you two must be the Killgores. Daddy is expecting you. Come with me."

If he had not been seething with anger, Marshall would have appreciated this young girl's beauty and charm. He would have liked the sweetness of her voice, her dancing eyes, her graceful walk. At that time, however, he had no interest. He was there only because his father and her father, the renowned Geoffrey Hathaway, had agreed that Marshall and this person, Louellen Hathaway, this person whom he had never seen before, were to marry. Their marriage was designed to cement a merger between the two, family businesses, "to create an empire," both fathers had said.

The three men and Louellen sat in wicker chairs on the porch, chatted, and drank cold sodas. When the business conversation finally began between the two older men, Marshall realized that the girl knew nothing about the parents' proposed plans. He noted that tears filled Louellen's eyes before she whispered, "May I be excused?" and turned to run into the house. She did not return to hear the plans finalized.

Within weeks, the businesses merged and Marshall Kilgore took his bride home. At first, the two tried to be civil, but both knew theirs was a marriage of convenience. For the sake of their parents, day by day, they worked out a tolerable existence with each other.

Perhaps, their relationship could have developed into something better if Marshall had responded differently when Louellen flitted into his office one day five months later. Her face aglow, she stood before him, smiling so broadly that dimples deepened on both cheeks.

Annoyed, Marshall looked up from paper work and said curtly, "Yes? And what do you want?"

"Sir, (as he had told her to call him), Sir,...... I...that is, we're going to have a baby!"

With sarcasm, he demanded, "So?" and turned abruptly to

the papers on his desk. Again he was angered by this marriage that had been forced upon him. He cringed. He wanted no baby with Louellen Hathaway. No, he had planned to marry Gil Garner, his childhood sweetheart, and to father her children; but because of Louellen Hathaway, all his dreams had been shattered.

Louellen was unprepared for the reaction to her announcement. Tears blinded her as she backed out of the office and, without stopping to get a coat, ran sobbing into the snowy woods behind their house.

Yes, that was the time that sadness entered Louellen's eyes. She left the room that day and never mentioned the baby again. During the next twenty years, there were five more babies born into their family; yet Louellen never again announced a pregnancy. Marshall knew only when the shape of her body changed.

Except for being mindful that the four boys would carry on the Kilgore name and that the two girls could bear grandchildren, Marshall paid little attention to the children. He spent all his time building the Kilgore-Hathaway Empire.

And now, Marshall sat close to his wife's bedside and touched her ivory cheeks. He lifted her small hand and noted the tapering nails. He caressed her pretty hands, hands he had never once held. He stood and stooped to kiss her fingers, her brow, and her cold mouth. He groaned, realizing he had never kissed Louellen's lips.

Why had he not been able to tell her when he realized he really did love her? Why didn't he let her know that his pet name for her became "Lou" even though he never allowed himself to call her that? Why, oh why had he spent 20 years venting the anger he felt for their two fathers on poor little Lou and their children?

Suddenly, he was on his knees by the bed, sobbing, "Oh, Louellen. Beautiful Louellen. My little 'Lou.' Please don't leave me. Please don't. I need you. Honey, I 'm so very sorry for the way I've treated you. I love you. I love you, precious 'Lou.' I love you."

But, unless God in his mercy, allows the departed to hear mortal man, Louellen never heard a word Marshall Kilgore said.

~ ~ ~

PREPARED FOR NAUGHT

Effie Edgefield was a meticulous planner. Everything in her home had an assigned place, and always every item was in that designated place. The seasonings in her cabinets were alphabetized and stacked in order. Closets were organized with proper places to hang each garment. – shirts here, slacks there, dresses, coats, blouses, housecoats: all color coordinated and in a specific place. Innumerable shelves had been built and labeled to store sundry household items, like detergents, toiletries, linens, fans, sleeping bags, cameras, etc. Picture albums were arranged according to months and years. Tapes and discs were properly stored in an "Electronics" cabinet. In truth, the Effie Edgefield systemization was the epitome of perfection.

Effie's good-natured husband, Hal, smiled at his wife's obsession. He had served in the military and liked keeping things in place. At home now he found it helpful, knowing every item he needed would always be in the same place.

Sometimes, however, he did question her overboard planning for possible disasters. Among her innumerable disaster supplies, she had boxes of all sizes of batteries; a year's supply of paper towels and toilet paper, a pantry filled with canned goods, staples, jellies, and olive oil. On a shelf in the master bedroom, she had a box labeled, "Important Papers" and another labeled "Funeral Arrangements."

When she discovered that she could not read without her glasses, she visited her optometrist and purchased two extra pairs of glasses. One pair she put in her top dresser drawer; the other, in the car.

Once when she visited a sick friend, it dawned on her that neither she nor her husband would be prepared to spend time in a hospital. Hurriedly, she bought three gowns with matching bed jackets, a housecoat, and slippers. For Hal, she purchased three pairs of pajamas, a bathrobe, and bedroom shoes. Carefully, she stored all these things away in a "Hospital Stay" container.

All medications were divided into enough pill boxes to last the Edgefields for one month or longer. In the basement, dozens of bottles of water lined top shelves, five-gallon water containers sat below. Other emergency items, like a new kerosene heater, a propane stove, first-aid kits, and battery radios, waited in readiness.

Yes, Effie Edgefield had everything a thoughtful person could have to perpetuate safety for a family. She and her docile husband rested in security.

Perhaps, that is why when hurricane Rita threatened to come ashore in their coastal town, the couple decided to stay put. Even when the evacuation became mandatory, they opted to stay. The Edgefields and their next-door neighbors, Drew and Mattie Darwin, had built their ocean-front homes at the same time with each man trying to outdo the other with safety precautions. The two builders added extra steel braces, pylons, and thousands of extra nails and screws. Both men were confident their elevated structures could withstand any fury the ocean could heave.

Earlier Effie had placed decorative shutters on all windows. Now, she simply called her handyman and had shutters closed and latched. For an extra measure, the front shutters were overlaid with unsightly plywood.

Effie was pleased to know that neighbors Drew and Mattie

had also decided to ride out the storm. Both families had discussed their plans and felt certain that they were doing the right thing.

Her sense of security was shattered, however, when the storm roared ashore in the middle of the night with pounding, howling winds that, mockingly, made their reinforced home creak and wobble dangerously upon swaying pylons. With a thunderous crash, the well-secured bay window coverings were ripped away, allowing funneled wild waters to surge through the house and shatter windows. Effie clasped her hands over her ears, terrified as the winds howled and screamed, banging flying street signs, trash cans, tree limbs, house sidings, and bricks against their teetering home.

The water was up to Hal's waist before he made it to the hallway to pull down steps to the attic.

"How can we pull the ladder back up?" Effie cried as she climbed in front of her husband.

"We probably can't!" he shouted over Rita's thunderous roar.

In a seemingly thick, black darkness, the soaked couple cringed together, mindful that the attic was barely more than a crawl space with mere two-by-fours and sheets of plywood covering the sheetrock ceilings below. The ever rising, gurgling waters grew louder.

"We've got to get out of here," Hal yelled and then muttered under breath, "Effie, how I wish you had stored an axe up here!"

Not able to see through the darkness, he became mindful of rain pelting against the small window at the end of the building. "We've got to edge to the window and get out on the roof, or we're going to be drowned," he said as he pulled Effie. As they crawled along, Hal silently tried to figure how he could break the one window, ironically, still intact. He was barefooted and there were no loose objects in the attic. By the time he reached the outer wall and ran his hand over the pane, he had formulated a plan. He took off his shirt and wrapped the wet garment around his right foot.

"Effie," he instructed. "Cover your face and stay against the wall. I am going to kick out the widow to see if we can climb up onto the roof." In paralyzed fear, Effie obeyed, sobbing and praying aloud.

She heard the crash of the window and clutched an attic's jutting two-by-four for support, as violent wind gushed through the opening, spraying icy water and glass missiles.

Laboring to remove shards of glass from the shattered window pane, Hal said finally, "Effie, listen to me. I'm going to climb out now. I'm going to see if we can get out onto the roof."

Struggling to see through sheets of rain and foam, he blinked repeatedly, gazing toward his neighbor's home. He groaned. His poor neighbor was clinging to a vent with one hand and waving a flashlight wildly, screaming, "Go back! Go back, Hal! Effie will not make it on the roof. My Mattie's gone! She's gone; she's gone!" he cried. "I couldn't hold her! I couldn't," he sobbed.

Hal edged back into the attic, hopeful that Effie had not heard Drew, knowing for sure, that he would not tell her if she had not heard. How could he tell his wife that her childhood friend, her college roommate, her closest friend was gone? How could he tell her there was no hope?

He pulled his wife into his arms and tried to cover her shivering body. She cuddled against his chest, making a pitiful whimpering sound. Hal began quoting scriptures aloud. *"The Lord is my shepherd. I shall not want...yea, though I walk through the valley of the shadow of death, I will fear no evil."* He prayed the Lord's Prayer. He talked to Jesus.

Tormenting hours dragged by. The waters below gurgled to the edge of the ladder's opening, but only the rain from the window soaked the floor.

When a lull came, Hal knew they were in the eye of the storm. He loosened Effie's grasp, explaining he needed to look outside. Yet, he had but one desire. He wanted to see if Drew still clung to his roof. Noting that his neighbor still held on with only one arm, he yelled, "Drew! Drew!" In a daze, Drew slowly turned his drooping head.

"Drew, can you try to swim over and stay with us? You'll be safer inside. The water hasn't reached us. Try it, Friend! Try!"

He was relieved to see Drew, like a zombie taking orders, painstakingly slide down into the murky water, his arms flailing helplessly. Instantly, he sank beneath the gushing waters. Hal leaned halfway through the narrow window, yelling instructions and praying aloud. "Drew! Drew, come up, come up!" *Oh, dear Lord, help him. Help him, please."* In moments, Drew's head bobbed to the surface. Disoriented, he jerked his head around until he spied Hal. His wide, pale eyes registered panic.

Hal frantically waved him forward. "Come on, Drew. You can do it. Come on!" *Father, help him. Help him. Oh, why don't I have something here to throw to him? Help me to know what to do, Lord.* **"Lean not unto thine own understanding... acknowledge him and he will direct thy path."** Hal was thankful for the verse that played across his brain. Instinctively, he looked around, expecting something (he knew not what) but something. And there it was! Within his reach, a long tree limb had snagged his roof. *Thank you, Lord. You are so very good to me. Now, help me.* He squeezed farther out onto the roof until his fingers touched the frayed end of the limb. He was now past his waistline from the window. If he lost his balance and was swept away, Effie would be left alone. Effie could not survive alone.

He looked down at his friend, battling the water, inching closer much too slowly. Unless he did something quickly, he knew that Drew would not make it. He made one last stretch, wedging his buttocks tightly into the window frame. Struggling, he strained and strained until he grasped the limb, only faintly aware of lower pain and scratches and cuts along his arm. *Thank you, Lord,* he cried with tears rolling down his cheeks. With a shout, he jabbed the long limb out toward his friend. "Grab hold, Drew! Grab!" Zombie-like again, Drew hurled himself forward. Eerily, the limb's leafy branches seemed to embrace Hal's drowning friend as he wearily pulled up between two v-shaped limbs and collapsed.

Hal knew that part of the battle had ended. Now, it was up to him to drag the heavy limb toward him to rescue his unconscious friend. The wind was beginning to whip up again, giving notice that the worst was yet to come. Hal talked to himself as he sought to inch back through the window. *I'm going to have one more problem. Drew is 20 pounds heavier than I am. I don't know whether he can squeeze through this window. If he can't, we may have to anchor the upper part of his body inside and trust that the lower part can weather the rest of the storm.* He began the arduous pull, wishing that Drew would awaken. His dead weight made it almost impossible for Hal to make much progress.

"Hey, Drew, buddy, wake up. Wake up. I need your help. Can you push with your legs? Can you help me? We need to get you inside."

In anguish, Hal knelt on the inside of the window, one arm anchoring the limb. He heard Effie crying out, "Hal, where are you? What are you doing? I'm afraid." She sobbed.

"I'm here," he answered, trying to make his voice sound

strong. "I'm helping Drew. I'll be there in a minute. Just hang tight a few more minutes. I love you, Honey."

When he called her "Honey," it dawned on him that poor Drew had just lost the woman with whom he had shared his life for over 35 years. Perhaps his friend would rather die. Perhaps Drew would rather go, too. *If I had lost my Effie, I know I wouldn't want to live. I would.....*

Hal shook his head, dismissing this thought. It was his responsibility to bring Drew to safety. Drew would have to make his own choices. He bent forward, and with renewed effort, began to tug the branch toward the window. Once or twice he heard his friend groan. "Hold on, Friend. You're almost here. Hold on! You're safe now." A surge of wind whipped against the branches and slung the limb a foot to the right. Drew moaned. *Oh, my, he must have some broken bones. I must get him inside.*

There was no way to tell how long it took to bring Drew to the window frame. Hal reached through the narrow space and began tearing off tree limbs. When, at length, he had cleared enough debris so that he could touch his friend, he let he head fall so that their cheeks touched. He cried, hot tears rolling down his face onto Drew's clammy skin. *Thank you, Lord. Thank you for taking care of my friend. Now, help me get him in.*

The process was less a problem than Hal had expected. True, Drew weighed more than Hal, but most of his weight was in his upper body; hence, Hal tilted the bulging shoulders up and down, easing his friend sideways through the narrow window frame.

Hal patted Drew's cheeks. "Drew, stay alert. I have you partly through the window, but I'm going to need your help when I pull your legs in. I'm not sure whether you have broken bones on the lower part of your body."

Drew opened his eyes widely with a vacant expression that

let Hal know that he could barely respond. He closed his eyes and tears oozed out as Hal began the painful tugging. Drew winced but made a groaning sound only as the last, rigorous yanks were made.

Hal sat with his back against the wall, cradling the shivering man in his arms. Slowly, he moved his right hand up and down Drew's drenched legs and feet, once noticing a stickiness that indicated bleeding. "Drew," he said moments later, "thankfully, I don't think you have any broken bones, but we need to get as far away from this window as we can. I want you to climb on my back. I'm going to crawl to where Effie is. Do you think you can do that?"

Drew barely whispered, "I'll......... try."

Effie called out as she heard them moving toward her. "Hal, are the Darwins all right?"

Quickly, Hal pressed his mouth close to Drew Darwin's ear and said, "Don't tell her about Mattie now. She couldn't take it. Please don't tell her. I'll say you sent her away before the storm. Please, Drew. Do you understand?"

Drew nodded and buried his face on Hal's back, stifling his sobs.

Hal knew his wife was in shock when she hunkered between the two men, and made no mention of Mattie. Pressing their heads upon their knees, the three cowered together, suffering again the fury of Rita's return. Hal was thankful for the screaming and hissing wind at times, for the clamor covered Drew's uncontrolled wailing. At times, the distraught man would screech, "Mattie! Mattie! Mattie!"

Effie would whisper, "Don't cry, Drew. Don't cry. Mattie's safe. She's here by me."

~ ~ ~

It was noon the next day when Hal squeezed through the attic window and frantically waved his pajama top, trying to attract the attention of the helicopter searchers above.

"They see me! They see me! They're coming for us! Effie. Drew. We're safe!" *Thank you, precious Lord Jesus. Thank you.* In guarded glee, he kept waving his make-shift flag until the helicopter was close enough that he could see the expressions of the relieved, rescue crew.

Effie was the first to be sky-lifted into the helicopter. Hal followed and then Drew.

A jubilant Hal, wrapped so tightly in a blanket that only his face showed, cried as soon as his friend was brought inside, "Oh, Drew, Mattie's safe! Mattie's safe! Drew, it was a miracle! She was washed onto an upper porch and was able to hold onto a banister. Praise the Lord, she was rescued three hours ago. She's going to be all right."

Hal slowly made his way to his wife's side and knelt to kiss her face and her lips. "Oh, Effie, I'm so glad you're all right. I love you. I love you." He buried his face close to her neck. He might have given in to exhaustion and slept in that kneeling position had not Effie stirred and tried to talk. "Hal." she slurred. "Hal…"

"What, Effie? What?"

Her eyes opened, gleaming. "Hal," she whispered in broken phrases, "the next thing…. I'm going to do…. is to stock…. our attic. You wait…. and see. I'll…I'll fix it right. You…. make me a list… and I'll….I'll do the rest." We'll be ready the next time."

Hal laughed aloud as he yielded to the helicopter attendant who began leading him to a place to rest.

WHAT WOULD YOU DO?

Theodore Hanson III should have been the envy of his neighborhood. His eight-columned house was the biggest; his luxurious Lexus, the latest model; and his tailor-made clothes, the best.

Almost six feet tall, Mr. Hanson possessed a full head of graying hair and bushy eyebrows that accented ice blue eyes. He was always immaculately dressed, wearing a suit and tie, even when he walked his prize-winning dog twice a day.

Walking his dog, also, earned him a punctuality accolade. The neighbors agreed that, in case of an electrical failure, they could set their clocks when Mr. Hanson stepped out on his porch precisely at 6:30 in the mornings and 6:30 in the evenings.

Yes, Theodore Hanson should have been the envy of his neighbors, but he was not: all because of one, annoying quirk. The elderly man was obsessed with finding a workable solution for every natural, or man-induced, calamity. "A Way to Escape" was his mania.

He constantly posed escape questions to men, women, boys, and girls. Once he asked five-year-old Bobby Barnes what he would do if he came out on his porch and found his house surrounded by water.

The youngster thought only for a moment before he replied, "I'd run back into the house. I can't swim!"

Undaunted by the child's answer, Theodore Hansen sat down on the doorsteps and patiently explained what should be done. From behind the screen door, the boy's mother listened to the conversation. She, like other parents, had learned that what Mr. Hanson told their children could be beneficial.

Adults, however, would have been insulted, had they not been amused, by the scenarios Hanson presented them: "What would you do if a dirty bomb exploded one mile from your home? What would you do if you were trapped in an upstairs bedroom during a fire? What would you do if you were in a car that was being quickly submerged in a murky lake?"

No one knew exactly where or when the nickname for Theodore Hanson III originated.

Behind scenes at some affair, Mr. Hanson was jokingly referred to as "Mr. What-Would-You-Do," and the nickname stuck.

Unaware of his new name, "Mr. What-Would-You" diligently continued his search for possible, dire circumstances, and day by day, bombarded listeners with questions.

-. Now no one ever asked Mr. Hanson a personal escape problem; that is, until the Rev. Charles Carrier moved into the community. The young minister eventually encountered the eccentric "Mr. What-Would-You-Do," having been stopped and asked, "Dr. Carrier, what would you do one Sunday morning if five armed men suddenly appeared in your congregation and demanded money from your parishioners?"

It was then that the minister fully understood the nickname he had overheard. He, himself, had been asked a What-Would-You-Do question.

He extended his hand, and smiling said, "I'll think about that and get back to you,"

Two days later, Dr. Carrier arrived at Theodore Hanson' home with his answer. The two men talked for an hour. Being pleased with the young minister's well, thought-out plan, Mr. Hanson interrupted two or three times to express his agreement.

In time, Dr. Carrier arose to leave, but stopped to say, "Mr. Hanson, you have asked many, thought-provoking questions about escape. Now, I would like to ask you one. If a doctor told you that you had only three months to live, what would you do? Could you escape death?"

Mr. Hanson mused for only seconds before he answered, "Perhaps I could. You see, I would immediately go to other experts in similar fields for additions diagnoses"

"That would be wise," the minister said, "but suppose all the physicians gave the same report?"

"Then, I would do research to see if there are alternative, natural cures being practiced somewhere else in the world."

"Excellent," the minister said, moving his chair closer to Mr. Hanson, "but suppose you could not find a record of any cure and all the doctors were adamant about your approaching death, how could you escape?"

"Well, Dr. Carrier, honestly, that is when I would come to you for the answer. I believe the Bible teaches something about everlasting life, and you would become my source of information."

The minister arose, chuckling. "That is a perfect answer, Mr. Hanson; however, I hope you will not wait until the proverbial death sentence before you discover the answer to your question."

They had reached the front door when Mr. Hanson said, "Preacher, what would you do if I came to your church Sunday?"

"I would tell you how to escape death and have eternal life. I do have the answer to these questions, Sir."

Theodore Hanson extended his right hand, promising, "I'll see you Sunday, Reverend."

CHERISHED BOX

Waking suddenly from fretful sleep, frail 90-year-old Nellie Little pulled covers up to her quivering chin and tried to adjust her eyes to the faint light. Having lived with one daughter and another and another for the past year, she found it confusing to know where she was, especially at night.

Soon, however, the nightlight helped her make out surroundings. She breathed more easily, having spied the tall posters of her bed and the big dresser across the room. She was in Martha's home. She liked being in Martha's home, mainly because Martha had let her bring her own bedroom furniture.

She loved this massive mahogany suit, for it was the last thing she and George had purchased together. Just running her palms over the polished dresser, chest of drawers, or night table made her feel close to her late, beloved husband. She missed him so greatly that her heart ached. She pressed her left hand over her chest; and with her right arm, eased herself upward.

Squinting, Nellie thought she saw a strange, shimmering glow on the dresser's top. Fascinated by swirling yellow and blue lights, she crept slowly from the bed, reminding herself that the doctor had told her never to get up quickly. Holding on to the bedpost for a few seconds, she eased her feet into her slippers, then, slowly shuffled across the room, strangely drawn by the mellow glow.

Something was on her dresser. Nellie could not understand. She did not remember placing anything on that elegant piece of furniture. She closed her eyes and shook her head. She did not always remember things lately, but she knew she was always so very careful with her furniture, not wanting to mar its beauty. Yet, as she grew near, she noted two boxes rested on the dresser top - a large dress box on the left, and a small box on the right.

Trembling, Nellie placed her hand over her chest. The boxes seemed to be throbbing, vibrating much like her heart. Eerily, she felt led to the smaller box. Carefully she lifted the lid. Tears slid down her wrinkled cheeks as she lifted a little, worn New Testament, the Bible her mother had always carried in her apron pocket or purse so that she could read whenever she had moments to spare. Nellie hugged the small book to her heart, slightly startled by a soft clicking sound that accompanied a gentle flutter within. She laid the small Bible down.

Automatically, her attention shifted to the large box. The soft clicking and the strange movement in her heart still did not disturb her. Placing her hands on the dresser to steady herself, she edged toward the big white box, the box with the strongest pulsating pull. She smiled as she laid aside the box's lid, opened the white tissue papers, and gazed upon a beautiful, flimsy, blue dress lined with blue satin and adorned with tiny, pearl buttons from neck to waist. She unfolded the sleeves, knowing what she would see. The gossamer sleeves were edged with blue satin ribbons and ruffles. She remembered this dress. She had loved the way the ruffles always fell upon her mother's folded hands.

Smoothing the garment, Nellie covered it again with tissue and tucked in the little New Testament. She replaced the top and bent over to kiss the lid before she struggled to slip the box onto her bed and climb in to lie beside it.

~ ~ ~

Martha and her two sisters stood by Nellie's bed, sobbing as they held each other.

Annette slipped around to the other side of the bed and whispered, "I can't do it, Martha; I can't. Will you, please, open the box to see what's in it?"

Martha hesitated and softly moaned as she bent to lift the cold, frail arm that rested upon the box. She laid the top across her mother's legs as though upon her lap. Gently, she turned back the tissue paper, and reverently caressed the blue dress and the little leather testament.

"Oh, Sister, look," she cried. "Bless her heart. Our little mother picked out her own shroud. Just like her. She didn't want us to have to do that. See. She wants to be buried in her mother's Sunday dress and she wants Granny's Bible to go with her, too. She wants...." Her voice broke.

She bent to brush a curl of white hair from her mother's brow and kissed her cold cheeks. "Goodbye, Mama," she cried. "Thank you for taking care of everything the way you always did."

"We love you, Mama," the other two daughters whispered," as they kissed their beloved mother goodbye.

Each promised: "I'll meet you in heaven."

SHORTCUT TO LOVE

I should have known something was "up" with my daughter. "Come on, Mom," she had said. "It's only a birthday party and you need to get out more."

"Why?" I said. "I don't know your friend. Why should I go to his birthday party?"

"You know why, Mom. Since Dad died, you've done nothing, that is, nothing that's fun. Face it, Mom. Dad has been gone a year. He's with the Lord, and he's not coming back."

I nodded but did not speak. It was true, but what Kathryn didn't understand was that when Jacob died, the true joy of living left me. Oh, I automatically went to the gym three times a week, ate at our favorite restaurants, and sat where we always sat in church; but after 35 happy years with Jacob Janson, nothing was the same. I constantly fought loneliness, even when surrounded by people.

And now, I absolutely had no desire to go to a birthday party. I had a novel to read. I planned to sit across from Jacob's recliner and sense his presence as I read.

This time, however, Kathryn would not take "No" for an answer. "Now, Mom, for once I am putting my foot down. I want you to go with me. If the weather permits, the party will be outside in the most beautiful flower garden you've ever seen. You know how you love flowers."

Perhaps it was because it was late spring with everything in bloom that I finally yielded to Kathryn's persistence.

"Wear your frilly, pink, floral skirt, Mom, and that matching lavender, straw hat. I want to show you off. Since I have come back to Keyville, you've never met any of my new friends."

I wanted to protest. I did not want to go to a fussy affair, but Kathryn seemed so excited that I smiled and said, "Okay, I'll look my best. I do want my only daughter to be proud of me."

The weather was perfect that May afternoon. I was elated with the view of plush green lawns and walkways that wound through beds of variegated hostas, golden daffodils, pink peonies, and late-blooming purple and yellow pansies. At strategic places, stone benches were stationed beneath pink and white flowering dogwood trees, inviting people to sit and drink in the beauty.

That is what I was doing, just sitting and admiring the scenery, when I saw my daughter, her friend, and a handsome, gray-haired man approaching. I knew immediately that this was a setup.

Kathryn spoke first, "Mom, this is Donald Nelson, Gina's father. He has recently moved to Keyville to be near his children. Sadly, to say, his wife died two years ago."

I looked at the dignified Donald Nelson and raised my brows, conveying a message which he acknowledged with a smile. After minutes of small talk, as was expected, the young women dutifully excused themselves and left the two of us alone.

"Well, Donald Nelson," I said, "I'm sorry but I think we've been set up for a blind date."

He laughed. "For more than a year, I have endured Gina's blind dates. I have gone out with tall women, short women, skinny, fat, loud, shy, giggly – you name it." He paused and sat down beside me before he added, "I only wish you had been the first."

"You are my first!" I said.

"Good," he said. "Let's do this right. My name is Donald Nelson and I'm glad to know you, Megan Janson. I've heard a lot about you."

"Oh, I'm sorry about that. I've heard nothing about you."

"That figures. You probably wouldn't be here if you had known what was in the making. Now, tell me, what do you think we should do to please our doting daughters?"

I thought for a moment, and then a devilish plan evolved. "Donald, would you like to teach our kids a lesson?" He grinned and nodded. I continued, "Why not pretend we have become so quickly involved that we want to get married right away with no pre-nuptial thoughts or wedding plans?"

He laughed a hearty, contagious laugh. "We'll do it, Megan. Are you aware that our daughters and their friends are watching us now? What do you say? Let's give them a great show!"

We turned to face each other on the bench. "No matter what we say to each other, let's pretend we are looking deeply into each other's eyes and saying sweet things," I said.

"Gotcha," he said, looking down at me with the most beautiful blue eyes I had ever seen. Jacob's eyes had been dark brown.

"My husband fought cancer for two, horrible years before he died."

"I'm so very sorry. My wife had a heart attack," he said, moving closer and whispering, "Would it be wise for me to take your hands now?"

"I think so." He reached over. I was startled by the thrill I experienced when he cradled my cold hands into his warm hands.

"You have soft hands. What kind of work do you do?" I said, trying to keep the conversation casual.

"I'm a real estate broker. That is why I could move my business here," he said, lifting my face and looking into my eyes. "You have beautiful eyes, Megan. In fact, you are beautiful."

I cannot explain my reaction. I said, "Do you think we should kiss now since they are watching?" I must admit I wanted to be kissed by this man.

He put his arms around my waist and pulled me close to him. "I actually think I love you," he said before he kissed me with a gentle, lingering kiss.

I did not want to, but I pulled away, baffled by my quick, emotional response. Stammering, I said, "I..I.. think we must have impressed them enough. Each time I've glanced around I've seen rows of staring eyes. Let's go and give the final treatment."

He took by hand, helped me stand, and took me into his arms for an extended kiss. Feeling weak, I placed my head upon his chest and rested in his embrace.

~ ~ ~

Our daughters stood with their jaws dropped when we announced that we loved each other and were going to be married right away. Before they could protest, we hurried across the lawn to Donald's car and sped away.

Once out of sight, Donald pulled over to the curb so that we could laugh together.

Finally, wiping tears from his eyes, he chuckled, "I've laughed until I've cried." Then he added, "Megan, perhaps we've hit upon a truly great idea. Let's get started right. I don't know about you, but I'm hungry. Now, I know a good steak house. How about sharing a meal with me?"

"I'd like that," I said, using a tissue to dab carefully under my eyes.

~ ~ ~

The meal was great; the conversation greater. Sometimes we laughed; at other times, we became somber as we shared sorrowful times in our lives.

Later, when we stood at my door, saying goodnight, Donald said, "Strange, isn't it? It's as though we belong together."

"How can that be?" I said. "Until today, we knew nothing about each other."

"Don't worry, Megan. Our children knew. They both checked us out thoroughly before they let us meet. I think I told you I knew a lot about you before you came to the party."

"But I didn't know anything about you."

"You didn't, but your daughter did. She had talked with me for an hour or so last week. Take my word for it; she thinks we are perfect for each other. She said so."

Again, I touched his arm, strangely confident that our children were right.

A SPLASH OF CLASS

Amy Cantrell draped her shivering body across the broken mast, digging her fingernails into the drenched canvas. Across from her, Scott Murphy clung, ever watching Amy and pleading with her to talk to him.

"Amy, dear, you must not give up. Help is coming, I 'm sure. Look at me, Amy Marie! I need you. I love you. Don't give up, Amy. Please."

How could this horrible thing happen? Both had just received their college degrees and were celebrating by sail boating Without warning, a squall had swooped down upon them and capsized their boat as easily as a person turns a cup down on a saucer. Only, there was no saucer. No place for the boat to rest. A loud crack. The forward sail broke, falling ten feet from where Scott was grappling with a disoriented Amy who flailed and fought. It was with difficulty that he reached the wooden mast pole and pushed Amy's body over the rough debris. In an instant, he ducked beneath the pole and stationed himself across from her, grasping her arms.

It seemed they had fought the frigid water for hours. Angry wave after angry wave crashed upon them. The last wave had hurled a mass of slimy seaweeds that clung to Amy's face below the nose. She made no attempt to shake away the slime. Her icy gaze was accentuated by the green, clotted mass covering her mouth and neck. With difficulty, Scott held more tightly to one of Amy's arms, using his free hand to yank the slime away. Tears burned as he stared at Amy. Her glazed eyes, the limpness of her arms, and her slack grip on the canvas frightened him. He clutched her forearms tightly, not trusting Amy's will to hang on. He was right. Amy had given up. Her face fell forward, and she slipped into dark oblivion.

Grabbing her, Scott threw back his head and screamed, "Lord! Dear Lord! Father, we are your children. Help us. Help us, please."

~ ~ ~

Amy Cantrell slowly regained consciousness, reveling in warm blankets tucked tightly around her entire body. Painfully, her eyes blinked, rebelling against the light. A soft voice gave instant comfort. "Amy. Amy Cantrell. You're safe."

Groggy, Amy whispered. "Scott. Scott. Is Scott all right?"

"Scott is fine," the voice replied. "You'll see him soon. He's being cared for in the men's quarters. Now, you rest. We have some good news for you."

When the word, "good news" registered, Amy stirred, trying to rise. She widened her eyes slowly and gazed around, taking in the whiteness of the room and the smiling, uniformed attendants. These white-clad women were not ordinary nurses, Amy slowly reasoned. Something was different about their uniforms. They were dressed in fitted, white suits trimmed with gold braid and wore white patent leather heels.

"Wait, Amy. Let's raise your bed so that you can see," the kind voice said. "As soon as possible, the Captain would like to come in to speak with you. You may tell us when you're ready."

The Captain. The white walls. The portholes. Instinctively, Amy knew she was on a ship. Then, she remembered.

"Ooooh," she cried as she sank back against the elevated bed. "Please, may I see Scott or the Captain now

"Of course, you may. The Captain will be glad to speak with you," a nurse said as she picked up a phone and dialed. It seemed only moments before there was a rap on the door. A tall, elegant man entered the room. With a slight bow, he removed his white Captain's cap, revealing thick black hair with distinctive gray temples. His broad smile was disarming.

"Amy Cantrell," he said, "you are aboard the Desiree Adorra Luxury Liner headed for the Bahamas. We had traveled from the New York Harbor to Norfolk when we rescued you and Scott. Now let me explain: our liner is on a honeymoon cruise and will be out to sea for another two weeks. Now, Miss Amy, we have been in contact with Scott's parents and your parents and have arranged for you and Scott to be our guests until we return you to a Norfolk port later this month. We hope this plan will meet your approval. Scott is well pleased. You see, this is the Desiree Adorra's gift to you two brave young people."

Tears slipped down Amy's cheeks. "But we have no clothes."

"But we do," the Captain smiled. "You'll be taken to our clothes boutique and fitted with everything you need. You see, I want you and Scott, as my personal guests, to sit at the Captain's table this evening with the brides and grooms."

With a bow from the waist, the Captain smiled again and turned, leaving as quickly as he had appeared.

~ ~ ~

As soon as the Captain left, a uniformed young lady approached the wall that appeared to be one big mirror running the length of the room. Almost magically, she slid back the mirrored wall, revealing a walk-in closet with a long rack of plush terry-cloth robes, ranging in colors from milky white, pale yellow, pink, and blue to deep maroon and hunter green.

"Choose a color, my dear, and we'll bring you a robe and matching slippers. We need to get you dressed enough to take you to the salon."

While Amy donned the perfectly fitted undergarments and the yellow robe, a wheel chair was rolled in. "Now, Amy, you may not feel you need this wheelchair, but we must go down a long corridor. We feel it would be too long a trip for you to walk right now."

With a smile of understanding, Amy took her seat, glancing down at her new, yellow bedroom slippers.

~ ~ ~

In the salon, Amy was rolled to a station for royal treatment. A book of hair styles was placed in her hands. "Choose any style, Amy, and our stylist will give you a perfect cut. In the meantime, you'll receive a manicure and a pedicure."

With the last remark, a huge, colorful artist's pallet was held before her. The array of colors ranged from pale rose to vivid red. Each dark shade was surrounded by multiple lighter shades of the same hue. The attendant asked that Amy choose the color group that appealed to her, explaining that the lighter shade would be for fingernails and the darker for the toenails.

~ ~ ~

At length, with a bouncy, new hairdo, perfectly manicured fingernails and toenails, and her terrycloth belt pulled tightly around her slim waist, Amy was again wheeled down long passageways filled with joyful people, who called her by name and wished her well.

"Everyone was a part of the rescue effort," the attendant explained.

"Ohhh," Amy said.

The two paused in front of a huge white door which opened automatically. In awe, Amy was wheeled into a huge lime-colored room with touches of dark green and soft mauve. A partially draped stage featured two long walkways surrounded by velvet-covered love seats.

"You may leave the chair now and sit where it is more comfortable if you would like," the attendant said.

"No. If you don't mind, I think I'll stay where I am."

"That's fine," the attendant said, turning to pull a long, gold tassel.

In a moment, soft music filled the room. Billowy curtains parted and a gorgeous model took center stage, swirling a long flimsy skirt of a sequin-bedecked, royal blue. As she made her way down the runway, the attendant stooped and whispered, "You are to choose anything you want to wear, compliments of the Desiree Adorra."

Amy felt as though she could not breathe. At times, her mouth fell open as model after model paraded before her in the most luxurious clothing she had ever seen. In time, two quaint white carts, stenciled with bright red and blue flowers, were rolled before her with a display of varied colored shirts, shorts, bathing suits, and slacks. Amy had only to point to the garments that appealed to her. After all selections had been made, the fashion show emcee approached Amy and placed a long-stemmed red rose on her lap.

"You have chosen wisely," she said. "Your wardrobe will be sent to your room."

~ ~ ~

Dressed in white slacks and a lavender shirt, Amy was led to an upper deck to see Scott for the first time. He was standing at the rail, looking across the horizon. She breathed deeply and then called his name softly, for the deck was filled with many other people. Even with the distant music, the chatter, and the laughter, Scott heard Amy's voice. He turned, both relieved and stunned, to see her unharmed and so very beautiful.

They ran to each other. They did not kiss; they simply held each other tightly. Amy did not know why, but she put her head against Scott's chest and cried.

"Amy, my dear Amy," Scott whispered at length. "Dry those tears. You don't want swollen eyes. Did you know, we eat at the Captain's table tonight? Oh, yes, and I have a tux to wear," he added.

"You have a tux and I have an evening dress," Amy said in wonder. She tilted her head for a sweet, tender kiss - a kiss cut short because of sudden applause from deck onlookers. Scott and Amy, embarrassed, but pleased, laughed and turned toward the rail.

Glancing sideways, Scott took Amy's hand and said, "I have something I want to ask you at the Captain's table tonight."

Amy smiled and thought, "In my heart, I know what you're going to ask; and in my heart, I know what I'm going to answer."

WHEN THE TIME IS RIGHT

With disgust, Alex Detrick shoved the reference books spread out upon the library table. He had already been annoyed, finding that all study carrels had been taken, and he had to settle for a table facing the ever-busy checkout desk. And now, a silly giggle had jarred him from his forced concentration.

Frowning, he raised his eyes. A person, whom he instantly sized up as a "jock," blocked his view of "the giggler" seated at the desk. The athlete, seeming to realize they might have disturbed someone, turned to look at him and mouthed, "Sorry."

At that moment, Alex glimpsed a pretty desk clerk pressing her fingers across her lips and shrugging her shoulders in a gesture of apology.

Alex feigned a smile and returned to his books. He was finishing his last term paper for the semester and was having difficulty analyzing two opposing views. He knew he needed to concentrate, but he found himself constrained to look up again and again at the blonde girl at the desk. His view was no longer blocked; the hulk had gone. Once, when he glanced up, his eyes met her eyes and she smiled. Embarrassed by his sudden nervousness, Alex pushed aside one book and opened another. For the next 30 minutes, he busied himself, refusing to allow himself to lift his eyes to the checkout desk.

He had started gathering his books to leave when he gave

a brief glance at the desk and felt a strange disappointment, for the giggler was gone.

For years, Alex Detrick had paid little attention to girls. He had dedicated himself to his medical studies. That was the way his dad and granddad, both physicians, always wanted it. The two older men had stressed that, at just the right time, God would present to him the right wife. They used themselves as examples, pointing to their own divinely- selected wives.

Many times, his grandfather had told him the story of how he met his wife, and he always ended by saying, "And, Alex, my boy, when the time is right, the Lord himself will provide just the right wife for you."

Grandfather Detrick had been careful to explain why he was certain that God would do this. He, as a young man, was finishing his internship when he twisted his right knee playing touch football with several other doctors. He had been sure he was all right, but an orthopedic specialist had insisted that he stay off his feet for a day or two, promising to send an occupational therapist to his home to administer help.

To Grandfather Detrick's delight, the therapist was a lovely, young lady named Lucinda Gray. Grandfather said when Lucinda entered the room and spoke, he knew at that very moment she would be his wife.

Years later, when his son Theodore was studying to become a surgeon, Grandfather Detrick had steered Theodore away from "wasting his time looking for a bride."

"At just the right time, Theodore," he had insisted, "God will provide a wife for you just as he did for me."

And it happened that way.

It was during an operation that Dr. Theodore Detrick looked across the operating table into the beautiful, blue eyes of an assisting nurse. For a moment, he held her gaze, aware that his heart had begun to beat fast.

When the operation was over, he washed up, keeping an eye out for the appearance of the nurse. He wanted to see the face hidden behind the mask.

When she walked out from the operating room and slipped off the surgical cap and face protection, he felt his heart speed up again. *Dear Lord, what is this? Was my father right all the time? Is this the person you've picked out for me?*

He walked over to the nurse and said, "Hello. I don't think we've met. You have never assisted me before, have you?"

"Oh, no. I've just moved here from Detroit."

"Well, I'm Theodore Detrick. I hope you'll like it here and will be assisting me again." She smiled, revealing perfect, white teeth and a dimple in her right cheek. Again, he was aware of his rapid heartbeat.

"How did you happen to come here from Detroit?" he asked, hoping to keep a conversation going.

"My parents needed me near. In our family, I'm the only child not married and able to make a move." He liked that she had come to aid her mother and father; and even more, he liked she wasn't married.

He surprised himself by saying, "I'm not married either. Would you care to go eat dinner with me?"

She laughed, thinking how absurd this meeting was, but she answered, "I'd like that very much."

And that was the way Alex's parents started their courtship. He had heard the story many times. His dad always ended it the same way, "Yes, Alex, and that's the way the Lord will choose a wife for you. I know, because I have prayed for that since you were a teenager."

From as far back as he could remember, his family had

groomed him to be a physician. For several generations in the Detrick family, the first son became a doctor. Knowing this, his grandfather and father had brought him up learning the bones, muscles, and nerves in the human body. His play things had been models of hearts, lungs, brains, and other organs. He had listened to discussions of procedures and cures at the dining room table, in the living room, and on road trips.

When he became a teenager, he was so thoroughly entrenched into the medical profession that he had little time for outside activities like sports (although he possessed an athletic body), drama clubs (his first choice of clubs), or any other school activity. Skillfully, his parents had steered him away from getting involved with girls, assuring him that God had a person for him; and at the right time, God, himself, would bring that girl into his life.

And Alex had waited, completely satisfied with his professionally driven life; that is, until the day he raised his eyes and glimpsed the pretty giggler at the check-out desk. Things changed after that brief eye contact.

No longer did he race to isolated tables or private carrels next to reference books. When possible, he sought to claim the table in front of the check-out desk, knowing the days Rachel Whitner would be there. He had learned her name and schedule.

Sometimes Rachel was such a distraction that Alex accomplished little; but at those times, he reveled in the gazing hour and delved into the books at home. He was aware that Rachel lifted her eyes often and smiled at him. This eye-contact ritual might have gone on indefinitely had not Rachel disappeared. For two weeks, Alex claimed his spot and waited, but always someone else occupied Rachel's place.

One day the head librarian, an elderly lady who had been friends with his mother, sat at the desk. Alex walked up to the desk and when the attendant glanced up, he said, "Excuse me, Mrs. Miller. I'd like to ask you something."

"Yes, Alex. What is it?"

He bent lower, hoping that no one else could hear him. "A girl named Rachel Whitner is usually here. I've noticed she has been gone for a couple weeks. Do you know why?"

A smile flickered across Mrs. Miller's face. "Yes, Alex, I do know why. Rachel's mother, who is fighting cancer, is having difficulty with chemotherapy. Rachel has gone home to help care for the family."

"I'm sorry to hear that," Alex said. "One more question: do you happen to know where she lives?"

"Yes. You see, Rachel is a local girl," she said, opening an address book. "Let's see. Yes, here it is. She lives at 1008 Oakland Drive." She wrote down Rachel's full name and address and pushed it across the desk.

"Thank you, Mrs. Miller. I may go to see her mother."

"You do that, Alex Detrick." She smiled again as Alex sheepishly gathered his books and prepared to leave. She smiled, for she knew the Detrick Family stories about their unusual love affairs; and now, she wondered if the young doctor's appointed time had come.

Alex hurried from the building, hardly mindful of blustery winds that pelted icy snow.

Once inside his car, he sighed. *What's wrong with me? I'm acting like a kid.* He berated himself; and yet, he automatically activated his GPS and gave the Oakland Drive address.

Learning he was 20 minutes away, he noted the clock. He would be reaching Rachel's home at about 4 o'clock. He wondered if that would be a convenient time. He wondered how he would explain his visit.

He mounted the steps, rang the doorbell and stepped back.

He took another step backward when the door was opened by Rachel. Strangely, she didn't seem surprised to see him, for she said quietly, "Do come in."

Just inside the foyer, he asked, "How's your mom doing?"

Tears flooded Rachel's eyes and her lips quivered.

In an instant, Alex had moved forward and Rachel had slipped into his arms. With her head nestled upon his chest, she sobbed. He held her close, knowing instinctively that he wanted to hold Rachel Whitner close to his heart forever.

While in this consoling embrace, Alex and Rachel eased apart when they heard Mr. Whitner's soft, "Ahem. Ahem."

Rachel turned, seemingly, with no embarrassment and said, "Dad, this is Alex Detrick."

She knows my name, Alex thought as Rachel added, "Alex is a friend from college."

Alex extended his hand and the two men shook hands as though it were a normal introduction; even though the older man had found his daughter in the arms of someone he had not met; and even though Alex Detrick had embraced a girl he, instinctively, knew would be his wife.

"The doctor is with your mom," Mr. Whitner said to his daughter. "He wants to talk with the two of us when he finishes his examination."

"Good, Dad. Alex comes from a family of doctors and he is finishing his medical training. Would it be all right if he met with us?"

"Of course. I can't think of a reason why he shouldn't, but we'll check with Dr. Stone to be sure."

It was then that Dr. Stone came into the room. As soon as the doctor eyed Alex, he said, "Hello, Alex Detrick. I didn't know you were a friend of the Whitners. I was just getting ready to ask Mr. Whitner to contact your dad. I really think our patient has need of an Oncologist specialist now."

Alex replied, "If Mr. Whitner agrees, I'm sure Dad would be happy to come to see Mrs. Whitner. He keeps abreast of every new treatment. If anyone can help, he can."

~ ~ ~

For the next three months Dr. Detrick and Alex concentrated on Mrs. Whitner. At night, both Alex's father and grandfather explored books and medical journals, trying to find similar cases and various treatments. Alex googled for the latest procedures and medications. The three men viewed ex-rays and read reports.

During the day, Alex scheduled his activities so that he always spent at least one hour in the Whitner home.

One day, when Mrs. Whitner slept, Alex and Rachel slipped outside to the flower garden. Under a shaded arbor, they sat, admiring the purple petunias and pink begonias. Birds tweeted around them. In this relaxed setting, Alex took Rachel's hands and slipped down on one knee.

"Rachel. This is about as beautiful a place as I can imagine. I need to ask you something." He hesitated, trying to read the expression on Rachel's face. Taking a deep breath, he continued, "Rachel Whitner, will you marry me? I love you, and I truly believe it has to be God's divine providence that has brought us together."

Tears glistened in Rachel's blue eyes. In merriment, she cocked her head to one side and said, "Alex Detrick, I'll have to think about it." In the next second, she tilted her head the other way and said, "I've thought about it, and the answer is 'Yes.' Yes!"

A little surprised, Alex said, "How could you answer so quickly? Don't you need to pray about it?"

"No," Rachel said with her delightful giggle. "Wait a minute and I'll tell you why."

She ran into the house and soon returned with a small, decorative box. She sat beside Alex and opened the lid. From her treasure chest, she took out a 4X6 picture that had been cut from a newspaper. Holding it to her heart, she said, "I've been praying about this day since I cut this picture out many years ago." Teasingly, she said, "Would you like to see the picture?"

"Yes, of course," Alex said, still puzzled.

Slowly Rachel turned the picture. Alex gasped. "Great day, Rachel! That's a picture of me. That's the picture they put with the newspaper story when I received my Eagle Scout reward. I was only fourteen."

"I know. I cut the picture out, but I didn't keep the write-up. In fact, I didn't even notice your name, but I took the picture to my dad and said, "Daddy, this is the person I'm going to marry when I grow up. I'm going to pray for him every day and I want you to pray for him, too." She laughed. "Do you know, I periodically went to Daddy and held the picture up to remind him to pray."

Baffled, Alex sank back. "Wow! I thought I was going to have an amazing story to tell my children about how God brought you into my life; but, Rachel Whitner, you've out-topped every story in the whole Detrick's collection."

Still shaking his head in disbelief, he added, "Rachel, when did you know that I was the boy in the newspaper clipping?"

"The day in the library when you looked at me with a mean scowl, a scowl that softened the second we made eye contact. I cannot explain it, but I recognized your eyes. I knew you were the person I had kept in my prayers for years."

Alex stood, shaking his head in amazement. "Rachel, I've always known that God is a loving God; but, at the risk of sounding sacrilegious, I must say He might, also, be a top-notch matchmaker. I believe my grandfather; my father; and, now, I might be absolute proof."

THE REAL ME

You don't really know me. If you did, you would hate me. You know me as Reginal Keefaufer, the son of a prominent doctor. You know me as a family man with a beautiful wife and three ideal children. A community leader. A good citizen.

Yes, outwardly, I'm a fine man; but inwardly, I'm not a good person. I truly am evil. My past is shameful, despicable. I now confess I am guilty of vicious, unconfessed crimes. I have been a cruel, dastard, ungodly (it grieves me to say the word) "arsonist." Yes, a merciless, sadistic, hell-deserving arsonist.

For years, without remorse, I watched distraught family members cringe in disbelief as all they owned and cherished went up in black smoke. Yes, I closed my ears to their pitiful cries while I watched their fiery disasters with secret glee. May God have mercy. I have been heartless.

Perhaps, I should tell you how my unspeakable, obsession with fires began. It all started when I was a third grader living in an affluent neighborhood. I dwelt in an elegant home, wore brand-name clothes, and attended the best private schools. I had everything, that is, everything except acceptance. I wanted to "belong," but the cliquish boys on my block shunned me. They called me "runt" because of my small body frame. They scorned me, refusing to let me take part in their neighborhood activities.

In a huge oak tree in the Simpson's backyard, these bullies erected a tree-house club which, of course, was off limits for me. Often, I hid in the bushes to watch them as they removed a thick sailor's rope from a hiding place. Skillfully, they tossed the rope's looped end to drape over the stub of a cut-off limb. Then one by one they grasped the rope and walked up the side of the tree. How I longed to try that walk.

It was then, in my angered mind, I formed a plan, a plan that was easy to carry out. At midnight, when my parents were asleep, I crept through the house, slipped outside and sneaked across the Simpson's lawn. For several minutes, I crouched, surveying everything. When confident I was alone, I uncovered the hidden rope; and after several attempts, lassoed the protruding limb. With a loaded book bag on my back, I side-walked the trunk of the tree as I had seen the club members do so many times. I reveled at my feat. How I wished the club members could see me master the climb. Once inside the forbidden club house, I relished probing around, seeing the many choice things that had been stored in their lofty hideout. Multi-colored pillows. A butcher knife. Board games. A calendar of pin-up girls. Three decks of cards. A baseball bat, perhaps, to conk anyone who intruded on one of their meetings.

Taking the heavy bag from my back, I put on a pair of my mother's disposable rubber gloves. You see, I had thought everything out. Slowly, I drenched pillows, pictures, books, and furniture with the kerosene I had brought, being careful not to let any of the smelly liquid spill on me. When the room was saturated, I backed out and closed the door. It was more difficult to stay dry while wetting the bark as I came down the tree trunk, but I was ever so careful. Once on the ground, I soaked the tree trunk until all the kerosene was gone.

It was not easy to wobble the heavy rope up and down to

lift the loop from the limb's stump. I almost despaired. When the rope finally fell to the ground, I wound it around the trunk. I didn't want to leave a way for someone to get up into the tree to stop the fire. Trembling, I dug into my pockets for the box of matches. This job might have taken me only fifteen minutes, but it seemed like hours. My heart was racing as I scurried away. From a distance, I threw a burning twig to the base of the tree. Angry flames leaped upward as I sped away.

Shortly afterwards, when the sirens of the fire trucks were heard in our neighborhood, I slipped from bed, pretending to be coming out of a deep sleep. My dad looked out the window and called to my mother, "Oh, Honey, it looks as though there's a fire at the Simpsons. Put on your coat. Let's go see if we can help." He turned and saw me rubbing my eyes. "Get your coat, Reginal. You'll have to go with us."

The fire was a beauty! Wild flames licked the sides of the tree and engulfed the structure above. Ned Simpson and his club buddies huddled together and cried. I slipped close to my dad's side and faked empathy.

And so, that was the beginning. At first, there had to be a reason for my actions. For instance, the burned-out vacant lot was filled with bramble and weeds and really needed to be cleared. Then, later, my crowded, fourth-grade classroom needed to be destroyed so that my classmates could have one of the nice, mobile units being used at the back of the school.

Year by year, my obsession grew. I torched bigger fires without any reason other than my personal excitement in watching devastating, glowing flames shooting upward; bewildered fireman laboring in vain; and gaping onlookers bemoaning the fiery scene before them. A scene I had created!

And now, to the last fire I set and, hopefully, the last fire I will ever witness. This last fire changed my life.

It happened at the beach in early spring. While few people were on the island, the owners of a six-unit condominium were having some renovations done. Out of view, I studied the habits of the workers. Noting that when the city's fire whistle blew at noon, the crew would immediately stop work and leave for a two-hour period, I devised a plan.

The plan worked well within the two-hour frame. Shortly before two o'clock, several loud explosions were heard; and, almost instantly, the huge condominiums roared with fire from one end to the other. Local firemen raced to the scene. They unrolled their hundred feet of hoses and began pumping water from the ocean and inlet waterways, but their equipment was gravely inadequate. It was as though they were trying to put out pulsating blazes with water pistols. To me, their futile efforts were comical; yes, laughable. Steadily, sirens wailed as fire trucks rushed from neighboring towns to assist. Every available parking space soon was taken for blocks as early beach goers and local people gathered, grieving openly. My heart pounded as I listened to their comments.

Enraptured, I stood, watching the biggest, most colossal inferno I had ever seen. Rapidly, the inner structures disappeared, leaving only a twisted skeleton of framework from which red and yellow flames clung and belched out billows of black smoke.

Onlookers stared in horror, and then it was that I heard a comment that jolted my attention. Someone near me said, "Think how awful hell must be! There the flames will be eternal." I heard words like "lake of fire, fire and brimstone, and worms that die not."

I backed farther away from the heat which, previously, I had enjoyed. Strangely, I remembered things I had heard in my childhood. Back then, I went to Sunday school and church. I heard about the fires of hell; but until now, I had never associated the fires of hell with me. Standing there with the wretched holocaust before me, suddenly I saw myself as I was - a wicked human being, a detestable person, a horrible sinner. I hated myself and knew that God must hate me, too. I believed that I deserved to be punished. *Hell must have been made for people like me.* The thought was horrifying.

With my head lowered, I edged through the crowd to my car. I put my face on the steering wheel and began to cry, a thing I had not done since I was a child. Horrible pictures flashed before me. It was as though every fire that I had ever set was etched upon my brain to torment me. I saw faces of sobbing people and heard their cries. I wept with them. At length, I knew what I had to do. With all my heart, I wanted to make amends. I wanted to pay for my vicious crimes.

Today, I have written a letter to the local FBI, documenting all the destructive fires I have set. Tomorrow they will come for me. I know I will pay dearly for my despicable pyromania and for the immeasurable hurt and damage I have caused. I confess to you that I am terribly, terribly afraid of life in prison; but, as a miserable sinner, I am far more afraid of the eternal fires of hell.

I have written a letter to my family members, begging forgiveness. I have, also written a letter to mother's pastor. I have asked him to come to see me. I hope that he will come when I am imprisoned. I need to ask him if there is any hope for a wretch like me. I do not want to go to hell.

BY THE WAY OF WATER

Although the house was quiet as an empty tomb, Molly Hunter did not hear the car when it crunched upon the graveled driveway, nor did she hear when her husband noisily unlocked the door and came into the house, calling her name.

Benjamin Hunter placed his briefcase on the foyer table and entered the living room. In despair, he gazed down upon his gown-clad wife who sat in the center of the floor, surrounded by picture albums. Rocking back and forth, she sat crossed legged with a framed picture clutched to her chest.

"Molly," he whispered as he knelt beside her. "Honey, let me help you get up. You need to get dressed." Her skin looked blue beneath the flimsy, cotton gown.

In anger, she turned dull blue, red-rimmed eyes toward him. "Get away from me! Get away," she screamed.

In his squatting position, Benjamin moved slightly away, resting his body upon his heels. "Molly," he said. "You can't mean that. I'm your husband. I love you."

"I hate you," Molly mumbled. "I hate you. My Tricia is gone. My poor little Tricia is gone, and it's all your fault!"

Benjamin groaned Then slowly his demeanor changed. For three months, he had endured his wife's cutting accusations, never defending himself, never letting her see his own personal agony. Now his brown eyes, closing to a mere slit, appeared black. His jaw twitched. Rising to his feet, he spoke in a firm voice. "Molly, I've heard you say that over and over. For the past three months you have accused me, but what you are saying is wrong. Tricia's death was not my fault. No, it was not my fault. It was yours!"

"Mine?" Molly choked back the words in disbelief. "How can you say that? You know I begged you not to buy that pool."

"I bought that pool with the understanding that Tricia would take swimming lessons. I enrolled her in the four-year-old class. I made all the arrangements, but you...you wouldn't take her!"

Molly's voice became high pitched. "You knew I was thirty pounds overweight and didn't want to wear a bathing suit before those people! I told you and told you. Why? Why couldn't you take her?"

"You know very well I had to be in court every morning." He glared at her. "Your stupid pride. Your stupid pride caused our daughter to die. It was your fault. Your fault! Do you understand?"

Molly slumped to the floor and opened her mouth to speak, but Benjamin cut in, "Where were you?"

Molly yelled. "You were at home, too, when it happened."

Benjamin eyed her with disgust. "I can't take this anymore," he snarled. "The house looks like a pig sty and you haven't cooked me a meal since Tricia died. I'm leaving. I'm going to David and Donna's house to stay for a while."

"To David's house? Dr. David Jordan! How could you even speak to him again? He let Tricia die!"

"For crying out loud, Molly, David is a pediatrician, not God! You know he did all he could. He never stopped working on Tricia until the paramedics arrived."

Molly suddenly began to sob, rocking back and forth again.

Benjamin stood for a few moments, once again staring

down at his distraught wife with pity. Despite her disturbing demeanor, he loved her and longed to help her; but he no longer had the will to do so. "I'm sorry, Molly, but I'm leaving for now. Call me if you need me. I'll be only two houses away."

Walking unsteadily to the foyer, he picked up his keys and briefcase and left. He did not need to take the car. He and David had gone through high school and college together; and when they had set up their practices in law and medicine, they had chosen to live in the same neighborhood. Thus, for several years, their two families had been very close. Benjamin needed his closest friends, David and Donna Jordan, now.

~ ~ ~

He sank down upon the couch in the Jordan's living room and buried his face in his hands. His body shook as he fought to stifle long-controlled emotions. David slipped to Benjamin's side, sat beside him, and read several passages of scripture. When he sensed no other words were needed, he laid aside his Bible and placed his arm around his friend. This kind gesture gave Benjamin the freedom he needed. Dropping his stoic resolves, Benjamin finally allowed himself to weep, a thing he had not done since Tricia's death.

When Donna, who had been standing quietly nearby, covered her mouth and rushed from the room, David leaned against Benjamin and cried softly with his friend.

After this overwhelming grief session, an unexplainable peace slowly soothed the suffering. David arose and left the room. Benjamin, sensing he was alone, whispered aloud, "Thank you, Lord," lay down upon the couch, and succumbed to a peaceful sleep he had not known for months.

David and Donna did not intrude upon Benjamin's need for

rest. Instead, they knelt by their bed and prayed. When they arose, Donna noted the last, lingering sunlight filtering through the sheer curtains.

"David," she whispered, tracing her fingers across the shadows on the bedspread, "See. It's getting late. I need to prepare dinner. Benjamin and Molly will need to eat."

"You're right," David agreed. "You go cook, dear. I'll go back to Ben."

When David slipped into the living room and flipped on a lamp, Benjamin raised his reddened eyes and opened his mouth, planning to apologize for his weakness, for his bringing sorrow into the Jordan home; but David stopped him.

"Don't be sorry, Pal. You needed to cry. You've kept that misery inside too long. Your body could no longer cope. You should feel better now. In fact, we'll all feel better. Donna is fixing us a meal, and she is going to take Molly a tray, too."

Benjamin nodded his head in appreciation but did not speak.

"Would you like to go to the guest room and freshen up, Ben? I'll call you when Molly is ready for us."

Benjamin stood, nodded again, and headed for the Jordan's spare room. He knew their house almost as well as he knew his own.

~ ~ ~

After much persuasion, two days later, Benjamin and Molly sat in David Jordan's Buick, heading to the North Carolina coast. In the back seat, Molly sat close to her window, far away from Benjamin, staring blankly out at the countryside. At first, David and Donna tried to keep a lively conversation going but soon learned that silence was a blessing.

It had taken careful finagling to get Benjamin and Molly to

consent to go to David's beach home. Even though the law firm had granted Benjamin a leave of absence and had urged him to stay as long as was needed, he had deemed it wise to work.

"Benjamin, listen to me," David had coaxed. "Your marriage is on shaky ground, and you know Molly's health is deteriorating. You really need to get away for a time of healing. Our beach house is large enough for you two to have your privacy. Too, I've found that sitting in a rocking chair on the porch or walking along the seashore can calm the most troubled mind."

And so, the four were on their way with David and Donna planning to stay only one night to get their friends settled. The car trunk was filled with staples, frozen foods, canned goods, boxed snack foods, and sweets. David and Donna had planned thoroughly so that shopping would not be necessary for Benjamin and Molly. At the entrance to Topsail Island, they stopped to purchase perishables - milk, bread, and ice cream before going the last mile to their ocean-front home.

~ ~ ~

Benjamin spent much time walking on the beach, collecting shells, studying sand fiddlers, feeding sea gulls, and watching shrimp boats being trailed by schools of dolphin.

Molly never responded to Benjamin's invitation to walk with him. Instead, she sat on the porch, watching from a distance. Slowly, as the waves repeatedly pounded the shore, spitting up snow-white foam and leaving a lace border across the sands, Molly seemed to be relaxing. She no longer clinched and unclenched her fists, and her rocking chair movements changed from a jerky thumping into a quieter, even rhythm.

In a few days, tenseness seemed to ebb from both grievers. At least, that is what Benjamin thought was happening. Little by little, he had noted more tranquility in Molly and, now and then, she smiled. She still did not respond when he placed his arm around her or called her by a pet name, but he was sure she was making progress.

It was three days later when he awoke and found Molly gone from the house. He rushed to the porch and screamed; for he saw two horrifying things – a gaping, pyramid-shaped rip tide and his distraught wife heading into the ocean, her wet gown flapping around her legs, her hair swirling wildly. Benjamin ran, screaming Molly's name over and over, but Molly could not hear. As in a trance, she was headed directly into the tide's center, plodding steadfastly ahead.

As he sped down the dunes, he kicked off his flipflops and sought to pull off his pants. He knew the best swimmers were no match for rip tides. Molly would drown. In dismay, he saw her stumble, stagger to her feet, and then attempt to move forward again. He groaned as he saw a mammoth wave lift Molly high and toss her around like a floppy, rag doll.

Having seen what was happening, a tall man ran toward the beach, shouting to Benjamin to swim out on the right of the rip tide; motioning he would swim out on the left. Though distraught, Benjamin understood the plan. All true island residents knew it was almost impossible to swim in the center of a ferocious rip tide. The life-saving procedure was to swim straight out perpendicular to the tide's broad base and then to cross where the pyramid shape peaked.

The initial thrust through the waves was maddening, far more difficult than Benjamin had expected. Powerful surges slung tons of foam into his face and battered his body. Across from Molly, he caught the panic in her widened eyes and feared he would not reach her in time. He turned to swim across to her when he saw the tall man, also, heading inward. Again, the fight against the waves and the tug outward demanded all the strength he had.

Struggling, he grabbed Molly with his right arm just as the stranger lifted her from the other side. He numbly obeyed when the helper motioned for them to return by Benjamin's route.

With each of them clinging to Molly's limp body and battling the waves with one free hand, they headed toward shore, seeking to ride with the waves whenever they could.

When after, what seemed like an eternity, the weakened men felt the shell-crushed bottom beneath their feet. In exhaustion, they stumbled to the shore. Benjamin wanted to collapse, to free his tightened chest, to close his eyes, to lie still; but he could not. He turned his ashen wife over and sought to empty the water from her body. He did not cease pounding her back and calling to her until he heard her cough and saw her eyes blink. Then, and only then, did he fall prone upon his back and close his eyes.

A throng of terrified people had gathered on the beach now, bringing a stretcher, blankets, and cell phones.

Someone bent close to him and asked, "Where are you staying?"

With effort he mumbled, "Jordan's Place." Then darkness closed in.

~ ~ ~

He did not know when they were carried into the house. He did not know when the doctor came. Nor did he know when the telephone rang and someone conversed with David. He only knew that they were safe, warm, secure.

~ ~ ~

Thoughtful neighbors and visiting beach goers took turns sitting by Benjamin and Molly as they slept. They awaited the arrival of David Jordan and his wife. who had been notified and were in route to the beach.

~ ~ ~

Two days later, as the four friends lingered after an evening meal, David cleared his throat and waited for his sorrowing friends to look at him. "Benjamin and Molly, I have something to tell you," he said. "Perhaps, I should have told you sooner, but I could never seem to find the right time to do so."

Not understanding, Benjamin and Molly stared in amazement. "What? What do you have to tell us?" Benjamin asked.

David sucked in a deep breath. "Ben and Molly, you know how Donna and I loved little Tricia. We loved her as our own. Now, what I have to tell you has brought a measure of comfort to us, and we hope it will do the same for you."

He moved closer to his friends and knelt before Molly, taking her hands. "Molly, you know I've always been Tricia's pediatrician. Do you remember, Molly, that you brought Tricia in for an examination a few weeks before she died? I questioned something about her condition and had you bring her back for some additional tests."

"I thought nothing of that," Molly whispered. "You were always very careful, and I knew you would tell us if there was something wrong." Tears welled into her eyes. "There was something wrong, wasn't there? Why didn't you tell us?"

David looked at his friends with a painful expression. "You remember that you were concerned about Tricia's lack of appetite and her paleness? Those two things and several other things prompted us to do some extensive blood work. I got the reports back and called in three specialists to confirm what I thought was wrong."

"Specialists?" Benjamin muttered, "Why? What did you find, and how could what you are telling us now bring comfort to you or to anyone else?"

David lowered his head, his lips trembling. "You know no one understands how or why precious little children become ill; but as a pediatrician, I know it happens."

"What? What?" Molly whimpered. "What was wrong with Tricia?"

David blinked back tears. "Molly and Benjamin, your little Tricia had an incurable blood disease. An awful disease." His voice broke. "It's a rare form of cancer. Tricia's life expectancy, in probability, would have been only months, and the treatments would have been painful. I hope you can understand this. When I learned that Tricia had drowned, I felt as though the Lord, in His mercy, had let Tricia walk through an open door and out into the water she loved so very much."

Benjamin pulled Molly into his arms and they clung to each other, remembering their little girl's attraction to water. As a small toddler, she had fearlessly scampered into the ocean, unmindful of the pounding surf. Often Benjamin had scooped her up into his arms while she squirmed and giggled. "Swim, Daddy. Swim." At times he had bent over, and holding her two hands, had let her walk and splash in front of him until the waves were almost to her chest. Molly had videoed the scene, and family and friends had viewed the tape countless times.

In a soft voice, David broke a long, tearful silence. "Benjamin, who knows why the door was open, and who knows whether Someone held Tricia's hand as she walked out into the water? She bypassed so much suffering, doing the thing she liked best-- being led into the water." In their minds, Benjamin and Molly could visualize the scene.

Looking at Molly, Benjamin whispered, "*Yea, though I walk through the valley of* the *shadow of death, I will fear no evil.* She wasn't alone, Molly. I know she wasn't. He was with her. She had no fear. We dedicated our Tricia to the Lord long before she was born. From the time she could talk, she expressed her love for the Lord, remember?"

David spoke softly, "In this sin-cursed world, diseases occur. Precious children get sick. Little Tricia was sick. Perhaps God did what was best for her. By way of the water she enjoyed, He took her home. He kept her from months of suffering."

They spoke no more, but the two couples held to each other, resting in God's love, recalling Tricia's childlike faith and fearless love of water.

CANNOT DECIDE

Perhaps it is my age, my background, or my many eccentricities; but I now face a troubling dilemma that has me stymied. In one week, I must make a decision, a grave decision that would challenge Solomon's wisdom. I've spent sleepless nights, pacing the floor and praying. My days have been filled with writing and re-writing pros and cons. I do not know what to do.

I mentioned my age. I am now 80 years old. Having lived through the Great Depression, I have known "hard times." Because of necessity, I've been forced to learn survival skills. Through the years, I've learned to be happy and content with very little.

I suppose, at times, I do rationalize. For instance, when I labor, digging into the soil to plant flowers or vegetables or when I strain, yanking out stubborn weeds, I often wipe my brow and think, "I really should be thankful that I have the joy of gardening. If I were wealthy, I would hire a gardener; but then, I would never know the soothing feel of damp soil in my hands, the satisfaction of planting seeds and watching them burst forth or the pleasure of nurturing roses or growing green beans.

In like manner, if I were rich, I would never know the art of preparing a delicious meal, surprisingly, even from meager supplies. No, like Oprah Winfrey, I probably would have a personal chef to shop, select, bake, stew, roast, and serve my meals. The kitchen would be off-limits for me.

Even more devastating, if I were rich, I would find it hard to have weekly fellowship with my friends in my local church. On weekend, I would surely be touring American shrines or flying abroad to view other cultures.

Had I been rich when I was bringing up my five children, I probably would have missed much of their childhood. Like many famous celebrities, I would have hired nannies and tutors to free me from responsibilities.

I probably would not know how to tread a sewing machine or even to hem a skirt. My clothes would have been tailor made.

I would not know the thrill of getting a new vacuum cleaner or a riding lawn mower.

Perhaps, my rationalizing could go on and on and on, but I must stop. I need to share with you the dilemma I face.

You see, my youngest grandson recently finished college with highest honors. After graduation, he came to spend several days with me before going to be interviewed for three outstanding positions. He is away now but will be returning in one week.

While cleaning his room last week, I found a lottery ticket on his dresser. I picked it up and smiled at the unusual numbers 22334455. I placed the ticket back with his things, regretting that a brilliant young man like my grandson would waste his money in such a trivial way. I had completely forgotten the ticket until I heard the winning numbers being read on television. Even before I checked to see, I knew that he had won $150 million dollars.

One hundred fifty million dollars!

Since that hour, I have been tormented, thinking how being a millionaire could ruin my precious grandson's life. I love this young man dearly and want the very best for his life. Unfortunately, I think that an excess of money will not bring him happiness; it may even bring him misery. At the present, he is facing a rewarding future, earning a great life for himself. And now, I have in my power to see that nothing stands in his way.

I must confess that I almost tore the ticket up immediately, but I restrained myself. Yet, in time, I seriously considered flushing it down the commode or burning it in the fireplace. I wanted its intrusion to go away.

Alas, I have debated and debated what I should do; however, I have not been able to come to a decision. I honestly do not know whether I should protect my grandson by withholding this winning ticket, or take a chance that wealth might ultimately enrich his life, not hinder it. As I have said, I love this young man dearly and want to do what is best for him; but I feel so very inadequate in making this decision for his life. That's why I need your help.

What would you do?

THE RETURN

Scattering gravel, the dusty Greyhound Bus slowed to a stop near the crossroads of bleak, deserted land that stretched down three other lonely roads. After minutes of activity aboard, the door opened and the driver backed down the steps, reached upward for two shellacked crutches, and then offered a hand to someone who thumped downward.

A darkly-tanned young soldier hesitated on the bottom step. Sergeant Hank Armstrong wore slightly rumpled khaki pants that folded neatly below his right knee. He hopped down the final step, squared his shoulders, eyed the road, and with a slight grin said, "You know, they never taught me how to walk on gravel."

"You'll do fine, Son," the driver said, trying to figure how to help.

With difficulty, Hank hobbled to the side of the road with the driver walking closely behind, carrying a big duffle bag. When the driver placed the bag near Hank, he said, "Son, would you like to sit?"

"No, Sir. I'll just stand."

The driver wiped sweat from his brow. "Are you sure someone is coming for you?"

"Yes, Sir," the soldier answered almost as though he were responding to a military officer.

Stepping close and extending his hand near Hank's right hand, the driver said, "God bless you, Son, and thank you." Pressing his lips together, slowly the driver walked back to the bus, lingering at the steps to glance back.

For fifteen minutes, Hank stood upon his left leg, bothered by the sweat that dripped down his face and nose. "Blasted, Hank," he scolded. "After being in Iraq for two years, you ought to be able to stand little ole Alabama sun."

He turned his back to the sun and waited and waited until the calf of his left leg began to cramp. Looking down at the duffle bag, he wondered if he could lower himself. He dropped the right crutch, and working his hands down the other crutch, edged downward. When he had flopped on the bag, he stretched out his good leg and rested before beginning to massage the sore spots.

While waiting, he took a New Testament from his shirt pocket and began to read. He had read three chapters in Ephesians before he heard the peculiar motor whir of his old Subaru.

The car skidded to a stop and a pretty young woman, wearing a long print dress and white tennis slippers, raced toward him. She knelt by Hank's side and, cupping his sweating face in her hands, kissed his lips, his cheeks, and his forehead.

From the car, three children tumbled out followed by a barking, yellow cur dog. The children ran, crying, "Daddy. Daddy!" The youngest squealed, "Dadee's home! Dadee's home!"

Hovering around their father, being careful not to touch the right leg's stump, the three children hugged and kissed him. Frantically, the dog circled the group until he spied the opening over the right leg. Not knowing better, he leaped up upon his master's lap. Yapping and licking, he worked his way up to Hank's chin.

"Oh, Honey," his wife whispered. "You're wringing wet. We're so very sorry we were late. The car wouldn't start."

"That's all right," Hank said. "You're here and that's all that matters."

"Let's go home," the wife whispered. "I have your favorite meal waiting."

Hank glanced down and said, "I don't know whether I can get up or not." He smiled.

"They didn't teach me how to get up from a duffle bag."

"No trouble," his wife said. "We can help you."

She stationed herself in front of him, took his hands, and bent her knees. "See!" she said. "I remember the way you taught me to lift heavy things." Laughing, she began the pull. Hank helped as much as he could and the three children pushed from behind."

Once he was standing and the crutches were stationed, the oldest child, eight-year-old Skeeter patted his father's back and said quietly, "I'm sorry about your leg, Daddy."

"Thank you, Son, but that's all right. When I get my bionic leg, I'll beat you across the field every time."

~ ~ ~

The faded old Subaru sputtered away with happy chatter, yapping, and a curly-headed toddler cuddled on her dad's lap, patting his chest and repeating, "Dadee's home. Dadee's home!"

CHRISTMAS TREE MAGIC

Trent Towers repositioned the last few remaining Christmas trees on the lot, barely mindful of the powdery snow that sifted through the branches, stinging his face and clinging to his woolen parka.

"Martha. Martha. Martha," he said. "What a wonderful season we have had," and then turned quickly to see if anyone could hear him talking. He grinned when he saw he stood alone. "Good, Martha," he said. "I don't want folks to think I'm ready for the 'loony farm.'"

Across the lot, he spied his partner, Matt, adding logs to the tall, metal fire barrel. Red, yellow, and blue sparks sputtered upward as though being chased by the white-hot flames. The warmth of the fire beckoned. Heading across the deserted lot, he stomped heavy clumps of snow from his black boots.

Matt sat on a big bale of hay near the fire barrel, alternately warming his hands and feet. Trent smiled at him without speaking and stretched his gloved hands near the roaring fire.

Having warmed the front of his body, he turned to toast back parts. He glanced across the lot, assessing the new arrangement of trees. It was then that he saw her.

She was standing beneath the scalloped row of lights strung around the lot, gazing childlike at the six-foot fir tree that loomed before her. The twinkling overhead lights illumined her pale, but perfectly chiseled face. Her face. Her face, Trent thought it looked exactly like the face of his mother's prized porcelain doll. How often, as a boy, had he traced his fingers over the smooth little face with the tilted nose and rosy lips. And now, he was looking at that flesh-and-blood face. The resemblance was uncanny.

The resemblance stopped with the face, however. His mother's doll had been adorned with blue satin puffed sleeves, ruffles, lace, and tiny pearl buttons. The Replica under the lights wore a red toboggan pulled down over her ears, allowing only a few sprigs of black curls to frame her pale face. She wore a faded green coat and clutched a big bag of groceries in her arms. Beside her stood two little children, holding to her frayed coat with ungloved hands and shifting from one foot to the other.

Trent made a step forward, but that slight movement seemed to startle The Replica and she turned and hurried down the sidewalk with the little ones running by her side.

"Did you see that lady?" Trent asked. "Do you know her?"

"Yeah," Matt said, standing again to warm his hands. "That's Sheila Sanders. That's a sad story. Happened five years ago, a short while before you moved here. Her husband was doing really well. Had his own electrical business and lived in Forest Hills. In a freak accident, the scaffolding at the bank building collapsed, killing young Sanders instantly. The poor guy left his wife with two little kids. Ain't that a bummer?"

"Where does she live?" Trent asked, ignoring the bummer question.

"She lives in that old house where Zed Coleman used to store his construction supplies. It's that red building on Hart Street. He lets her live there free."

Trent took out a roll of bills from his pocket and peeled off three twenties.

"Matt," he said. "Do me a favor. After I check the music, I'm going to call my brother, Ted, to see if he can come to close for us. I'd like for you to go to Walmart and get enough decorations to cover that big fir tree in the center there," he said, pointing to the tree that seemed to interest Sheila Sanders.

"For her?" Matt asked flatly.

"Yes," Trent answered. "I'm going to take her that tree."

"No electric lights," Matt said bluntly. "No electricity."

"No electricity? Why?" he asked, but the answer came to him before Matt could respond. "Oh, well, we'll take care of that tomorrow."

As Matt headed for the car, Trent followed and handed him additional money. "Buy some food, toys, anything you think those kids would want. Play Santa Claus."

Matt grinned. The last idea appealed to him. He patted his bulging stomach and grinned.

Trent went into the little house in the back of the lot to call Ted. "Silent Night" played in his mind as he busied himself, waiting for Ted to arrive. He whistled as he headed toward the elegant fir, enjoying downy flakes that danced around.

"Mr. Tree," Trent said as he lifted it and carried it to his truck, "I'm placing you in a deserving home tonight."

And for the first time since his beloved wife, Martha, and their little son were killed in a wreck, Trent Towers felt a warmness kindle his heart.

An hour later, he stood on the rickety porch of Zed Coleman's storage house. He hesitated, not knowing what he would say. He knocked and stepped back, waiting for the door to open.

It opened only a crack. "Yes?" a soft voice said.

"Mrs. Sanders," Trent said, "My name is Trent Towers. I

own that Christmas tree lot down town. Every year I give away a few trees to special people. I saw you at the lot tonight and thought your children might like this tree."

Little hands pulled the door open, and two children crowded in front of their mother. "Oh, Mommy, look. It's the tree you liked!"

"Can we have it, Mommy?" the little girl pleaded.

Sheila Sanders placed her hand over her heart, not saying a word but looking down at her children and then back at the tall stranger.

"I don't know," she finally stammered.

Trent stood the tree upright. "See," he said. "It's a perfectly good tree and it comes with lights and everything."

"Lights too!" the boy said, swinging open a squeaking screen door.

Trent said, "May I bring the tree in, Junior, or what...what is your name?" he said.

"Marcus. Marcus Sanders," the boy said, reaching through the lower branches to help carry the tree.

"Well, how about it, Mrs. Sanders? May Marcus and I bring the tree inside?"

Sheila stepped aside reluctantly, ashamed for this stranger to see inside. Trent took a quick glance at the barren room with its crude wooden table, two chairs and a box, an oil lamp, a sleeping bag at the foot of an iron bed, and a kerosene heater in the center of the room. Stationing the tree in an empty corner, he wondered what had happened to Sheila Sander's home and furniture.

"Mrs. Sanders, my assistant will be here soon. He'll be bringing the lights and some other things. Do you mind if I wait for him?"

Tears filled her eyes. "Of course, you may wait. Would you like to sit?" she said, moving toward the table.

She took a seat across from him, closing an open Bible. The two smiled as they watched Marcus and his sister dance around the tree.

"I know about your husband, Mrs. Sanders. I'm very sorry. If you do not mind, I would like to do something special for your family this Christmas....in memory of him."

Sheila turned her head away to hide the tears that ran down her cheeks.

"Thank you," she finally whispered, fingering her wedding band.

She still wore her ring. He liked that. He wore his, too. Close friends had sometimes asked him why he still wore his wedding band. He knew they could not understand, but Sheila Sanders understood.

Hardly knowing what to say, Trent was relieved to hear his partner kicking snow from his boots. He strode to the door and said, "It's about time! We've been waiting for you."

Matt entered the room, barely able to see over the top of the boxes he carried. Sheila removed the lamp from the table and placed it on a turned-up crate. Trent helped stack several boxes on the table, mindful of two, little wide-eyed, happy faces watching eagerly.

When Sheila spotted the boxes of stringed lights, she pressed her hand to her lips.

Quickly Trent said, "We hope you do not mind. We are having your lights turned on tomorrow." Again, she turned away. Trent noted the black, curly hair that fell upon her shoulders. *Just like the porcelain doll*," he thought.

Most of the evening was spent decorating the tree and enjoying Matt's purchases - roasted peanuts, chocolate candy, and milk. Later, while Matt and the children added icicles to the tree, Sheila and Trent sat, talking as though they had always known each other.

Trent glanced at his watch. He knew it was past the children's bedtime; and yet, he knew they could not go to bed so long as he and Matt were there.

"I've had a really nice time," he said as he reached for his gloves and hat, "but we need to be going."

Sheila extended her hand, so tiny, so soft. "Thank you so very much, Mr..., that is, Trent. You have made my children very happy tonight."

Trent looked down at her, knowing that he wanted to make Sheila Sanders and her children happy forever. "May I come back tomorrow night?" he said. "To see if the lights work, you know."

Sheila smiled The Replica's sweet smile and said, "Yes. Yes. Please come back."

As Trent backed out the door, he smiled and said, "I'll be back. You can count on that."

Little Sheila, I'll be back.

SMITTEN BY A NAME

Horace Emory Hamilton IV stood looking at himself in the mirror. He noted his unruly, yellowed gray hair, his bushy eyebrows, his furrowed brow, and rugged features. All his life he had been noted to be plain, nothing but plain; yet, all his life he had received unusual, admirable attention. For all his sixty years, he had been the recipient of day-by-day preferential treatment.

"Why?" he asked himself. He had always asked why. "Why did people bow and scrape before him?" He asked himself repeatedly, but he always knew the answer: he was Horace Emory Hamilton IV! Horace Emory Hamilton. Everyone knew that name. Rich or poor; educated or unlearned; refined or uncouth: all reacted to the Hamilton name in awe.

Yes, they revered the Hamilton name, but Horace hated it. He hated all it had entailed for him during his entire life.

"No, no, Horace Emory Hamilton, you mustn't do that," his mother had often cautioned. "My dear, you are a Hamilton. A true Hamilton would never do that."

"No, Horace, you cannot go to that camp; you must go to Europe for the summer," his father had said sternly when he had begged to go to a local camp with classmates.

He was not allowed to go to church. The first Horace Emory Hamilton had frowned upon organized religion. In fact, he had claimed to be an atheist. He instructed that all his descendants must refrain from dependency upon, what he called, a fictitious supreme being. He was adamant that his non-religious views must be followed; and of course, no one dared cross the great Horace Hamilton.

Often Horace, the fourth, had watched the chauffeur's children playing church. In secrecy, he had listened to their childish preaching and singing. He knew the words to "Jesus Loves Me"; and when he was alone, wondered if there really could be a person named Jesus who loved him.

His happiest moments were spent, not with his strict governesses and instructors, but with the ragtag children of the staff who managed the Hamilton Estate. His favorite secret playmate was Pug Powers, the son of the stables' caretaker. Red-headed Pug was simply called "Stable Boy."

Once while Horace was watching, Stable Boy skinned his finger while cleaning a saddle. In pain, he screamed out, "Owwww! Horse manure!"

Shocked, Horace jerked his head around to see if anyone was near enough to hear such a crude, crass expression. Crude and crass, yes, but ten-year-old Horace loved the wording. He had never been able to say even a slang word. Once when he had exclaimed, "Durn that fly!" his mother, aghast, scolded, "No, no, Horace. "No Hamilton would ever let such a word come from his mouth." Years after Stable Boy spit out that crude, crass, obscene word, Horace often thought the words "Horse Manure," relished the sound, and boldly uttered them in his mind. "Horse manure! Horse manure! Horse manure!"

Now, looking at himself in the ornate, gold-rimmed mirror hanging over his mahogany desk, Horace frowned, thinking again of all the things he had been denied because of his birth name. That name had kept him from marrying the one girl in the world he loved. Unfortunately, he had fallen in love with Miriam Moore, the petite, demure governess who taught his nephew and niece. When he professed his love for Miriam, his parents, however, ridiculed his choice. Miriam was immediately dismissed, and he never saw her again. Horace learned his wife had already been chosen. In time, he married the highly esteemed Eleanor Ellington from Vermont. Yielding to parental pressure, he and Eleanor, in a loveless union, produced three children – all girls, the one thing that Horace counted a blessing. At least, to his satisfaction, the Hamilton name was not being carried on. He, himself, was not guilty of placing the Hamilton albatross upon a son. All three daughters fortunately had married and changed their names - all to his delight.

Horace opened the desk drawer, took out a hidden picture and pressed it to his lips. From a drawer, he picked up a pistol and placed it to his head, watching himself in the mirror. With a satisfied smirk, he reached over and swept the elegant, marble Horace Emory Hamilton IV nameplate from his desk. He smiled at himself in the mirror while his finger tapped the trigger. With one pull, he knew he could end his never-ending bout with the Hamilton name.

He took a deep breath, steadied his finger on the trigger, but…….

What irony. A song, sung by the chauffer's children, played upon his brain. He could not explain it. He lowered the pistol and looked around. No radio or television. The house was as silent as an empty graveyard.

Yes, the house was silent, but he heard the voice of the children singing, "There's a new name written down in glory, and it's mine. Oh yes, it's mine."

As though in slow motion, Horace eased to his knees and bowed his head. He cried, a thing he had been cautioned never to do. "Hamiltons must never yield to crying! Do you understand? Crying is a sign of weakness," his father had said.

Now, Horace chose for himself. For the first time, he sobbed and prayed, "Oh, dear Lord, please give me a new heart and a new name. Write my new name down in glory. I believe everything the Ransom children preached. The way they taught me, I now repent of my sins. I believe in Jesus. I want Him to have my life."

The soft shadows of evening were falling when 60-year-old Horace Emory Hamilton IV walked out of his elegant office a new man, a new man with a new name written down in heaven. He hummed another song the children used to sing:

Jesus loves me
This I know
for
The Bible tells me so.

THE GREAT REVELATION

Oscar B. Brighton bolted upright in his feather bed, his icy blue eyes wide open, his lower jaw dropped. Jarred awake by a frightening revelation, Oscar clasped trembling hands to the sides of his head, leaped up, and danced around the room. Strong, frenzied thoughts bounced within his brain, making him fear his skull might explode.

He gasped for breath, sank down upon the bed and rocked back and forth, whimpering, "The revelation! The revelation! What could it mean? What could it mean?"

Slowly the light came. He knew. He knew his destiny. He, Oscar B. Brighton, had been chosen. He had been given a divine appointment Humbly, he bowed his head and whispered, "I'll do it." He knew, without a doubt, he had been challenged to change the world.

Change the world! Already, he knew he could do it. He had thought about it many times. Now, he could save the world.

1. First, he would trade hate for love - - the kind of love that makes people smooch instead of fight.
2. He would heal all body ailments from ingrown toenails to bellyaches.
3. Every family would have a car and a bicycle and, maybe, a scooter.

4. No one would ever be hungry. Big Macs and fries would be free.
5. Anyone caught fighting would be beaten to a pulp.
6. Plastic surgeons would make everybody look good or, at least, better.
7. Teachers and policemen would trade salaries with actors and football players.
8. He would pay someone to invent cars that could run on water.
9. He would remedy the race problem by dying everyone green. No, not green. Purple!
10. He would make fat people "thin as a rail" and skinny people "pleasingly plump." He would ban dieting.

He thought and thought. He had millions of ideas, and he knew every single one would work. Yes. He, Oscar B. Brighton, would accept this new challenge. He would change the world; but, right now, the roosters were just beginning to crow and it was still dark. He would sleep for two hours and twelve minutes. Then he would begin the job.

Contented, the appointed Oscar B. Brighton sank back into his feather bed and slept until noon.

Twelve-year-old Johnathan Mims had just typed THE END when his mother came into the den and said, "Have you finished the assignment, Johnathan?"

"Yes, Mom. I just finished and was getting ready to highlight the whole thing and hit delete."

His mother came and stood behind him, looking down at the final page. "Why would you do that, Johnathan? I thought the assignment was due today."

"It is, and I'll have to work like crazy to write something else; but I just don't feel right about printing this story."

Mrs. Mims moved to face her son. "Why, Son? I thought you told me the guys in your class were liking the parts you had been sharing with them."

"That's just it, Mom. They laughed, but they were laughing at the Oscar Brighton character I had created; and that reminded me of something that happened at school today.

You know, we have a Special Ed class, and the kids in that class have some forms of handicap. Well, in the hall today, a group of us boys were passing a student from that class. One of our guys twirled his forefinger around and pointed to his own head, indicating a mixed-up brain. They laughed. I looked at the Special Ed student; and, Mom, I saw hurt in his eyes. That got me to thinking. This story makes light of someone whose thinking is strange. Sure, the kids in my class will laugh at it, but I wonder if it will cause hurt to anyone in the Special Ed class or to someone who has a handicapped family member."

Mrs. Mims touched her son's shoulders. "Oh, my son, how thankful I am that you are sensitive to others' feelings. I've been standing here reading your last page; and, Son, I think you are right. Delete this story and we'll pray for inspiration to write something much better. I do want the say, however, that I thought you did put something positive in this story.

"I did?" Johnathan said.

"Yes, you did. You see, you didn't let your character grieve over his handicap. He went back to bed and slept peacefully. In his mind, he had accomplished something."

"Yeah, he was happy, wasn't he? I like that." Johnathan said as he highlighted the story and hit the delete key.

HUMOR

TRAVELING WITH HATTIE T.T.

The stocky, young bus driver smiled as a spry, little, gray-haired lady quick-stepped toward him, wearing a red turtle-neck shirt, a blue jean vest decorated with sequins, a matching skirt edged with frayed fringes, and shiny cowboy boots sporting silver spurs.

With a twinkle in her blue eyes, she whispered, "Thank you, Sonny," as he touched her elbow to assist her up the steps.

At the base of the steps, the driver lingered to hear his new passenger say, "Hello, everybody! My name is Hattie T.T. Hatfield. I am 92 years old, and this is my first time to ride a Greyhound Bus. Yep, my first time, and I aim to have a super great time. Anybody want to help?"

A male voice from the back of the bus said, "Yes, Hattie T.T. Hatfield. I'll help."

Sitting up, a weary traveler rubbed his eyes and squinted. In spite of the fact that it was 10:00 p.m. and he had 100 miles more to go, he smiled at the talkative elderly woman. He felt compelled to say, "Me, too. I'm with you, Little Lady."

"None of that Little Lady stuff. My name is Hattie T.T. Hatfield," she said as she took her seat behind the bus driver who had just closed the door and revved the engine.

As the bus glided from the station and wound through the

traffic, Hattie T.T. leaned forward and talked quietly with the driver. At times, he chuckled.

Once they were on the highway, suddenly Hattie stood; and with her back resting against the iron partition that separated her from the driver, yelled, "Hey, Bus Driver, turn on the lights. I want to see who's on this bus."

The lights came on. A soldier removed the folded jacket he was using as a head rest and grinned. Middle way back, a young married couple, who had been necking. straightened up and giggled. Amused, a heavily-bearded man wearing bibbed overalls said, "Okay, Hattie, You did say Hattie T.T. Hatfield, didn't you? Well now, tell us something about yourself."

"Thank you, Sonny," Hattie said. "I thought you'd never ask." An outburst of laughter assured Hattie she had a trapped audience.

"Well," she continued. "I have thirteen children. Yep, thirteen."

Gracious, it would never do for them to know I have only one child.

"My first husband, rest his soul, gave me six boys, not a single girl! He named them Bible names. We had Abraham, Isaac, Jacob, Joseph, Mohammad, and Moses. She paused to enjoy the snickering. "Now, that Moses was something else. He was very talented. His gift was music. Yep, he is well known. Yep, he's the one that wrote that famous song, 'Let My People Go,' you know."

My second husband, rest his soul, gave me a mixture – two girls and two sets of boy twins. He named the first boy twins Eenie and Meeny; but when we got the second set, I put my foot down. I refused to name them Miney and Moe. We compromised with Meecum and Moecum.

Now, my third husband, whose soul can't be resting

anywhere, gave me one puny girl. He was a rascal, he was; but I loved that man! He loved me, too. Yep, he loved me and fifty other women!

The driver laughed more heartily than everyone.

"Now, since I had all them children spread from Maine to California, I've had to keep the sky hot. I've flown in everything from a creaky two-propeller plane to a jumbo jet." *It would never do to tell them that, other than a car and this bus, I've never ridden even a taxi cab, or a bicycle.* She clapped her hands. *"*Yep, I like those fast Concords best of all."

A prime little lady, dressed in a faded plaid dress and a floppy hat, asked, "How could you afford all those trips?"

"Oh," Hattie said. "Money is no problem for me. Why, I've got $3000.00 pinned to my underwear even this minute." The driver bent over with laughter.

Periodically, the bus stopped to let someone off. Each time, those departing gave Hattie a hug or shook her hand. Hattie's eyes sparkled as she bade farewell and always said, "God bless you."

Every time a new passenger boarded, she extended her hand in greeting and told him or her where to sit. Newcomers seemed amused at the unusual welcome and took the designated seats. At midnight, however, Hattie sank down in her seat and said, "I think I'll get a little shut eye."

"Good idea," the driver said. "We have another hour to go."

Soon, only the hum of the motor and an occasional snore could be heard. Even as Hattie dozed off, she earned a chuckle when mumbling, "Did I tell you about the time I danced with Franklin Delano Roosevelt?"

It was after 1:00 when the driver slowed to a stop. He gently shook Hattie and whispered, "We are at your stop, Hattie T.T."

Slowly, she gathered her things. Some on the bus riders

awoke because of the muffled whispers; some, because of the station's lights.

"Bye, Hattie," someone called. In a second, another voice rang out, and then the bus came alive with, applause, well wishes, and a racy whistle.

Hattie grinned and did a curtsy before the driver took her arm and gently escorted her off the bus.

With his arm around her shoulders, he led the giggling, petite lady into the station where a pretty young woman hurried to meet them. Laughing, the open-armed greeter stood on her toes and kissed the driver's lips before whispering, "You're a wonderful husband."

"No. You are the wonderful one," he said, "taking your grandmother so far away to different stations just so that she can ride back on my bus and put on her show."

"I do it because she enjoys it so," the driver's wife answered, taking Hattie's empty suitcase. "How did she do?"

"Just like usual. She had them rolling in the aisles."

They kissed again.

"Thank you, my Dear," Hattie said, patting her granddaughter's hand as they left the station.

"Honey, just wait 'til you hear what I told them this time!"

GERBER GOOCH

Gerber Gooch was an amiable man, and yet, he was offensive. Truly offensive. He had a broad smile, unfortunately, with teeth that looked as though they belonged to a mule and squinting green eyes that glinted in darkness as well as in sunlight. His face was clean shaven except for the one spot that circled a large, brown mole on his left cheek.

But these features, though troubling, were not what bothered folks.

Gerber Gooch had a strange odor, an odor unlike any body odor anyone had ever smelled. It was not a reeking stench. It was just eerily strange.

Old codgers sat in the barber shop or on their porches and discussed it. Gentile women, secretly in the Ladies' Garden Club meeting, tried to analyze it. Children, with no restricting adult couth, held their noses and called any unusual smell a "Gerber scent."

Almost everyone was trying to pinpoint the precise, descriptive word for the Gerber scent.

Once, a neighbor was peeling Irish potatoes and called out to her husband, "Edgar, come smell these raw taters and see if they are what Mr. Gooch smells like."

Farmer Funk declared Gerber smelled like a watermelon just slit open; whereas, Zimmerman's chief shoe salesman vowed he smelled bacon when he fitted Gerber's boots. Town's folks automatically sniffed (some boldly, some more discreetly) when they encountered the rotund Gerber in a store or even on the street. Each sniffer hoped to be the elite one to discern the true odor.

No one ever considered Gerber to be unclean. The man was always immaculately dressed. His favorite clothing was bizarre, but clean. Once when Hyman's Department Store had a sale on shirts, Gerber purchased eight identical shirts. They were all the same pattern and color, looking much like a red and black checker board. Since the clerk had only six in his size, Gerber said, "I'll get two more in a larger size; and, maybe, I'll grow into them."

Without thinking, the clerk said, "I hope not." Then, noting Gerber's pudgy body, he squirmed from his weight blunder by adding, "You're right. Sometimes when it's cold, you might need to wear the shirt over a heavy undergarment."

"Good idea," Gerber said, giving his broad-mouthed grin.

And so, thereafter, everyday Gerber appeared on the main street of Gallatan, wearing creased jeans and one of his starched checker-board shirts.

Alas, when he was 65, Gerber Gooch upped and died before the town folks distinguished his unique odor. I say odor, for no one ever used the words "aroma" or "fragrance" to describe whatever they considered the body odor to be, no matter how pleasant the scent they detected.

The strangest of all things happened when Gerber's remains were sent to the Miller Funeral Home. The Miller sons, who had been in the embalming business for twenty years, confessed that the aroma of freshly baked apple pie filled the facility as they worked on Gerber's body. They had no explanation for the aroma. The Miller women were away visiting in Maine, and no one else was cooking. Sheepishly, the brothers admitted that they stayed hungry all the time they were doing the embalming.

Their report of the kitchen scent was verified in several years that followed. Often during a funeral, suddenly the tantalizing aroma of apple pie wafted throughout the chapel. In truth, stomachs actually began to rumble so loudly that some ministers suffered humiliation; for, to their chagrin, even with a corpse lying before them, they found it hard to keep from laughing.

Dr. Ben Kettle, who was known for minute details, always asked the funeral directors to use a floral spray before the service began and to keep air ventilation flowing.

Yes, Gerber Gooch was an odd man with an odd peculiarity, but his memory is etched upon the brain sensory of every person who ever met him.

Sometime, even today, when some neighbor is peeling potatoes, she suddenly thinks of Gerber Gooch. Others are affected by the aroma of watermelons, bacon, fruits, and especially apple pie.

Who knows? Gerber's presence may be permeating heaven now.

It is certain his fragrance lingers on earth, at least in Gallatan.

MR. BRYANT PULLEY

For my first five years in public high schools, I reveled in teaching. I loved my students, and I believe they loved me, too. I had great rapport with the faculty members; and like the 78 other teachers, I adored Mr. Jerry Trenton, our amiable principal. Day by day, he mentored and encouraged his teachers. He inspired us to teach.

Yes, those initial years in my teaching career were ideal. Perhaps, that is why I grieved when my husband was asked to transfer to another state. Tearfully, I tried to cope. I reasoned there would always be other likeable students, faculty members, and principals.

An optimist by nature, I sought to find the positive aspects of the situation. The move would be made after Christmas; therefore, I could start a new semester with ease. Kind Principal Trenton had already written a letter of recommendation and secured me a new teaching position in the Chesterfield High School.

The superintendent of schools had sent brochures of the sprawling, yellow-brick school, nestled in the center of Chesterfield, Iowa, a small picturesque town with a grand population of 12,000 people. I reasoned that going from a school with 78 faculty members to a school with only 25 teachers would be beneficial. Surely, I would make friends quickly.

School opened January 2, with the principal, whom I had not met, stranded in Vermont in one of the state's worst snow storms. I was greeted warmly by the faculty members on my hall. Two or three fellow teachers popped into my room to chat briefly as I arranged desks and fashioned a colorful bulletin board.

Most of my apprehension was allayed when I met my students. I knew immediately that we would get along well together. Aside from a slight difference in dress and accent, these teens were similar to the beloved pupils I had left behind in North Carolina.

The fourth day in Chesterfield, I headed for the teacher's lounge to eat my lunch. In my eagerness to get organized, I had been eating in my classroom. Now, I wanted the fellowship of other teachers. Surprised by an empty teacher's lounge, I noted the absence of a drink machine, microwave oven, and coffee machine -- things to which I was accustomed. I sat at the long fold-up table, opened my lunch bag, and removed a ham and cheese sandwich, a bag of potato chips, and a Little Debbie. I had just poured coffee from my thermos when the door opened. Instinctively, I stood as the hugest man I had ever seen filled the doorway. He stood with his feet wide apart, his arms folded over his massive chest.

With a scowl, he said gruffly. "I am Mr. Bryant Pulley, the principal, and I must assume you are Mrs. Stewart, our new teacher.

"Yes," I said timidly, extending my hand, which he ignored. His black eyes squinted beneath bushy eyebrows.

"Mrs. Stewart," he said gruffly. "I'm sorry I was not here to inform you of school rules. We run a tight ship here and expect everyone to comply. As you can see, you are the only teacher in this room. No teachers ever eat here. They eat in the cafeteria.

If the food is good enough for the children, it's good enough for the faculty. In the future, I will count on seeing you in the cafeteria." He turned to go but stopped at the door. "There will be information in your mailbox to be studied by tomorrow."

And so, began my association with Mr. Bryant Pulley, whom I later heard referred to as Mr. "Tyrant" Bully, mainly by students, but sometimes by whispering teachers.

Cafeteria mealtimes were menacing. All teachers sat behind long tables that faced the students, causing both teachers and students to feel uncomfortably on display. Mr. Pulley stalked around the room for all three lunch periods, pointing his gigantic finger at someone who was leaving something on his plate, or thumping someone on the head if he talked or laughed aloud.

In spite of, or perhaps because of the daily cafeteria disaster, I endeavored to make my classes light and happy. Once my classroom door was closed, the atmosphere changed. The students seemed to relax. They were easy to teach. I must admit, however, that I could not forget that one teacher had cautioned, "Be careful, dear. These walls have ears."

Students seemed to delight in one assignment I made. I asked for an oral report that could be presented with props, video films, drama, music, or guest speakers. I was astounded by their creativity. Policemen and firemen came with equipment. Two representatives from the local community theater came and conducted tryouts for an upcoming production. The class enjoyed musical combos and dramatic skits. The week was filled with excitement, but the last presentation topped them all.

Mike Pendelton brought in a tape which he wished to show. He chuckled as he inserted the tape for the television. I propped my arms on my desk and leaned forward, expecting a treat from one of the school's brightest students.

I caught my breath, however, when the film began with

the opening of the heavy oaken door of the principal's office, a place "off limits" for teachers and students unless they were being chastened. The camera scanned the room -- the huge mahogany desk covered with a glass top and nothing else; two chairs; and a huge double-door with a small chain and lock. The scene went dark for a few moments.

I trembled, aware that Mike had hidden a camera in the office. I should have stopped the presentation; but, somehow, I couldn't. The film started again. The door opened, and the dreaded Mr. Bryant Pulley entered the room, carefully locking the door behind him. Everyone knew that the principal always went to his office after lunch each day, making it clear to his secretary that he was not to be disturbed. No one knew what he did. They speculated he took a nap.

The students leaned forward, almost fearing to breathe aloud. They watched as the principal went directly to, what was called by anyone who ever entered the office, the "secret double doors"; used a key from a chain tucked inside his shirt; and swung both secret doors wide open, revealing a huge, well-stocked pantry. All gasped. At one end of the long shelving there was a small refrigerator and at the other end, a microwave oven. The center shelves were stocked with a variety of cheese crackers, peanut butter, candy bars, canned foods, and small cakes.

From the stuffed refrigerator, the grinning principal snatched meats, cheeses, mayonnaise, pickles, and mustard which he placed on his desk. In a frenzy, he made a triple-decker sandwich, opened a big bag of potato chips, grabbed a Pepsi; and like a starved man, dived into eating action. Hunched over, he crammed food into his mouth, sometimes stopping to lick his huge, pudgy fingers. Another sandwich. Another Pepsi. At length, he wiped his greasy lips, leaned back in his chair, patted his bloated stomach, and gave a gross belch. The screen went black and Mike's false voice sounded: "And now, you have met the real Mr. Pulley, who, perhaps, should be called 'Mr. Fully.'"

The students' suppressed tittering erupted into uncontrollable laughter. I laughed with them until tears ran down my cheeks. Mike slipped to my side and handed me the tape. "I have a copy," he said, "just in case we ever have to blackmail."

At that moment, the door banged open. Filling the whole door frame with his massive body, Mr. Pulley bellowed, "What's going on in here? I'll not have it! Such hilarity cannot be a learning process."

He was wrong. I looked at Mr. Pulley with feigned attention; but inwardly, I was laughing, for I knew my students had learned a lot. In fact, I was sure they had both learned and stored away much knowledge for a later day.

KOOTA TOWN

Our township is probably the smallest one in the whole United States of America. My name is George J. Koota; and, perhaps in the outset, I should tell you why Koota Town is named after me. You see, my rich uncle, Colonel Calvin Koota, died and left me hundreds of acres of undeveloped land. As a young man, I had absolutely no idea what to do with that vast spread of fertile soil until three guys from my former high school came up with an idea.

Billy Markham spearheaded the plan. If I would donate the property with no cost, these three former high school jocks, with whom I had played basketball, baseball, and football, would pool their talents and build all three of them a house, and one for me, too.

Guy Johnson claimed to be an electrician, having worked as an apprentice with an electrician for a full year. Paul Pittman had worked for his father's plumbing company all through his teen years; and Otis Overton was a self-proclaimed carpenter, having worked in construction work for two summers. And as for me, my dad always said I was the "Jack of all Trades." Yep, we had the perfect setup. Without question, we had the brain power, the on-the job "know-how" and as hulks, the "physical prowess" to tackle the job.

It took us two years and three days to complete all four

dwellings. Every day as we worked, onlookers stopped and watched in awe. I must admit, we were awesome. Soon people began to ask if they could build around us. It was then that we renowned builders decided that, perhaps, we should build a town. Since I owned the property, the guys voted to name the town after me. And that's the way Koota Town began.

As of today, we have 28 houses and a population of 152. We have a grand town, boasting at least one of everything. On Main Street, we have one grocery store, one furniture store, a library, post office, drug store, café, doctor's office, a make-shift hospital with five beds, and one movie picture theater. Oh yes, and we have one church the preacher calls "Ecumenical," whatever that means.

We have some unusual families with some unusual stories. Now, there's the Graham Family. I mention them first, for this family is the biggest in Koota Town. Erwin and Erotica are only in their forties, but already they have ten kids. Secretly, neighbors have dubbed Erotica "The Baby Machine." It seems that every time we turn around, she has "one or two buns in the oven." They have three sets of twins. The sad part of this story is that the Grahams built a house with only three bedrooms; and their lot is so small that the only way they can add more bedrooms is to stack them one on top or the other. That accounts for their strange looking house. People, who drive into our town to check it out, always stop and stare at the oddity of a house that looks like stacked building blocks.

Then there's the Pequits. Only two people live in their ten-room house. I say two; but, perhaps, I should change that, for they have two live-in Labrador Retrievers, three cats, a parrot, and a monkey –all who have the run of the house. Outside, the Pequits have rabbits, ducks, chickens, and a pet pig. The proud owners have their yard fenced in; and when their menagerie is allowed to play on the lawn together, children gather to cling to the chain-link fence and watch what they call the "Koota Zoo." The Pequits do not seem to mind.

Then there's Emmit Moore. I must mention him; for in our town, he's Koota's most Godly man, even counting the pastor. Whenever anyone has a spiritual need, you can bet he or she will end up in Emmit Moore's kitchen getting counsel. Maybe this does not seem strange, for all communities seem to have this kind of leader, but I need to tell you what's strange. You see, Emmit used to be a pitiful sot. Yes, sir, he spent half of his time holed up in some ditch, wallowing in his own vomit. In neighboring Kerby Town, Emmit used to be called their "town drunk." He might have died in that pitiful condition had it not been for a dear old black lady named Ms. Mamie Mae.

You see, Ms. Mamie Mae was the live-in maid for Kerby's Mayor Joe Hart for many years. She helped bring up the five Hart boys. Since the Harts didn't have any girls, the Hart household was always filled with lots of boys, and Mamie Mae doted on every one of them. Those boys really loved her; and even the very rowdiest of them let Ms. Mamie Mae boss them around, and they would even listen to her talk to them about Jesus.

Emmit Moore was one of those boys that hang out at the Hart's house when he was young, but he quit going there after he went off to college and he started drinking. In his junior year, he dropped out of college and soon became a low- down drunkard. Yeah, he was a miserable wreck, and that's the way Mamie Mae found him one day. He was sitting propped up against a park tree, his shaggy head drooped upon a grimy shirt that was crusty with dried puke.

Mamie Mae, dressed in the typical starched white dress she always wore, sat on a park bench near Emmit; took her frayed

Bible from her big brown purse; and began reading and praying, ever watching the drunk man. At dusk, when he awoke, Mamie Mae moved to the dazed figure, slipped right down on the grass in front of him and began talking quietly.

Startled, Emmit tried to focus his swollen eyes. When he recognized Ms. Mamie Mae, he began to sob. Yeah, he sobbed like a baby. On her knees, Ms. Mamie Mae moved with open arms to hold Emmit close for a long time. With tears running down her black cheeks, Ms. Mamie Mae hugged Emmit and began telling him how much she loved him and how much more God loved him and that Jesus could save him from his drinking problem.

"Oh, Ms. Mamie Mae, you're wrong," Emmit protested. "Look at me. I'm a filthy, no-good (he started to say the SOB words but clamped his hand over his mouth) no-good rascal. Excuse me, Ms. Mamie Mae. Just look at me! God could never love me."

"Don't you tell me what God can and can't do, Emmit Moore. You listen to what the Good Book says," and then she opened her Bible to just the right place and preached him a sermon. To make this story short, in no time, she had him on his knees, crying out to the Lord. When he left that park, he left a different man. Yes, sir. He straightened up, opened a business, and a year later built a home here in Koota Town. The rest is history. He's the most Godly man in our city."

Now, having talked about Emmit, I must warn you I'm getting ready to go from the sublime to the ridiculous. I want to tell you about Isaiah Isenberg. Something happened on the Isenberg property that everybody talks about.

First of all, we sold Farmer Isenberg our biggest mass of land, a seven-acre plot located on the very edge of our property. We knew he wanted to raise livestock; and to protect our other land owners, we were attempting to keep the farm yard stench as far away as possible.

Now, Isaiah could raise the biggest hogs, cows, horses, goats, and every kind of fowl anybody ever saw. We told him he ought to charge admission to all the folks who liked to go to his place just to gawk at his livestock.

There are a lot of tales about his place, but I want to share with you one true, funny story about his mule, Kicko.

First, I'll tell you how Kicko got that name. It started before he was born. Farmer Isenberg noted something eerie when his mare's belly suddenly poked out at places, causing the distressed, pregnant animal to rise up on her hind legs and let out a whinny that sent goose bumps down Farmer Isenberg's back. It was as though something was trying to poke its way out of the poor mare's insides. Isenberg called in resident Vet Foil. When the Doc Foil could get close to that frantic mare, he felt and rubbed and felt and rubbed. Sometimes he jumped back when a sudden jolt knocked his hand away.

Now, that went on until the day that ornery mule was born. It was a horrible delivery with that poor mare pushing and groaning, and that blasted long-legged mule kicking its way out.

A sticky red mess, tired Vet Foil grumbled, "Name this cantankerous animal 'Kicko' 'cause I've never seen anything like this birth before. There's something terribly wrong."

And he was right. That mule was different from the time its feet hit the ground. Those two back legs hiked up and gave a powerful punch every now and then. The mare had a hard time feeding him. The older the mule got, the more the annoying kicking isolated him. When all the horses and mules rested under the big oak trees, Farmer Isenberg had to find a shady spot for Kicko to be by himself, and you could always tell where

Kicko had been stationed because of an unsightly upheaval of red dirt.

Finally, Vet Foil declared that he had googled and checked things out. He was determined that Kicko's behavior would be qualified as a new Kicko Kicking Syndrome. He filled out the paper work and mailed it to the right people. Word spread and everybody came to see the kicking mule with a phenomenal kicking habit.

The farmer bragged that Kicko's syndrome had made a big impact. His mule was being recognized nationally. Now, I don't know whether it was that constant bragging or the aggravation of the many curiosity seekers; but one day, that mule got good and mad and took revenge. He edged up close to the yakking farmer, raised his hind legs, and banged both feet on his owner's behind. Of course, none of us ever saw the result of that kick because we never saw Farmer Isenberg naked; but our doctor swears that Isenberg has a purple imprint of the mule's hoofs, one on each buttock. The standard joke is that Vet Foil's diagnosis was right: Kicko did make a real impact. Farmer Isenberg's butts bear indelible proof.

At night, sometimes we gather under the street lamp at the end of Main Street. We've built us a little stage there with benches in a semi-circle. There's one chair up front; and anyone who has a story to tell takes that place. Once in a while, we shed tears, but most of the time, we laugh until we cry.

Some people have told us we should get a patent, a copyright, or something so that we could build Koota Towns all over the United States. We're looking into that. One of our residents used to study law, you know.

LET ME OUTTA HERE

For the past several months, my existence has been terribly humdrum.

Perhaps, I should not complain. I have a warm place, suitable nourishment, and constant security. Why should I fret about a simple thing like not being able to make menu decisions? How can I expect anyone to be concerned that onions do not agree with my system, that pizzas make me burp, or that I like cold foods rather than hot, and I hate caffeine?

I resent being confined in such a small area. I regret there is little I can do for exercise. I can do simple stretches but cannot perform a simple jumping jack or make a cartwheel. I loathe these rigid restrictions. Oh, how I long to break loose!

My greatest "beef," however, stems from the lack of light. The darkness of this place smothers me. Once, from a muffled discussion, I overheard someone talking about "light at the end of the tunnel." In my situation, I do not know what that particular light means, but I surely hope to see a tunnel that leads out of here - and soon.

I have tried to inform my doctor how I feel; but, unfortunately, he has paid no attention. Neither has my mother even though I nag at her all the time.

I wish these two grown, seemingly intelligent, people, would check their calendars. Surely, they would see I'm already two weeks overdue; and, drat it, I want outta here. I want to be born. Not tomorrow! Now!

FAT AND LIKING IT

Tillie Tillman smiled at herself in the mirror. She was fat. Yes, she was quite fat, but she did not care. Most of her life she had spent being skinny, yes, very skinny, even gaunt. She had been trotted by doting parents from one doctor to another, vitaminized, Ovalteen-ized, force fed, and stuffed: all to no avail.

What the medical profession and her anxious parents could not do, Nature had now supplied with a delightful "middle-age" spread. She was plump, plump, and in her eyes, "pleasingly plump."

Tillie could remember when she could wrap her hand around her upper arm and overlap her four fingers across her thumb. She pushed up her sleeve and placed her hand in the same spot, but now her fingers extended over a wonderful mound of flesh, circling only half way around.

She turned her body and grinned at her reflection. She was no longer flat chested and she even had bulging hips and a sassy derriere.

She liked what she saw. "Oh, yeah," she said aloud. "I've got lots of fat, and I love every ounce of it!"

KID'S STUFF

YOUNG LOVE

Eleventh grader Eric Richardson tried to pull his long legs inward when he saw so-called "Bungling Bill," stumbling down the aisle. In true form, "Bungling" stomped Eric's toe and grumbled, "Getcha size 13 outta the way, Richardson!"

"I'm sorry," Eric mumbled and turned his head. He had been deep in thought. This was his favorite class, not because he liked Algebra, nor because Mr. Hendrix was his favorite teacher. No, this was his favorite class because Angela Adams sat in the row to his left, two seats up from him; and he could watch her for a whole hour each day.

Eric Richardson already knew what he wanted to do in life. He aspired to be a journalist. He planned to enroll in the School of Journalism at the University of North Carolina. Yes, he wanted to be a writer; and on this day, he had been studying Angela's head for five minutes, trying to find words to describe her hair's curly strands. Angela's hair was not a solid-colored blonde, like a blonde that came from a bleach bottle, he reasoned. No, Angela's hair had a mixture of wheat-hued and spun-golden streaks. He smiled at his wording and promised himself to try again, maybe when the sun was not filtering through the blinds and playing tricks upon her head.

At that moment, his idol shifted in her seat and glanced over her shoulder. Their eyes met momentarily, but Eric felt they held for five minutes. His heart jumped. He could not breathe. Angela smiled, then demurely turned away.

Once again, he tried to pull his huge tennis shoes completely under his seat. He had to do something about those ratty shoes, he thought, comparing his appearance with that of Angela, the very personification of neatness. He heard his teacher talking and suddenly wondered if he could ever pass any subject with Angela, beautiful Angela, sitting within his view. He tried to concentrate, reminding himself that, as usual, he would, at least, manage to go through the door just as Angela did after the dismissal bell. Sometimes, he had accidentally brushed her arm as they exited.

That evening he placed newspapers on the counter in the kitchen while his mother prepared supper. As he started polishing his brown loafers, he said, "Mom, I think I'll wear these shoes to school for a while. I think they might look neater than my tennis shoes, don't you?"

Mrs. Richardson placed a pan of biscuits in the oven. She smiled and replied," Yes, Eric, they will be an improvement, and I must say I like the way you have been wearing your hair lately."

Eric looked a little embarrassed. "Oh, yeah, I got tired of the crew cut."

His mother came to stand opposite him at the counter. There was a twinkle in her eyes as she said, "Okay, Eric, are you going to tell me who she is?"

Embarrassed again, Eric asked, "What are you talking about?"

Mrs. Richardson laughed. "Eric, you forget you had an older brother. I've seen this happen before. Josh started polishing his shoes and styling his hair the first time he fell in love. I know all the signs; so, if you want to tell me, I would like to know all about her."

Relieved that he now had someone to tell, Eric pushed the shoes aside and leaned on the counter and started talking. "Mom, her name is Angela Adams. Isn't that a wonderful name? Yeah, her name is Angela and, Mom, she is the prettiest girl I've ever seen. She has long, silky blonde hair that glistens. I wanted to tell you about her sooner, but I didn't want Sue to know. You know how it is. Sis is at that bratty age, and I was afraid she might run her mouth or do something stupid."

Ten-year-old Sue had come into the dining room just before this conversation started. She had crouched down near the door and listened whenever her mother started her teasing questions.

And now, she arose, slipped from the room, and hurried upstairs. "So, he considers me to be bratty, huh?" she fumed. "I'll show him. I will." She flung herself on the bed and began considering a way to get even. Her big brother sometimes had a way of putting her down; and this time, she was determined he would pay for his remarks.

Downstairs, Eric continued his report to his mother, who smiled encouragingly and nodded approval. "Oh, yeah, Mom, and you will like this. Angela is a Christian. She goes to that big church on Midway Avenue. And did you know, Mom, all the teens from her church carry their Bibles to school. How 'bout that?"

~ ~ ~

It was not until Sue was brushing her teeth at bedtime that suddenly she remembered something. There was a boy named Andrew Adams in her homeroom. Was it possible that Andrew Adams could be Angela Adam's brother? Tomorrow she would find out. Maybe, if Angela was Andrew's big sister, Andrew might have a reason to want to get even with her. Maybe, together, she and Andrew could plot something. She went to sleep quickly with a devious plan in mind.

Sue hurried to her homeroom to note when Andrew Adams went to the pencil sharpener. She planned to talk with him there. She watched him unloading some things from his book bag. Perhaps he was not Angela's brother, she thought with a sigh. Her brother had spoken about Angela's blonde hair, and Andrew Adams had the blackest hair of anyone she knew. In fact, his hair was so black that earlier that year some boy had joked, "Andrew, your hair is as black as the Ace of Spades." Some of the boys had laughed and, from that time on, had called him "Ace." Once, the teacher even used his nickname.

The next morning Sue hurried to her homeroom to note when Andrew Adams arrived. She timed it so that she stood in line behind him at the pencil sharpener. "Ace," she said rather shyly, "Do you happen to have a sister named Angela?"

Surprised to hear a girl call him Ace, he turned with a quizzical expression, "Yes. She's in the eleventh grade. Do you know her?"

"Not exactly," Sue replied, "but she knows someone I know."

"Oh," Ace said and sharpened a second pencil.

It was her time to sharpen her pencils, but Sue bypassed the sharpener. Her teacher had a rule that all pencils had to be sharpened before the tardy bell. Sue now reasoned she could manage with what she had. For the moment, she wanted to talk with Ace Adams.

"Ace," she said, causing him to stop and look at her. "I would like to talk with you about something."

"Yes?" he said.

"First, is your sister named Angela?" When he nodded, she said, "Do you get along with your sister? I mean, has she ever caused you trouble so that you would like to play a little joke on her?" She hurried on, "You see, I have a big brother that I need to get even with, and I was wondering if you would like to help me. My brother and your sister are kinda liking each other."

Ace grinned. "Really? So, that is why my sister has been acting so strangely lately. You think, my sister and your brother really have a thing going?" He studied her face as she nodded her head.

"Okay. Okay. Let me think about it and I'll talk with you later," he said.

The next morning, Ace walked over to Sue's desk. "I've been thinking about your idea. Last week I begged Angela not to tell Dad that I got in trouble for skipping a class; but she told him anyway, and I was grounded for two weeks. I need to pay her back big time."

"Good," Sue said happily. "We will need to share information so that we can plan something." Ace agreed; and so, the planning began. Both tried to get to school earlier and to spend time plotting. At first, when Ace had a clever idea, Sue giggled, and Ace experienced an uneasy feeling. He had been "anti" girl for a good while, and often he had heard Sue's laughter and had grimaced. He had to admit that now, however, her giggle was almost melodic; and every time he heard it, he felt like smiling. Heretofore, he had considered giggling to be such a silly, girl thing, but lately he had noted Sue's giggle usually came because of something he had said. Strange, but her giggling response pleasantly registered as whole-hearted approval. He liked that giggle. He was aware that he looked forward to their scheming minutes spent together.

At last, their first plan was ready to be executed. At the

dinner table Ace was supposed to laugh and tell the family about an eleventh grader named Eric. He would say everyone was talking about him. He would explain that this guy's feet had a horrible, unbearable odor. His poor parents had tried everything. As a last resort, they had taken Eric's tennis shoes away and were making him wear loafers. Each night they fumigated the shoes and washed his socks in a special deodorant.

In her home, Sue would bring up something strange about an eleventh-grade girl named Angela Adams. She would say everyone was talking about it. This girl is a "neatness freak." She is obsessed with everything being perfect. She is running her family crazy with straightening pictures on the wall, re-arranging furniture, and restacking dishes. Her parents are considering taking her to a psychiatrist. And, of course, as she talked, Sue would mention Angela's name often.

The plan was an absolute success. The next day, Ace and Sue laughed heartily as they shared their table conversations and the shocked reaction of their older brother and sister. Then, they began to plan another attack.

For his sister's benefit, Ace once again was supposed to give a report about the eleventh- grade guy who was causing such a disturbance in his home. Not only did this guy have stinky feet, he had the worst table manners in the world. His family could not eat at the table with him. He chomped, and slobbered, and gulped until they could no longer stand it. He had to eat in a room alone.

Ace's parents were appalled at their son's talk and reprimanded him for passing along such terrible gossip. Ace pretended to be repentant, but inwardly he congratulated himself.

In Sue's home, the conversation ran once again to the

unusual girl in the eleventh grade. According to Sue, today everyone had been talking about Angela Adams' obsession of bathing over and over and over. Sometimes she took six showers in one day and washed her hands at least one hundred times.

Mrs. Richardson had stopped Sue in midsentence and had demanded that she no longer repeat anything she had heard anyone say.

It had taken only two plots for Ace and Sue to see a change in their older siblings. Angela had stopped singing and flitting around the house. Eric had stopped wearing his polished loafers and had almost shaved his hair. Both were sullen and, seemingly, unhappy.

Ace and Sue were surprised that they did not delight in what they had caused. Their plans had worked and had worked quickly, but their victory was not what they had expected. They had already formulated another attack; but for some reason, they were reluctant to proceed.

Ace said somberly, "You know, Sue, somehow I don't feel good about what we've done. We accomplished what we set out to accomplish, but I don't feel right. I guess it's because I'm a Christian."

He did not need to say more. He had put into words what Sue was thinking. There was no light-hearted giggling now. Instead, tears wet her long lashes and she turned away.

She blinked, wiped her cheeks and turned again. "We have made a mess. Now, we must find a way to straighten things out," she said.

They worked out a new plan. Sue would ask her big brother to meet her after school at the stone wall surrounding the left side of the school campus. Ace would ask his sister to meet him at the same place. They would insist that it was urgent because they needed help. Sue and Ace knew their older brother and sister would come.

The two fifth graders arrived at the wall meeting place early by racing to the spot as soon as the dismissal bell rang, thankful that the middle school classes were dismissed 15 minutes earlier than the high school classes.

The two schemers sat on the stone wall, miserably quiet, waiting for Eric and Angela. They heard the high school bell; and Ace said grimly, "It won't be long now."

He was right. Almost immediately, they saw Eric running over the grassy hill; and at the same time, Angela coming down the sidewalk. The two upperclassmen looked at each other in wonder as they approached their kid brother and sister.

Ace and Sue slipped down from their seats on the wall. They stood with their heads lowered, not able to look at Eric and Angela. Ace began the explanation. His voice sounded low and quivery. Sue cut in to explain it was her awful idea. She had asked Ace for help. Then, the whole ugly plan tumbled out.

For a few moments, Eric and Angela stood in mute astonishment. As soon as the plan and the results fell together in their minds, they felt so very relieved that, at the same time, they began to laugh. The two younger siblings lifted their eyes in amazement. Eric and Angela were laughing; and yet, they had just been told such a terrible thing. How could they laugh?

Eric pulled his little sister into his arms. "Sue, you are such a brat; but I'll have to admit, you're a smart brat. You really pulled this thing off. I'm angry at you, and we will have to take care of this later; but, at least, you have tried to make things right."

Angela touched Ace's arm to make similar remarks and then looked up at Eric to say, "Eric, let's leave these two conniving rascals and go to McDonald's. I need some French fries." She made light talk, for she was afraid she was going to cry. She did not know whether it was because she was angry or because she was glad things could once again be right for Eric and her.

The ten-year olds sat quietly upon the wall as they watched Eric and Angela walking away with Eric carrying both book bags.

At last, Ace spoke. "You know, my dad always says, 'When you have a lemon, you can choose to hate the sour taste, or you can choose to make lemonade.' Now, you and I have made a real mess. We have a big lemon, but I do see some way to make lemonade."

He slipped down from his seat and stood looking at Sue. "At least, you and I have had a chance to get to know each other, and I like that. I even like to hear you giggle; and…and I don't know whether I should say this, but I think you are the prettiest girl in the fifth grade. I hope after all of this, we'll be friends. Friends forever."

Sue smiled sweetly, "Friends forever. I would like that. You know, Ace, I like the way your dad has taught you to handle sour lemons." She paused and slightly blushed. Her blue eyes sparkled. "And, Ace," she said with a soft giggle, "I really like the way you make lemonade. I really do."

KATHARINE'S CHANCE

Katharine Klee Kayton. What a beautiful name. How easy it conformed to perfect penmanship. Katharine wrote the three words again, noting the three lovely K's and the easy flow of the other letters. Unlike some of her teenage friends who claimed to hate their names, Katharine had always loved hers. She liked the Katharine she got from her grandmother and the Klee that came from a distant aunt. And, of course, she liked being a Kayton, for the Kaytons had been respectable citizens of Greenville for years. Yes, Katharine Klee Kayton liked her name. Very much.

She folded the gold-edged stationery and slipped it into the top desk drawer. From her bookbag she took out a history book and began her homework. She had read only a few pages when, little by little, she became aware of a strange glow that seemed to be filling the room like vibrating, pink and deep rose clouds. Startled, she lowered the book and glanced around. A soft, but radiant light encased the entire room, encased her. She looked down at her blouse and shoe strings that had become a bright, glowing white. Lifting her eyes, she stared at the center of the room where a more dazzling mist seemed to swirl and swirl and swirl until a figure began to emerge. Katharine clasped her hands to her throat. Frightened, she gazed in awe upon the most beautiful creature she had ever seen. Surrounded by a mellow light, the petite, lady-like figure, adorned in a shimmering, gauze-like fabric, floated around the room before she finally settled on a nearby chair. Her shining cream-colored hair was bedecked with tiny yellow flowers. Her face was perfect; her complexion, flawless. When she spoke, her melodic voice was unlike any earthly sound Katharine had ever heard.

"Katharine Klee Kayton," the voice intoned like tinkling bells, "you are right; you do have a beautiful name. Now, how would you like to be far more beautiful than the name?"

Katharine did not answer the question. Instead, she whispered, "Who ...who are you?"

A smile played upon the creature's face, revealing perfect, pearl white teeth. Again, her voice floated like music from her lips. "Katharine, I am your fairy godmother, and I have come to do something for you. But first, I must see the sketches you have drawn."

Amazed that this dazzling creature knew about her artwork, Katharine did not move.

"Come, come, Katharine. Bring me your sketch books," the being said impatiently. "I know that you specialize in drawing beautiful women. Show me your latest work."

Katharine moved almost mechanically to the bookcase and took down a huge sketch pad. Timidly, she offered it to the godmother.

Like a dream, the godmother and Katharine moved to the desk where the creature opened the book. The first picture was the head of a gorgeous redhead with green eyes. No word was said, but the two studied the picture. The next page appeared, and there was a blonde with soft, curly hair. She wore a blue ruffled dress, but the creature did not seem to notice the clothing. "See how symmetrical the features are," she said.

The two eyes are identical. The nose and lips are perfect. Is she not beautiful?"

Katharine was afraid not to respond; she nodded her head. The godmother smiled as she flipped to another page. Katharine knew that the book contained only pictures of glamorous women, for she spent all her art time sketching women, trying to master the art of drawing eyes, noses, and mouths.

The new page produced an entirely different type. The girl could have been a Mexican or an Italian, for the hair was jet black and the brows and lashes thick and dark. Katharine had enhanced those dark features by using charcoal instead of pastels or colored pencils.

The godmother noted, "This young lady would never have to wear eye makeup, would she?"

Again, Katharine responded by nodding. The book contained at least 25 pages which were examined one by one with comments by the glistening creature.

At last, the creature closed the book and looked intently into Katharine's eyes. Katharine stared back, entranced by the lady's piercing gaze. She felt as though her innermost thoughts were being read.

"Katharine Klee Kayton," the brilliant being said, "I have come to you with a proposition. I have something that I can do for you. You draw beautiful women – beautiful in face and in form. I'm going to give you two weeks to study all your creations. Then I will come back to you. You'll get out a sketch pad and will draw the most beautiful girl that you can draw. I must warn you, however, you will not be able to erase or change anything you have drawn. Whenever a stroke is made, it will be permanent. You may take all the time you need to finish your work. Once you have finished your drawing, however, your part will be done. I will then perform a miracle - a permanent miracle. You will become as beautiful as the sketch! You will become the exact image of the person you have drawn. You will have the hair, eyes, nose, mouth, body, hands, and feet of the masterpiece you have created. You will no longer look like the Katharine Klee Kayton you now are."

The luminous being flitted across the room. "I leave you now. Take your time and consider how you would really like to look. Check every picture, note every feature, and make wise selections. You may be transformed into another person when I see you next."

And then, without a gradual fading away, the glittering light was instantly gone, and Katharine stood alone in a dimly-lit room. The wonderful dazzle had disappeared.

For the next few days, Katharine found it hard to think of anything other than the splendid creature and her bizarre proposition. She kept going through her sketch books and studying her best masterpieces. She tried to determine which of the ladies had the most beautiful eyes, the most perfect noses, and the most desirable lips. She studied the hair color and the styles. She noted bodies, hands, and feet.

She studied her own features. For the first time, it seemed that she was seeing herself. She squinted at the mirror. She had always thought her eyes were blue; but now, as she looked closely, she saw tiny flecks of gold radiating from the black center. Her lashes were longer on her top lids. In her paintings, she always made her women have long, rather dark lashes on both top and bottom lids.

Her nose was nothing special. It seemed ordinary. She had to admit most of her prettiest women had small, slightly turned-up noses. Only rarely did she draw a very straight nose or a nose with a hump in it. Whenever she did, she was careful to make the other features extremely outstanding.

And now, she gave special consideration to her lips, to her teeth, and to her smile.

She experienced an inner concern as she tried to determine what she wanted to change about her appearance. Would she choose bigger eyes, drooped lids, longer lashes (for sure), or would she try beautiful slanted eyes?

Would she opt for the perfect little tilted nose? Would she choose fuller or smaller lips? Would her mouth turn upward or downward? Would she add dimples?

Would she be taller or shorter? Would she choose to be thinner or plumper? Would her legs be longer or fatter? Would she trade her size seven shoe for a size six?

She doodled hundreds of features and settled upon none. When she compared her drawings with her own peculiar features, she could not understand; but, seemingly, she could not bring herself to make a trade.

The first week flew by and the second was almost gone; and yet, she had not reached a decision. She did not want to forfeit such a wonderful opportunity, but she could not make up her mind.

Once she examined her own eyes again and said to herself, "I really like my eyes all right. God gave them to me." At times, she felt the same way about her nose, her lips, and her smile. She kept coming to the same conclusion: "This is the way God made me. Why do I need to change?"

As the last few days sped by, the same thought troubled her as she studied and assessed her prized drawings and frequently looked at herself, sometimes in a hand-held mirror and sometimes in a full-length mirror.

The day before her visitor was to return, Katharine made her decision. She packed up all her sketch books and placed them neatly on a shelf. She peacefully awaited the godmother's return.

She knew exactly what she would say. "Thank you, Beautiful Being. Thank you for your offer, but I have decided I like myself just as I am. I'm sure I could draw someone far more glamorous than I am. I'm sure I might enjoy looking different, but the truth is: I want to remain Katharine Klee Kayton, just as God made me. I do hope you understand." She would curtsey to show her respect.

The brilliant creature, however, did not reappear as she had promised. Katharine waited day by day. She spent much time at her desk, waiting for the swirling lights and the majestic appearance, but her wait was in vain. At length, Katharine wondered if the vision had only been a dream. Had the Being been only a figment of her imagination? Had the godmother really existed?

One thing, however, erased her doubts. On her pillow one evening she found a silver-edged piece of stationery with a beautifully penned message written in silver glitter. It read, "Katharine Klee Kayton, you have made a wise decision. You have chosen to love yourself as you are. Because of your contentment and your sense of self- worth, you will live a happy, successful life. I am proud of you. You will bless others."

Katharine blinked back tears; and, glancing around the room, whispered, "Thank you. I shall really try." She tucked the silver-edged note into her desk drawer next to a strange, glittering silver-writing pen. She whispered, "Thank you again, Fairy Godmother. I will keep this note as a reminder. I not only like my name, but I'm, also, happy being the person I am. God made me this way."

FEAR WORKS

Boy Jay gulped down the wiggly, slippery worm his mother had dropped into his gaping mouth. He smacked his tiny beaks, trying to eat slowly, oh so very slowly, hoping to delay what he knew was about to happen.

"Boy Jay, look around you," his mother scolded. "Your brothers and sisters are gone. You are the only one left. Now, Boy Jay, it's time. You must leave the nest!"

"I can't," Boy Jay squeaked, hunkering down into his safe place. "I can't, Mama Jay. I have height-a-phobia."

"Nonsense. Where did you ever hear such a thing?"

Boy Jay thought fast. "A little worm told me," he whispered, trying to explain. "And besides, I've looked down."

Stretching out his skinny legs, he whimpered, "Mama Jay, look at my tiny legs. Down below, I've seen tall things with two long legs and big feet, pecking the ground. Always pecking the ground. Maybe, they might peck me. And that's not all. I've seen four-legged things a lot bigger than I am."

Mama Jay scooted down into the nest and, using her strong wings, pushed Boy Jay upward. When his head reached the nest's rim, she said, "Put your fears aside! Now, Boy Jay, you watch me. I'm going to show you how it's done."

She flapped her wings and soared peacefully through the sky, returning to swoop down on the grass beneath the tree.

Suddenly, a four-legged creature sprang from the bushes and swatted angrily, barely missing Mama Jay.

In a second, Mama Jay soared upward and plopped down deep into the nest, her heart beating wildly.

"See, Mama Jay, it's dangerous down there," Boy Jay said, "but we're safe up here. Come and cuddle with me."

It was then that Mama Jay heard a scratch, scratch, scratch. She edged upward and screamed, "Boy Jay, the THING, the THING! It's climbing our tree. Oh my, it's coming out on our limb! Oh, Boy Jay, it's now or never! You've got to fly!"

Boy Jay peered over the nest, horrified to see two glinting, yellow eyes, long whiskers, and a mouth like nothing he'd ever seen before.

"Fly, Boy Jay! Fly," Mama Jay screeched as she flew upward. "Fly!"

And fly Boy Jay did! And fly he did!

WINK'S NEEDED FRIEND

Wink Wagner slumped in his porch swing, slowly pushing himself back and forth with the tiptoes of scuffed tennis shoes.

"Wink?" Wink Wagner. Few people knew Wink's real name was Winifred Warren Wagner, a very dignified name, a name befitting the President of the United States. The insignificant "Wink" was bequeathed to him by his doting grandfather who taught him to wink his right eye before he could talk. At first, only the family adopted the name; then the neighbors; and by the time he entered school, even his records accepted him as Wink Wagner.

Today Wink was glum. Horace had gone away and Wink was lonesome.

"Horace," he grumbled to himself. "Why did you have to be gone? I get in trouble when I'm not with you. That's what my mother says."

Already Wink had had one dilemma. It had happened at breakfast. He had to admit, though, that Horace could not have helped that. Wink had spied a can of, what he assumed, was whipped cream. The can was blue just like the can in the refrigerator. He looked at the stack of golden pancakes on his plate and suddenly thought of the specialty he once had at a pancake house in Pigeon Forge, Tennessee. Those pancakes had been topped with peaches and a mammoth glob of whipped cream. They were great! He had cleaned his plate that day with no coaxing from anyone.

And so, he shook the can vigorously and sprayed a mountain of snowy white on his pancakes. He dug in and quickly crammed into his mouth a heaping fork filled with pancakes, Maple Syrup, and frosty cream; but, to his dismay, the taste was horrible. Covering his mouth, he raced to the bath room to spit out the awful concoction and gag. After rinsing his mouth, he returned to the table and, embarrassed, read the wording on the blue can of his dad's SHAVING CREAM! His dad had left it on the counter when he returned from shaving.

His mother had tried to pretend that it was a natural mistake, but he noticed that she held her apron up to her mouth so that he could not see her laughing. She would probably tell his daddy and the two of them would laugh when he was not looking.

Wink slid from the swing and ambled across the yard to the fence that separated his big yard from the neighbor's big yard. He looked to the right and to the left, but all he could see was the neighbor's house and a lot of rolling green land.

"Horace, when will you be back?" he asked, glancing around one more time. He trudged back home.

Seated on the porch, suddenly Wink had an inspiration. He would go gather eggs for his mother. That would be helpful. He surely did not need Horace to help gather eggs. He ran around the house and took an egg basket from the back porch. Once in the hen house, he poked into the straw nests, surprised that all nests were empty, except for one. He could not check that one, for a big brown hen huddled there, covering the whole space.

"Move," Wink said, but the fat hen clucked angrily at him and seated herself more firmly. When she changed her position, however, Wink spied some eggs beneath her.

"You selfish chicken!" Wink scolded. "I bet you hid those

eggs from my mother this morning. Now, you get up and I mean it!" Taking a broom from the corner, he swung it over the hen's head, being careful not to hit her. Frightened, the ruffled hen squawked, flew down from her perch, and scurried out the door.

Wink was proud when he entered the kitchen, eager to show his mother his collection. He was surprised, however, at the look that came to her face when she saw the eggs.

"Where did you get those eggs, Wink?" she asked with a troubled voice.

"In the henhouse. I bet mean ole Ms. Henny was hiding them from you this morning."

Mrs. Wagner was about to explain when, suddenly, a shell made a clicking sound; and from a cracked shell, something seemed to be trying to get out."

"Look, Mommy," Wink said, "There's something in that egg!"

"Yes, yes, yes," Mrs. Wagner said, gently scooping up the basket of eggs and hurrying toward the henhouse. Wink followed, taking two or three steps to his mother's one.

"Wink, the hen was sitting on these eggs to hatch some biddies. I had not told you, for I wanted it to be a surprise. Now these little ones will need their mother. One is already on the way.'

"Wow!" Wink shouted. "We're gonna have chicks. Horace will love that!"

"I am sure he will," Mrs. Wagner said as she carefully placed the eggs in the nest. Now, let's stand back so that the mother hen can come to her eggs."

It seemed that immediately there was a rustle of wings and the brown hen flew upward and seated herself dutifully upon her eggs.

Resting on the front door steps, Wink frowned, trying to think of something to do to pass time. Again, he walked to the fence. He kicked one of the newly painted white slats. It was then that an idea came. His daddy had built this picket fence just to make their yard pretty. Yet, he had made a mistake: he had painted all the slats white. Wink thought of the red paint they had used to paint the barn and blue paint they had used to paint the shutters. He knew where the leftover paint was stored. He envisioned how pretty it would be if he painted the slats in a red, white, and blue order. He was so delighted with his idea that he raced back to the swing. He sat and looked at the white fence. How much better it would look after he finished his painting. When his mother took her afternoon nap, he would get started. He could hardly wait.

His planning was interrupted, however, when his mother opened the screen door and said, "Wink, I'm getting ready to pack a good lunch for your daddy. I wonder if you might like to take it to him. He's working in the lowest meadow and wants to work until sundown".

"Sure, Mommy, I'll do that," Wink said, eager to pass the morning. He could hardly wait for his mother's nap time.

"I'll call you when I'm ready," Mrs. Wagner said, wiping her hands on a damp paper towel.

In the kitchen, Mrs. Wagner busied herself, getting together Mr. Wagner's favorite lunch foods. She opened two cans of sardines, placed them in a plastic container, and sprinkled the little fish with vinegar. She fastened a plastic top over the container and set it aside. Next, she placed several crackers in a sandwich bag. From the refrigerator, she took two boiled eggs which she peeled and salted. These she put in a container. She filled another container with cherry JELL-O, put a dab of whipped cream on top, and fastened a plastic lid. Almost as an afterthought, she took two Hershey candy bars and added them to the collection. She smiled with satisfaction as she carefully packed everything into a huge brown paper bag. Folding down the top, she called Wink.

Wink darted into the kitchen, ready for his assignment. At last, he had something to do. He listened impatiently to his mother's last- minute instructions. He wanted to get started. He grabbed the big sack and was surprised at its weight. As he walked to the back porch, he thought of the distance to the lower field and was sorry that the bag was heavy and hard to carry. It was then an idea dawned. He set the lunch down and raced upstairs to his bedroom. In minutes, he returned with his empty backpack. Strangely, he had trouble getting the big lunch sack to fit into his backpack. The lunch should fit, he reasoned. From his backpack, he had just removed four big books, a sweater, a pair of tennis shoes, some baseball cards, and a softball. Yet, it took a lot of cramming and pushing to get everything moved around so that the lunch would squeeze into place. He paid no attention to popping and snapping sounds made as he endeavored to crush the brown sack enough so that he could, at last, fasten the Velcro flap.

He hoisted the bag to his back and was on his way. As he walked, skipped, or jogged, he thought of the pond. While his daddy was eating, he could skip stones across the top of the water. With that thought in mind, now and then he stooped to pick up a smooth stone to shove into his pockets. Each time he bent over, he heard strange noises in his backpack and once he thought he noticed a faint, but strange odor.

"Mommy must have fixed Daddy something very different today. I wonder what it is."

Mr. Wagner, who had already seated himself under a towering Oak, wiped the sweat from his brow and called out a greeting as Wink bounded into view.

"Hi, Daddy," Wink shouted, freeing himself from the

backpack as he raced to the tree. "I brought your lunch. I got me some stones, too, and I'm going down to the pond while you eat. Okay?" He did not wait for an answer, but he heard his dad call, "Be careful."

"He always says, 'Be careful,' and I've only fallen in twice," Wink thought as he neared the pond. "Parents surely worry a lot."

Mr. Wagner had difficulty getting to his lunch, for part of the soggy paper sack was wedged into some open containers. When he finally made an opening, he stared at a red-stained paper bag reeking with a strange mixture of fish, vinegar, boiled eggs, and JELL-O. What he saw and smelled made his stomach churn. He closed the reeking backpack immediately and hurried to the truck where he placed the awful mess out of sight.

He walked down to the pond just in time to grab Wink as he started sliding down the embankment to the water.

"Hey, hold it, Son," he yelled as he pulled Wink back.

"Wow. It's a good thing you came along," Wink said. "I threw that last stone so hard that I almost lost my balance. But it bounced just right! Did you see it, Daddy?"

"No, but I'll take your word for it. Say, Son, I need to go to the house for a little while. Can you leave now?"

"Yes, sir," Wink said. "I have something to do this afternoon."

Wink did not notice the backpack pushed into a corner of the truck. He was too excited to be seated in the big truck beside his father. "May I steer?" he asked, scooting over to Mr. Wagner.

"Yes, I think you might do that. You are getting to be a big boy now, aren't you?" his father said with a forced smile.

When they rolled into the back yard, Wink leaped from the

161

truck and ran around the house. "I'll be back," he said. "I'm going to see if Horace has come home."

Mr. Wagner was glad that Wink did not enter the house with him, for these few minutes gave him time to sneak the backpack to Mrs. Wagner and to whisper what had happened.

Mrs. Wagner stored the soiled backpack under the sink and promised to fix another lunch. "While you eat, she said, making a sandwich, "I'll take Wink down to see the chicks. That should keep him busy until you finish your meal."

Mr. Wagner walked down the hallway and went out to the front porch. He found Wink sitting on the top step with his head on his knees. Quietly, Mr. Wagner sat down and pulled his son over to cradle him against his chest. "Say, Son," he said, "your mother is going down to check on the chicks and she wanted to see if you would like to go with her."

As though his father had said some magic word, Wink blinked away tears and jumped to his feet. He might have lost his balance again had not his father grabbed him.

"Hold it just a minute," his father said, hoping he had given his wife enough time to make his second lunch. "Son, why don't you run around the house and be waiting on the back steps, as a surprise, for your mother when she comes out?" he said in a secretive whisper. Wink liked the idea and was off before his father could stand. Mr. Wagner shook his head and smiled.

Mrs. Wagner pretended to be surprised when she opened the screen door and saw Wink waiting for her. "Oh, Wink, how glad I am that you are here. I'm going to check on our chicks, and I would like to have someone go with me."

He skipped by her side as they made their way to the chicken coup. "Mommy, I'm lonesome when Horace is away," he muttered.

"I know," Mrs. Wagner said. "I think maybe you need someone else to play with."

"But we live away off from almost everybody," Wink said. "How could I?"

Mrs. Wagner said, "Wink, do you know this song we sing at church?" She started singing, "What a Friend We Have in Jesus."

"Jesus can be your friend," she said, "and He can be with you at all times."

"But I can't see him and talk with him, and he can't help me stay out of trouble the way Horace does."

"Oh, but he can," Mrs. Wagner said. "You can talk with him as easily as you talk with me or with Horace."

"Just the way I talk with Horace?" Wink asked in amazement.

"Yes, but maybe a little differently. You would want to show God reverential respect. For instance, you would want to speak to him as Lord Jesus or as Dear Jesus, but then you could talk with Him just the way you talk with any friend."

"Really?" Wink said as he considered this thought. Even as he and his mother played with the fuzzy little chicks, Wink seemed to be thinking about something else. He was glad when his mother was ready to leave.

"Mommy," he said, "I'll meet you at the house. I need to go out by the barn for a few minutes. I want to see if I can talk with Jesus - you know, the Lord Jesus."

"That's fine. You go," Mrs. Wagner said, giving him a gentle pat on the back.

She smiled as she heard him talking as he rounded the barn. He was explaining how he didn't always know what was right to do and he was complaining that Horace was often away.

"I really need Horace to come home or to get a new friend," he said.

Mrs. Wagner was seated at the table with Mr. Wagner, drinking a glass of tea when from the front lawn, they heard Wink's joyful cry. "Horace! Horace, you're back! You're back! Mommy! Daddy!" he yelled. "Horace has come home! I talked to Jesus....the Lord Jesus; and, Mom, you were right. Jesus heard me. He answered my prayer. He sent Horace back home."

The two parents hurried down the hallway to look out the front door. The father drew his wife close to his side as she placed her hands over her mouth and sighed. Both rejoiced, happy to see Wink laughing, hooping, and racing around the yard with his beloved Beagle Horace yapping at his heels. Mr. and Mrs. Wagner were, also, glad Horace was home.

THE FROG THAT
COULDN'T SAY, "NO"

Jig lay stretched upon a huge lily pad, enjoying the sun. Suddenly, a loud plop - plop jarred him from his dreams. He stared as a plump little frog headed his way.

"Hi, Jig," plump little Bobo croaked. "Say, the water is fine. Come on in! Come, come, come."

Jig wanted to say, "No." He liked what he was doing, but Bobo insisted. Finally, Jig slid off into the water. He tried to pretend that he was having fun. Splash—splash—splash he went, but he missed his sunny spot on the lily pad.

At last, plump little Bobo went away and Jig returned to his resting place, but it was no longer the same. The sun had disappeared. The water felt cold.

Jig decided to go home. Perhaps his mother had prepared something good to eat. He hopped along the bank. Near an old stump, he saw three of his pals.

"Come and chat with us," the three pleaded.

Jig didn't want to chat. He was hungry He wanted to go home, but he could not say, "No."

He stopped and chatted and chatted and chatted. At last, he said, "I'm sorry but I must go."

It was dark, dark, dark when he arrived at home.

"Oh, Jig," his mother said. "I had the best meal prepared for you, but it was late and I thought you must be eating with your grandmother. It was so very late. I allowed Floppy, Moppy, and Poppy to eat the last bit."

Jig hopped quietly onto the porch. He felt sorry for himself. He wanted to cry. That was when little Dingo came along. Little Dingo looked excited. "I'm running away from home," he said. Please come with me, Jig. We'll have fun."

Jig wanted to say, "No, no, no" but he could not. Reluctantly, he hopped away with Little Dingo.

They had traveled a long time. The land looked strange. The noises were strange. Jig heard a thud—thud—thud that he had not heard near his home pond. Suddenly, a long stick stuck into the mud right beside his body. He sprang to another spot. Another stick followed. Jig realized something was trying to get him. Poor Jig. He did not know that there were PEOPLE.

He did not know that some people thought frog legs made food.... good food.) Jig wanted to be in his safe home. He turned and began hopping and hopping and hopping.

Little Dingo yelled, "Jig, come back! Stay with me!"

"No," Jig answered. "No! No! No!" he kept saying to himself. "No! No!

"No!" He liked the sound of the word. For the first time, he had learned that sometimes it is a good thing to say, "No."

"No, no, no." he croaked happily each time he leaped. "No, no, no," he sang all the way home.

SAY NO

To a good Mommy
And a good Daddy
I never say, "No."
That's because
These two people
Love me so,
Love me so,
To a good teacher
And a good preacher
I never say, "No."
That's because
These kind leaders
Love me so.
Love me so.
BUT......
Whether young or old
I shall become bold
If asked to do wrong,
I'll sing this new song
It's NO, NO, NO
B e c a u s e
God's Word says so.

ILLUSTRATED....by the author's ten-year-old great granddaughter, Ava Marie Phillips.

BRIEFS

To illustrate the over-the-years' compilation of miscellaneous writings, I am including a few journal entries, essays, poems, my dad's bio, a newspaper feature, memorial service bios, and a short play.

JOURNALS

SNOW HONEYMOONING (1942)

My Air Force husband and I (to use a trite hyperbole) think we have "died and gone to heaven." We are honeymooning, 1000 miles away from home, in a whiteness we have never known.

In our North Carolina state, we've been fortunate to see one or two light snows a winter. Now, in Fort Wayne, Indiana, thick snow covers the ground practically every day. Icicles hung from eaves and trees glisten in sunlight. Nightly, icy snow crunches musically under our feet as we tread streets, awed by bright Christmas lights and gleeful carolers.

As two transplanted Southerners, we truly revel in this Northern Snow Heaven.

~ ~ ~

(THREE SHORT ENTRIES I FOUND HANDWRITTEN ON YELLOW PAD PAPER)

1. **Chester** went to Dean and Marilyn's, and for the first time, saw their miniature puppy. Being of a loving nature, little Corky went right to Pops. Later Pops said, "That dog attacked me; and if I find out she bit me, I'm going to be mad."

~ ~ ~

2. **Vince** was going to undergo oral surgery to remove an extra tooth that was coming in at the front of his mouth. Since the surgery would necessitate splitting the upper gum and removing the tooth, the dentist took time to explain the procedure to Vince. After the explanation, he asked, "Now, Vince, is there anything you would like to ask me?"

"Yes, Sir," Vince replied timidly. "How long will it be before I can eat pizza?"

~ ~ ~

3. Dated Mar. 16, 2001 (Day I received a pacemaker)

Kent, Marianne, and Vince, (9) came to see me the evening following the day I received the pacemaker for my erratic heart.

Vince came in with a dollar bill he had found in the parking lot. He pointed out to me that on the back it said, "In God We Trust."

When the three started to leave, Vince wanted to give me the dollar which, at first, I did not want to take. I consented, however, when I saw it was important to him. After he left, I noted he had propped the bill up to show the writing and to remind me: "In God We Trust."

SHORT REMEMBRANCES

It is now 2007. I tell you the date, for last week I picked up an old composition book that had been tucked away. I flipped open the pages and found short, personal stories that had been written 22 years ago. As I read them, I was mindful of convention speakers who always insisted that all writers should keep a daily journal.

I must admit keeping a journal was hit and miss for me. Now, I am mindful of the wealth of happenings I have long forgotten but could be recalled if I had taken time to write them down.

NICK AND APPLE

I smiled as a read the following account dated February, 1985

"Recently, I read a super magazine article about the great health value of the apple. Later, I was explaining to Nick, my first-grade grandson, how the apple possesses properties that purify the system, etc.

He quickly responded, "Well, that proves one thing."

'What?' I asked, interested in his observation.

"It proves," he said, "that it was not an apple God told Adam not to eat." (I had never thought about that, but Nick's proof was certainly sound.)

~ ~ ~

TYLER AND PRONUNCIATION

Another story dated **March 1, 1985**, read:

"Yesterday Dean and Marilyn made the announcement that they were going to have their fourth child. Chester and I were very happy with the news, and so were Nick and Tyler.

Before he went to bed, four-year-old Tyler asked his father, 'Did you know that Mommy is preg - geh- nant?

KENT AND HOSPITAL MISUNDERSTANDING

An April 12, 1985, entry stated:

"Last night at 1:30 Marianne call to report that Kent's nosebleed for an entire day made it necessary for him to go to the emergency room. Chester and I promised to meet them at the Medical Center to take 3-month-old Logan home with us.

As we waited inside the lobby, I asked Marianne, 'Doesn't Logan have to be fastened into his seat?' to which she replied, 'No, you can lay him on the floorboard in the back.'

Envisioning my infant grandson being placed on the floor, I said, 'If you don't mind, I'll sit on the floor and hold him.'

I thought that, in their haste, they had not been able to bring his car seat.

Then I discovered that Marianne meant that the car seat would be placed on the floorboard.

We both laughed at my misunderstanding and consternation.

I've had several, good, reflective laughs about this mix up, realizing what a picture I had conjured in my brain regarding little Logan rolling around on the floorboard."

Reading these stories jotted down in a composition notebook 22 years ago have re-enforced the fact that journal writing preserves precious memories. In 2007, I hope to try to make journaling a part of my everyday life.

THE HEART OF A GRANDSON

My grandson, eleven-year-old Vince, possesses unique qualities:

Though strongly athletic, he plays the violin.

Though witty, he displays seriousness.

Though intelligent, he shows no arrogance.

One of my son's businesses is a fireworks store which he opens only weeks prior to New Year's Eve and the Fourth of

July. Vince often clerks in the store with other family members and several teenagers.

In July, a man entered the store, wearing a t-shirt that caused quite a stir. The front of the shirt pictured a huge circle in which there was a cross. Over the cross there was a slanted line, the kind often used to say, **"NO."** Beneath the circle were the words, "False Religion."

While customers and clerks eyed the man and his shirt with sly glances of disapproval, Vince eyed differently. As the man stood in the checkout line, Vince eased up to him, placed his hand on the man's back; and looking up at him, quietly said, "Sir, I hope you change your mind about your shirt."

~ ~ ~

I FOUND THIS TRIBUTE TO MY SON WRITTEN ON A YELLOW, LEGAL PAD:

MY SON

It all started the day I pulled a robe over my still ill-shaped body and inched my way to the display window in Memorial Hospital, Smithfield, North Carolina.

Kind viewers glanced my way and allowed room for the "new mother" to move to a better viewing position.

I looked over the rows of metal bassinettes and spied your beautiful body squirming and stretching.

"That's my son!" I announced with exuberant pride.

And do you know, Son, I've been saying those proud words for years now?

"See. That's my son!"

SON,

You were such a perfect baby with big, shining eyes, soft strands of hair, and ever-moving lips.

I often made a spectacle of myself. When you did the least thing (like a gurgling proclamation or a meaningful gesture) I called in an audience and marveled., "See for yourself," I'd say, "That's my smart son."

SON,

You don't remember, but your appetite began early. I fed you and fed you and fed you. Because you were so very appreciative, I liked to watch you gulp your milk, relish you Gerber's, and skillfully smack your lips.

"See how well he eats," I'd beam. "That's my son."

SON,

Did you know you once made news when you displayed only one tooth? I called your grandparents and notified our friends. I held you up and pried your little mouth open to show to anyone ......everyone......that one beautiful tooth produced so very early in life.

SON,

You really wanted to walk long before I gave the OK. From birth, your legs pumped and pumped and pumped. Yes, you really wanted to walk before the tenth-month achievement came. I probably held you back, but you soon slipped from overly protective arms and took steps that made me so very proud.

SON,

Do you remember the plays and programs you starred in as a little boy? You were not too happy when you were asked to be a tree, a dancing box, or a talking animal, but you cooperated. And when the final day came, you outshined everyone. I'd sit among all the other doting parents and I'd proudly acknowledge,

175

"That's my son. That's my talented son. And do you know, they agreed."

SON, do you know how much I love you?

MY BELOVED CHILDREN

I was blessed to have three children – a girl and two boys. Over the years, I recorded many clever things they did or said. When they were grown, I collected all the clippings I had and gave them to each child, probably a foolish thing to do. I thought they would read them and enjoy seeing how smart, how adorable, how mischievous they were. I know they might have glanced through them but felt embarrassed to keep such recordings. They tossed them, I'm sure.

I wish I could share many more, but today I'm drawing from one account of each one.

CINDY

Tonight, when I had a bedside chat with my five-year-old daughter, I sensed that she wanted to talk with me about Jesus. After I had explained the gospel to her, she told me she wanted to let Jesus come into her heart. We prayed together and she cried as she asked the Lord to be her Savior.

When her dad came in later, I told him what Cindy had done, and he went immediately to her bedroom. She was still crying as she told him what had happened.

She said, "Daddy, I know I let Jesus come into my heart, but (she opened her mouth widely and pointed) look down there and see if you can see Him."

~ ~ ~

DEAN

Our children have been brought up in a sheltered environment. No one ever thinks of coming into our parsonage, cursing or exhibiting any kind of bad behavior.

That is why I was surprised this morning when I went to the back door and saw my five-year-old son, Dean, talking with a tough-looking little guy I had never seen in our neighborhood. I was more surprised when Dean asked him a very strange question. "Hey, little boy," he said. "Can you curse?"

I was shocked at the string of profanity that child used. He said,"blankity- blankity- blankity blank YES, " using a list of curse words.

My sheltered son said, "Oh, yeah? Let me hear you."

~ ~ ~

KENT

This morning I came out on my front porch and looked at the corner house across from me. A big moving van was parked close to the porch, and furniture was being carried into the home. I was bothered, however, to see my five-year-old son, Kent, standing near the truck with his arms around a little girl, kissing her right on the lips.

I called him home and said, "Kent, what where you doing kissing that little girl like that?"

He said, "I didn't think anybody could see me."

I said, "But, Kent, God sees you at all times."

He thought only a second or so before he said, "BUT God made me a loving little boy."

CHESTER: ONE HUNDRED TIMES

February 21, 2006

On the way to work early, often my husband would turn right on a one-way street to drop off his dry cleaning. He would then cut across the street, go through the bank's driveway, and turn left onto the parallel street.

One morning after his customary practice, he was shocked to see flashing blue lights. He pulled over to the curb and waited for the police office to approach his car.

After the officer had examined the driver's license, he said, "Dr. Phillips, do you know you made a left-hand turn from a right-hand lane?"

My husband said, "Oh, I've done that a hundred times."

"Ohhhh, you shouldn't have said that," the officer said, taking out his pen and ticket book.

CHESTER AND GUS

In college, Chester made friends with a young man who lived in that city. He had led the man to Christ and was trying to aid him. They had been discussing two problems facing Gus. One, Gus was needing to move his furniture from one home to another. Two, he had a desire to move his father from one cemetery and placed in another.

Chester used this story to show that two people can be having a conversation with each other with one thinking one thing; and the other, thinking something else. For instance:

Chester said, "Gus, we don't need to hire anyone. You and I can do the job ourselves. We'll borrow a flat-bed truck, and you and I'll load it. It will be easy to go right down main street." In his mind, he was thinking about moving furniture.

He did not know that Gus was thinking about something else - - digging up his dad and carrying his muddy casket down Main Street on a flat-bed. He did not know until Gus cried in dismay, "Oh, no, no! I couldn't do that. I couldn't bear to touch my dad's casket."

CHESTER AND CHET

I have heard my grandson Chet tell this story.

Our families were together at Topsail Island, North Carolina. Chester was sitting on the porch when young Chet came out, ready to go swimming. He tells that as he was heading to the beach, "Pops" called him said, "Chet, if you get in trouble out there and think you're going to drown, call me."

Musing on this kind thought, Chet turned to walk away. Then he heard Pops say, "Yes, call me, Chet. I've never seen anyone drown before."

OUR MEAL OF CHOICE

It had been a hot day, and I prepared Chester what he had requested for supper. We had just sat down to eat when Kent came by to check on "his elderly parents." He was bothered by what he saw us eating. He could not understand that this combination was something we actually liked: canned sardines in mustard sauce, un-heated Pork -N-Beans, soda crackers, and ice-cold Pepsis.

Sorry, Kent, but in years to come, now and then, this probably will still be one of our meals of choice.

ESSAYS

Perhaps, I should explain why most of these essays are very short. For over ten years, I headed a group of writers at the Senior Center in Johnson City, Tennessee. Our class ranged from ten to twenty each session. In order for all to read what they had written and get input, of necessity, we limited presentations to three typed, double-spaced pages. Since the writers liked assignments, often we wrote from as little as one word like SNOW, VETERANS, or DISAPPOINTMENTS. With varying backgrounds and interests, this plan worked well for us.

Writings were often informative; sometimes, humorous; sometimes, sorrowful..

LUCKY ME

Who says being the only girl in a family is fun? Especially when there are three boys!

How often some nincompoop said, "I bet you are 'spoiled' being the only girl in the family." How inane. Who likes a three-to-one ratio?

Every six weeks I caused my athletic-crazy brothers trouble. As a studious little girl, I came home with a glowing report card. Once, I hid my report card so that Daddy could not compare my grades with those of my smart, but cut-up, younger brother. Frankie knew what I did just for him; but he hated me anyhow because, in spite of my help, he got a whipping.

I was always very slim although I ate like an athlete, trying to keep up with my brothers. At our home, we always had hot meals to please my father. On Saturdays, however, when he worked, mother delighted us with sandwiches. She would make a long loaf of bread into sandwiches which were counted out – "One for you, one for you, and one for you" until all had an even number. I ate four or five right along with my muscular brothers.

To my detriment, I tried to be a tomboy. One Christmas my brothers got boxing gloves, and our front yard became the boxing ring for neighborhood boys. One day these boys had the brilliant idea that my friend, Maxine, and I should have a bout. They laced up our gloves.

I was sure I could lick Maxine, for I had watched my father showing my brothers how to hold up the left hand to guard and to punch with the right. I knew Maxine had not been privy to such training. The boys clanged a bell and Maxine came at me, ignoring all rules of boxing. She rushed into me with her arms swinging like a tilted windmill. She swung so rapidly that I didn't have a chance. My guard was knocked down and so was I within seconds. It was then I decided to be lady-like for the rest of my life.

Another disadvantage of having only brothers came at bedtime. I hated to sleep by myself. When my younger brother was a little fellow, my older brother and I fought over him. Bobby would grab the little fellow under his arms and I would grab his feet and we would pull until Mother responded to Frankie's cries. I am ashamed to admit that Frank had to have a spinal operation later in life, probably because of us.

On one occasion, Bobby won and I lay wide-eyed in my bed, hearing noises.

As I lay there shivering, the thought came that if I were hidden under my brother's bed and someone came into our house, he would not find me.

Quietly, I stole from my bed, dragging covers with me. After I was comfortable under the bed, I became pleased with my idea. I decided that I should share my smart plan with my older brother (who, incidentally was sleeping on the back side of the bed – scared like me, I bet). I reached up and felt around until I could grasp Bobby's hand. I gave it a hard yank. My idiot brother sprang up and screamed, "Mama! Mama!"

Now, I do not know why I did this, but I tried to change my voice and say gruffly, "Bobby, shut up!"

"Dorothy," he stammered, "Who's under there with you?"

I never answered his question, for lights came on everywhere: and in moments, my hiding place was discovered. In shame, I crept back to my lonely bed.

I did have one advantage as the only girl though. I really believe Daddy loved me best. Perhaps it was because my blonde hair and blue eyes made me so very different from my black-haired, brown-eyed brothers. Perhaps it was because he felt more protective of me, his little girl.

Often he gave me talks that he did not give to the guys. "Dorothy," he would say, "all a poor girl has is her good name. If she loses that, she loses everything."

I listened to him. I really tried to guard the Hicks' name until years later when I traded it off for a better name – Phillips.

I have thought and thought; but try as I may, I can think of only one lone privilege of being the only girl in my family. It's not much, but I didn't have to wear hand-me-downs.

COUNTING MY BLESSINGS

Many years ago, a lovely 23-year old lady nestled me beneath her heart for nine, long months; and then with only a few sips of whiskey for pain, labored to give to me my greatest earthly gift - the gift of life.

Her gift came with all benefits afforded to those born in America. When I reached the then "magical age of six," I entered school right along with boys, a privilege often withheld, even today, in many parts of the world.

Because I lived in America, I was guaranteed the right to pursue happiness. I could choose what I wanted to be. In addition to the earliest years of limited vocations, usually only nursing or teaching, I could aspire to be a doctor, lawyer, or astronaut.

I could wear what I wanted to wear, go where I wanted to go, and marry the man I wanted to marry.

Of greater importance, because of America's freedom of religion, I could consider all religious beliefs. Because of this freedom, when I accepted the Lord Jesus Christ as Savior, I had the joy of experiencing another birth – a birth into the family of God

Mother blessed me with a great gift; the Lord, with a far greater-- the Gift of Eternal Life. How blessed I am!

NAME DILEMMA

It was during a writer's convention that I discovered my Nemesis. A published writer named Dorothy (Blank Blank) noted that I signed my writings, " By Dot Phillips." In a sweet, helpful, but condescending way, she stated," I would never sign my name 'Dot.' 'Dot' is too very insignificant."

I smiled at her observation, for I had never thought of my name as being insignificant. Gradually, however, the author's thought began to plague my mind. Could she be right? Had I handicapped myself by choosing the label "Dot" rather than Dorothy? For most of my life, whenever I was introduced as Dorothy, almost immediately my new acquaintances dropped the formality and called me "Dot." I must admit I had always liked the switch. The shortened name seemed warm and friendly. I actually welcomed the uninvited "Dot" as a pledge of acceptance.

I began to wonder. Was Benjamin Franklin less respected for his witty maxims, his manifold inventions, and political endeavors when great and small dared call him "Ben"? Was one of America's best loved Presidents belittled when his constituents called him "Abe" Lincoln instead of Abraham Lincoln? Did being called Joe Namath instead of Joseph Namath affect the quarterback's game? What about all the other famous (or infamous) Joes, like Joe DiMaggio, Joe Stalin, Joe E. Brown, etc.? In every field of endeavor, one might point to famous nicknamed artists – many with names shortened to two or three letters. In keeping with Shakespeare's well-known lines, I have asked myself if a rose were called by another name (as "roe"), would it not smell just as sweet?

With regard to the insignificant Dot, however, I am delighted to see that little word displayed in many places. In my town, I often see a colorful road sign that says Tenn. DOT. I can even revel in similar unpaid-for publicity, even all over the other fifty states in America.

More importantly, today in a zillion places and for a zillion times, someone will think DOT com. What other name can top that?

I have reasoned all of these pro and con arguments in my heart, but my mind has not been cooperative. You see, I now sign all my writings " Dorothy Alease Phillips," just to be safe, you know.

Signed: By Dot Phillips

WARTIME FAREWELLS

Until World War II, I had said no sorrowful goodbyes. In my home we had said cheerful goodbyes when we left for school or went to some local event. We even had said a happy goodbye when my older brother went away to college, for we were glad for him.

Then came the war, and my patriotic 20-year-old brother

left college to become a Marine. After three grueling months of training to kill or be kill, he was headed for a horrible landing on Guadalcanal. My mother grieved each time she remembered how he kissed her goodbye and ran around the corner of the house so that she could not see him cry.

The war raged on, and in our neighborhood every young, single man and even several married men with children were called into service. Although Chester Phillips and I had known each other for over a year, we had not been dating but five months when his summons came. He was to report to Fort Bragg, North Carolina, in two weeks. Uncle Sam's letter stating, "Your friends and neighbors have selected you..."changed everything for us. Heartbroken, we decided to get married in a few days (with Chester promising that he would see that I got to attend college).

Chester, dressed in his Sunday's best; and I, dressed in a new navy blue dress with a white collar; and with no music or flowers and only one couple as witnesses, we were wed in our pastor's home. Our wedding was such a hurried affair that even our parents were not present.

Our first goodbyes said at Fort Bragg were not grievous, for we knew that I would follow him as soon as his basic training had been completed. In three months, he was shipped to Fort Wayne, Indiana; and I, an 18-year-old person who had never traveled alone, boarded a train and traveled 1,000 miles to be with my young husband. We reveled in our one-room, efficiency apartment with a foldup bed and window icebox. Snow perpetually covered the ground, making it perfect for two young, snow-loving Southerners to walk the magical, white streets and play.

Snow was still on the ground when, quite suddenly, Chester was transferred to Syracuse, New York, for another phase of training. And then came the last transfer. The 10th Air Force group was being sent to New Brunswick, New Jersey, for departure to points unknown. Young wives turned to each other to find ways to travel together to the final military base. Husbands were granted passes for only a night or two to say their farewells.

On departure day, alongside the panting train, couples hugged, cried, and kissed, fully aware that these would be the last embraces for many of them. I have no words to tell the deep, sorrowful trauma experienced as the soldiers reluctantly released their loved ones and yielded to the raucous "all-aboard" warnings. Once aboard the train, the men scrambled to the windows to throw kisses and mouth, "I love you."

For the two years that Chester was in Europe, this final farewell haunted my memories. We wrote to each other, but his letters were always censored. Even when Hitler was defeated, the men could not tell what was happening. Perhaps it was because they were still needed. It was on a ship taking them, not home, but to the Pacific that Chester's division learned that Japan had surrendered. With the 10th Air Force no longer needed in the South Seas, their ship now headed for America.

The jubilant servicemen landed in New York without parents and spouses to greet them but with cheering, appreciative citizens that daily lined the shores to greet all ships. Hurried telephone calls were made to families all over America, announcing that their loved ones were home at last.

Chester's parents and I had been looking for him to return all during the day. Night fell and he had not come. I had spent hours at the window, looking down the newly-cut road that led to his parents' recently- built, lone house. At length, I lay across the bed, crying. Then I saw car lights. I heard the roar of a motor. Chester's parents and I rushed to the front door in time to see our uniformed soldier getting out of a taxi. Amid all the hugging and crying, I noted the cab driver who stood leaning upon his car and saying over and over, "Praise the Lord! Praise the Lord!"

And now, as thousands of young men and women are bidding farewell to grieving loved ones, may the Lord enable many voices someday to cry, "Praise the Lord. Praise the Lord" as their brave ones someday return home.

LAST TRIP TO SEE GRANDDADDY

Unfortunately, I lived a good distance from my grandfather and seldom got to see him; but I knew he was my daddy's daddy and I loved him. Because of family stories, I knew him well.

He was a hard-working man, seeking to bring up ten children during the depression days. Guided by the philosophy, "Spare the rod; spoil the child," he was a strict disciplinarian, handling his children as his father before him had handled his. In spite of his strictness, or maybe because of his strictness, he was honored and loved by his children and his many grandchildren.

Yes, Robert Vance Hicks was a beloved father and grandfather. When he died in the mid 1930's, great sorrow fell upon the Hicks Clan. Most of his family lived near him in Richmond, Virginia; but those who lived a distance away sought to go to his memorial service.

My father, who lived in Durham, North Carolina, left right away on a Greyhound Bus. Buses were the main mode of transportation during that financially-strapped era. At that time, only two people in our middle-class neighborhood had cars. Most people either walked or rode local buses. Trains or buses, when available, took care of distant traveling.

Mother wanted to go to the funeral, but she was caring for

a newborn baby. After some consideration, she decided that I, only 13-years-old, and my eight year old brother could travel alone on a Greyhound Bus. (People did not have the same fear for their children that parents must have today.)

Having walked to the downtown bus station with our meager luggage, my little brother and I boarded the huge, magnificent Greyhound Bus! Even though we were traveling to a funeral, the trip was the highlight of our short lives.

We were in good hands. The personable driver cared for us. To our chagrin, my little brother became "car sick" after an hour of travel. Without much traffic on highways at that time, the driver pulled over to the side and led Frankie outside where the inevitable happened With compassion, the driver stood by and talked soothingly to his little sick passenger until they could return to the bus. With understanding, the driver then did some re-arranging so that Frankie could sit on a front seat.

In time, we reached our destination in good health, happy and grateful for the care given to us by a thoughtful bus driver on a Greyhound Bus.

MOTHER'S BLOUSE

My heart was grieved for the time had come to remove my precious 100-year-old mother from her thriving assisted living facility to a nursing home where she could receive added care. I knew the change would be drastic. My Friday was spent going through all of the necessitated red tape. By evening I was exhausted.

The day before, Mother had suffered a mini stroke, and it seemed that the opening in the nursing facility had come just at the right moment. I went to bed early, saddened by the abrupt change. Fearful of what the mini stroke foretold, I could not sleep. Much earlier, had gone to Morris Baker's Funeral Home to make Mother's final arrangements. I felt I had to do this while she was well and happy. Now, I lay in bed, thinking about her clothing. She had a new red suit she loved. In my fretful sleep, I reasoned she could wear this beloved suit, but she had no elegant blouse.

"Lord," I prayed. "When Mother dies, I will not feel like looking for a blouse for her. What will I do?"

In exhaustion, I finally fell asleep. Saturday morning, I awoke and began the customary straightening-up process. In my bedroom, I reached into my closet for something. Strange, but I noted a shirt box tucked back on the right side of the closet floor. I picked it up. It felt heavy as though there was something inside, what I thought, was an empty box. I removed the top, folded back the white tissue paper, and gazed in astonishment at a beautiful white silk blouse enhanced by delicate braid and tiny seed pearls.

It was late February and this lovely blouse was one of the gifts I had bought for my Mother for a Christmas present. I looked at the gorgeous blouse that I now needed and marveled. Was it not more than a mere coincidence that I had forgotten to give Mother this added gift on Christmas day? Had my personal Lord not saved this for this personal need at this personal time? I say, "Yes, and thank you, Lord."

> *"Delight thyself also in the ways of the Lord; and He shall give thee the desires of thine heart." Psalms 37:4*

HA HA MEDICINE

People often refer to King Solomon's words: *"A merry heart doeth good like a medicine," "A merry heart maketh a cheerful countenance,"* or *".... A merry heart hath a continual feast."* Medical doctors and psychiatrists, too, agree that humor has great benefits. As professionals, they laud laughter as an excellent medicine.

Without doubt, a good belly laugh works better than Alka-Seltzer, Tums, or Pepcid. At night, chuckles for an hour before going to bed will demand better results than Tylenol PM or sleeping pills.

This much- needed, humor stimulation comes in many forms – puns, jokes, poetry, comical skits, movies, cartoons, etc. Apart from these planned laughter enticements mastered by comedians, laughter is generated from ordinary people caught in embarrassing circumstances. A clumsy fall, a jump-out-of-skin scare, a slip of the tongue, a dumb misunderstanding: all can cause spontaneous laughter, sometimes to the chagrin of unfortunate persons. Who hasn't laughed at clips of people bumping into glass doors, sliding on ice or banana peels, or toppling off a stage?

Even innocent behavior can make the heart merry. Recently, I watched America's Funniest Videos' $100,000 award for the year's funniest video, a video of infant quadruplets lying on their backs and prompting each other to outbursts of gurgling, baby laughter. Their uninhibited, bubbly laughs were so contagious that no one could hear them without laughing.

Sometimes something as simple as persons mispronouncing words or, in ignorance, using the wrong word is amusing. Archie Bunker of "All in the Family" was a master of mixing words, like referring to an elderly person as decrap-et rather that decrepit.

At times, humor comes in the mail. Once, my husband received a letter from a mayor, expressing regrets that the mayor could not attend some function in our church. In error (or by a Freudian slip) the mayor's secretary had typed: "I regret that I cannot be there for this "monotonous" occasion instead of "memorable" occasion.

Perhaps puns, however, offer the easiest forms of impromptu humor. When a speaker prefaces a remark by saying "No pun intended," one can be sure a funny play on words will follow. These puns daily show up, even in headlines. Following a noted Bowl Game, won by the Pittsburg Steelers, a front-page heading was "Steeling the Show."

Such puns are delightful to all quick witted, from children to adults. Although puns are sometimes followed by groans, one has explained that the groaners do so because they are sorry they did not think of the pun first.

Jokes with surprise punch lines can cause outbursts of sustained laughter. How often have we heard the comment, "I laughed until I cried" or "peed on myself." Now, these admissions are complements to the person telling the story.

Jokes are usually best if they are short, never drawn out. Examples might be:

A father says to his son, "You have it easy. When I was your age, I had to walk all the way across the room to change the channels." Or, a father said to his son, "When Abraham Lincoln was your age, he walked 12 miles to school."

The son looked up and said, "When Abraham Lincoln was your age, he was President."

In addition to puns, jokes, and drama, humor is depicted in practically all newspapers and magazines through cartoons.

One of my favorite cartoons pictured an old Indian, draped in a colorful blanket, sitting cross-legged by a fire. In the distance, three puffs of circled smoke ascend into the sky. The old Indian bemoans, "Oh, I wish I had said that!"

Perhaps an article in the February 2006, *Ladies' Home Journal* best summarizes the importance of laughter:

> "...among proven ways to stay heart healthy: Regular exercise relieves tension and reduces stress hormones. So do yoga and meditation, breathing and relaxation techniques. A support network of friends and families helps. And laughter may be the best medicine, studies show."

A Yiddish proverb states, "What soap is to the body, laughter is to the soul; therefore, perhaps, to be healthy and blessed, we need to lather up and giggle all day.

WANTS BEING MET

In my elementary school, elite students could boast of having had appendicitis, pneumonia, or some other disease that had granted them hospital stay For the hospitalized, all classmates were forced to make colorful, get-well cards, and once our class even painted a huge mural to be hung in Betty Bowman's hospital room.

Other popular students knew the joy of having classmates standing in line to sign an impressive arm or leg cast.

Year by year, I trudged by, waiting for my turn; but alas, I was healthy and agile. I didn't get sick and I didn't break anything.

With the same luck, I sailed through junior high, senior high, college, and graduate school with no scars, no hospital tales, and no attention.

While bringing up my three children, I was far too busy to be sick. I kept coasting along.

And then, I hit what they call the "golden years" and, suddenly, I leaped to the front of the line. I made my debut by passing out twice in Sunday morning services before doctors pinpointed atrial fibrillation and suited me with a pacemaker. I was immediately satisfied. I thought my days in the limelight were over.

That is what I thought, but I was wrong. Recently, I added a painful, near-death experience with pancreatitis. This time, instead of adding to my physique, the specialists took something away from me. They pumped my tummy up as big as a basketball and as tight as a bongo drum and skillfully confiscated my gall bladder.

Now, those early starters in grammar school may still be able to boast of far more glamorous hospital bouts than I have had. That is fine. I no longer want to compete.

LIKE OR LOVE

Once I had an English teacher who stressed using "like" and "love" properly. She admonished the class not to use the word "love" when really we should be using "like."

Often since her lecture, I have questioned if it were proper to say that I like or love something. I must admit I'm the type person who feels strongly about most things and "like" is often too mild for me Oh, I may say, "I like spinach"; but to say, "I like chocolate" would be a gross understatement. I love chocolate!

To me, love is and always has been a powerful, all-encompassing, treasured word, a word I love.

Most songs carry a love message. My mother, who was born in 1899, used to sing to me the romantic song that was popular when she was young:

> "Let me call you sweetheart.
> I'm in love with you.
> Let me hear you whisper
> That you love me too.
> Keep the love light glowing
> In your eyes so true
> Let me call you sweetheart.
> I'm in love with you."

Elvis Presley's "Love Me Tenderly; Love Me True" is still being sung after a half century. An all-time favorite, "I Love You Truly," is used at this time, probably, more than any other song in weddings. Love songs like "Love is a Many Splendored Thing" and "Love Story," used as movie- theme music, are still lauded.

Love has inspired poetry, both trite and profound. When I was in the third grade, my first love, curly-headed Reams Hargis, sent me a rose-covered valentine that read:

> "The whole world loves a lover,
> So, they say.
> Then I hope it is true
> For the world is in love with me
> Because I'm in love with you."

After all the years, this simple poem has remained in my mind even though I have become acquainted with more sublime messages as in Elizabeth Barret Browning's sonnet,

"How Do I Love Thee." In the mid-1800s, Mrs. Browning wrote:

> "How do I love thee? Let me count the ways.
> I love thee to the depth and breadth and height
> My soul can reach, when feeling out of sight
> …I love thee to the level of everyday's
> Most quiet need, by sun and candle-light.
> …I love thee with a love I seemed to lose
> With my lost saints –I love thee with the breath,
> Smiles, tears, of all my life! – and, If God choose,
> I shall but love thee better after death."

Yesterday I listened to an advertisement for a male quartet who will serve as a singing valentine for $40. The demand for such performers has become so great in our area that there are now four quartets, one made up of all women.

I thought about this entertainment idea and I think I would LIKE a singing valentine, but I know I would LOVE a box of chocolates.

By the way, I like the word "Like," but I love the word "Love."

ALL I WANT

As a senior citizen, I usually try to be an alert, but cautious driver; but recently as the light was turning yellow, I said to my husband, "Shall I make it?"

"Sure," he said. "You have plenty of time."

I suppose he was right, for I sped up and got to the other side before the light turned red. Laughing, I said, "I did that just like a person driving a pickup truck, didn't I?" And that is when the thought hit me: at my age, I need a pickup truck!

I have two sons and three grandsons of driving age and all five of them would probably give up their citizenship before they would part from their beloved trucks. In these cherished vehicles, they haul hunting, fishing, golfing, and sports' gear. They transport their pedigreed dogs in style, and pull boats and campers from one state to another.

Now, I have no desire to use my pickup for hauling anything or for lugging something behind me. No, I want a pickup truck so that I can drive a little more like a flighty, teenage blonde. I want to experience the same high these gals seemingly possess when energized behind the wheel of this souped-up machine.

I plan to set certain limitations to my newly-found power, however. A friend of mine told me that last week she chose not to race under the caution light, and the girl behind her in a pickup truck became so very angry that she followed her for several blocks, making gestures and screaming obscenities. On my honor, I promise not to follow, gesture, or utter cuss words. I just need a LITTLE invigorating.

Now, it's too late for my birthday or a Mother's Day gift, but I am giving notice for Christmas. All I want is a powerful RED pickup truck with a set of steps to help me ascend and descend. I feel better already.

NEVER FOR ME

As a labeled "Senior Citizen," the other day a thought hit me: there are many things in this lifetime that I have not done.

Now, I'm not talking about way-out-there things like joining a nudist colony, wrestling alligators in Florida, or going over Niagara Falls in a barrel. I'm thinking about today's everyday challenges that have over shot anything I ever dared to do.

For instance, as a child, I could skate and even do a little fancy footwork; but, regrettably, I've never brought myself to cover my arms and shins with protective gear to go roller blading or skate boarding. What a shame. These two activities seem far more dangerous.

In those childhood days, I was proud that I could do the backbend, turn a cartwheel, and execute a half-way-down split (looking much like open scissors stuck in mud); but I've never studied gymnastics and will never know the thrill of leaping into the air and twirling three times before landing erect upon a mat, with a perfect curved back.

Early, I mastered the tricycle and later the bicycle; but until now, I have never sported a black leather jacket and straddled a Harley, speeding down a super highway, obliterating flying insects. I think maybe I've missed something.

I remember a requisite at my high school demanded that all students could swim the length of our inside pool. I learned to float and to dive from the poolside, but my expertise stopped there. I'm aware I'll never know the thrill of diving from a rugged cliff into a lake 100 feet below or surfing upon monstrous waves in Hawaii.

I've flown in both propeller and jet planes, but I probably will never fly in a hot-air balloon, ride a hang glider, or blast off in a space ship.

In amusement parks, I have dared to ride the Merry-go-round, Scrambler, and simple Ferris Wheels; but, up to now, no one has been able to persuade me to try the Bungee Jump. I may change my mind.

Now, in retrospect, I've heard old timers, completely satisfied with their past, say, "I've been there. Done that."

Been there. Done that. Not I. Considering the minuscule things I've done and the vast number of things I have not done, I have made up my mind. When the Grim Reaper comes for me, I'll say, "No, Kind Sir. Please wait. I can't go now. I have too many other things to do. Give me a little more time."

CONFUSING LINGO

I am a home-grown American. English has been my language from the first uttering of ooogar-bill and tah-tah; yet, I must confess, there are words and phrases in our day-by-day conversing that baffle even brilliant minds.

Take, for instance, "hogwash." Now, what do these two words mean when they are tacked together? Everyone knows that it would be ridiculous to wash a hog who has a mindset for wallowing in the mud. So I say, "Hogwash" to this made-up word.

Then there is "filthy rich." I have known many immaculate, well-groomed, expensively dressed rich people whom I have admired. As a matter of fact, I may have sinned and coveted their wealth; and yet, I hate filth. Would I dare be filthy rich?

Think about the "stone deaf," the "tear jerker," and "bald-faced liar."

Now, my husband once a military man, told me what "brown nosing" meant in the service. I cannot repeat the definition, but I am baffled that "brown nosing," "gold bricking" and "apple polishing" even though, extremely different, are all dumped together.

Where do we get "willy nilly," "dilly dally," or "hanky

panky"? Who in the world is a "fuddy duddy" or who can be accused of "skullduggery"?

Why can a person be labeled as a turkey, hog, goose, fox, snake, or goofball?

If these word woes beset me, pity a poor foreigner who tries to assimilate our American lingo. He's dead duck, for sure.

AROUND AND AROUND

If I were to say, "Sometimes I feel like a gerbil, running around and around on his wheel," I would have to pause and say, "But that is not always bad." Surely, that zealous little gerbil finds joy in racing around. The exercise is beneficial; the ride, exhilarating.

How like life! Thinking back to the days when I sought to motivate 150 high school students each day, fulfill all the duties of a minister's wife, be a loving helpmate for my husband, and give devoted care to my three children, I identify with the unending, going-going motion; yet my memories are sweet.

Only in later years have memories had a tinge of bitter sweetness. The proverbial race became less joyful in 1991 when my adored husband had a brain tumor removed, leaving a semi-paralysis on the right side of his body. The aftermath of the 12-hour surgery slowed the racing pace almost to a standstill. My heart grieved to see a man who usually bounded up steps two at a time endeavor to walk again; to see a minister who developed and delivered great messages to hundreds (and on occasions, thousands) of people struggle to talk again; and to watch a person with such a keen sense of humor that labeled him "the life of the party" suddenly sit quietly with isolated, humorous thoughts.

Getting back on the wheel has not been easy, but steadily

progress has been made. Chester walks, usually, with the aid of a walker; with effort, talks with a tongue that has only one motor nerve; and once again, displays his spontaneous, jovial wit.

As a minister, having been faithful in pastoring for 38 years, he realizes that, for some purpose, a loving Lord has entrusted him with a slight weight to carry as he continues his race.

Endeavoring to shoulder the load with dignity, he clings to scriptural promises and anticipates a good, long run.

Today we tread the wheel together, enjoying our time, jogging along. Like the gerbil, however, both of us still have fun the faster we go.

Yet, we know as we add the years, someday we may gladly switch to an enticing, melodic merry-go-round. That ride will be slower, but we'll try to make it great.

LOSING OUR CINDY

When cancer snatched my precious daddy from me, I experienced deep grief. In my daddy, I had reveled in unconditional love, respect, and admiration. He had always been my mentor and my greatest backer in anything I attempted to do. I smile as I think of an apropos illustration. I took piano lessons, but I never was skilled in playing. Surely, my daddy knew that I had no great musical talent as I plunked away, but I heard him say, "Doesn't Dorothy have a pleasant touch on the piano?" This assessment of my playing is symbolic of his way of constantly encouraging me. I loved him dearly and wanted to keep him forever.

Yes, I grieved when he was taken from me, but that grief paled in comparison with the drenching grief that engulfed me when our only daughter, our beautiful Cindy, was killed almost instantly in an automobile accident.

She had come to visit and had spent the night with us. She and I stayed up late with me, mostly listening and catching up with all that was going on in her life. She was 30 and held a high-paying position with Levi as their first woman salesperson. She had been a school teacher but had left the classroom for this more lucrative job.

I knew that I had to teach the next day, but I was enjoying her infectious enthusiasm so greatly that I could not bear to say goodnight. When I finally mentioned that I should go to bed, she started thinking about what she had that I could wear the next day. She asked if I had a black skirt and then she brought forth a classy beige blouse that was trimmed in black. Next, she brought to me her selected jewelry to accent the blouse.

She was up early the next day to iron the blouse, for this was true Cindy style: she always liked to iron whatever she was going to wear just before dressing. She asked if I had any black high heels and I admitted I had a pair in a popular style.

"Good," she said. "Wear them and give the kids a treat."

At lunch, I sat in the teachers' lounge, sharing with my teacher friends Cindy's visit and her selecting what I was to wear. I smiled as I recalled her coaxing me to wear high heels.

Following lunch, I was having my planning period, awaiting my journalism class. Two of my editors were with me, discussing the newspaper. Suddenly, the door opened and my ashen-faced husband spoke not a word, headed to me, enfolded me in his arms, and in a choked whisper sobbed, "Cindy was killed in a wreck in Boone this morning." The pain from his body coursed through my being. It was as though we were smitten and sealed within a horrid dome of sorrow. No one or nothing else existed.

Our beautiful, intelligent, talented, vibrant, thoughtful, caring Cindy was gone, taken from us without any warning -- taken so abruptly that we had not said, "Goodbye," but we had said our "I love you," for this is something we had always done morning, evening, and nights. The last thing I remember Cindy saying to me as I left for University High School that morning was, "You look really nice, Mother. I love you."

Now, we were Christians and were certain that according to scriptures, "To be absent from the body was to be present with the Lord." We knew that the Apostle Paul taught we have a great hope. He said, "If in this life only we have hope, we are of all men most miserable," but Paul rejoiced, knowing that Christians rest in Christ's promise that those who know him will be resurrected to everlasting life with Him.

Yes, we rested in these truths, but our hearts ached to hold Cindy close to us – to have her to love for many years. We were like most other parents. We never considered having one of our children precede us in death. Giving Cindy up was the greatest sorrow we had ever encountered.

Our love and grief were so mutual that for the next lonely months if one of us started suddenly to cry because we had heard music, smelled a special fragrance, tasted a certain food, or noted some small thing that reminded us of Cindy, the other joined in sobs unashamedly. We cried in our car, at our table, on our knees, in public and in private. We thought the grief would never cease even though thoughtful friends sweetly sought to assure us that time would help soothe our sorrow.

Cindy has been gone (as of October 4, 1978) many years; and yet, she is still so very much alive in our hearts and memories that it seems only days since she was snatched from us.

Shortly before she died, someone cautioned Cindy to drive

very carefully. She smiled and replied, "Well, if I die, I will go immediately to be with the Lord."

Her assurance is our assurance, all based on biblical teachings that if a person has personally accepted the Lord Jesus Christ as Savior, he or she will have eternal life. I remember the evening Cindy accepted Christ as Savior. I watched her, in childhood, grow in her faith. She attended her senior year in high school at Bob Jones University's Academy, was graduated from Bob Jones University, and taught in a Christian school. I know she loved the Lord.

Thus, we rest in the truth of God's Word:

> *"For God so loved the world that he gave his only begotten son that whosoever believeth in him should not perish but have everlasting life."* **John 3:16**

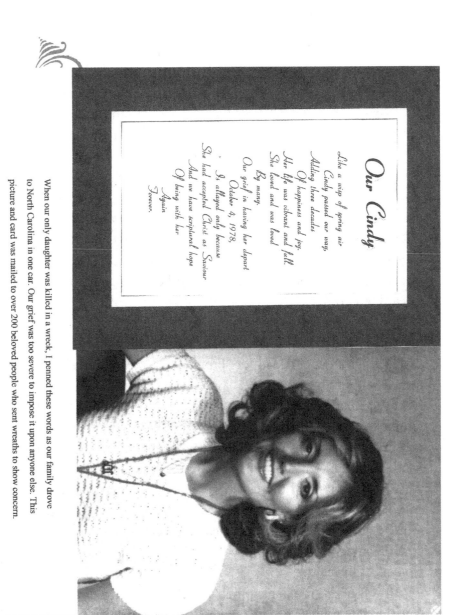

Our Cindy

Like a wisp of spring air
Cindy passed our way,
Adding three decades
Of happiness and joy.
Her life was vibrant and full.
She loved and was loved
By many.
Our grief in having her depart
October 4, 1978,
Is allayed only because
She had accepted Christ as Saviour
And we have scriptural hope
Of being with her
Again
Forever.

When our only daughter was killed in a wreck, I penned these words as our family drove to North Carolina in one car. Our grief was too severe to impose it upon anyone else. This picture and card was mailed to over 200 beloved people who sent wreaths to show concern.

MY CHILDHOOD LOVE

My first love affair lasted six years. Since his name was Reams Hargis and my name Dorothy Hicks, the alphabet kept us together from grade one through grade six.

Reams had blond, curly hair, blue eyes, and a dimpled smile. In truth, he was the cutest boy in school. In my childish way, I loved him. Yes, I loved him and he loved me; but in the third grade, Valentine's Day almost tore us apart.

In our classroom, the teacher fashioned a big box covered in white crepe paper and decorated with red, crepe hearts and ribbons. In the box top, there was a slit into which students could insert valentines for a week before Valentine's Day. The teacher saw to it that all children, regardless of popularity, got a card or two.

Senders could sign their names, using an alphabet code (like "From 4 -8" for Dorothy Hicks), or with anonymous wording such as "From your friend" or "From your secret admirer." The whole activity was fun.

The greatest celebration in our locality, however, came later in the evening. In Durham, North Carolina, in the 1930s, we observed a happy way of celebrating Valentine's Day. After dark, children were allowed to go around in the neighborhood, distributing cards. (I digress to say that in those days, parents did not have the same fears they have today.) A child would run up onto a porch, put down a card, stomp up and down, and then scamper to a hiding place before someone came outside to collect the card.

It was after I ran to my porch to pick up a card addressed to me that my troubles began. Oh, the card was fine. Now, I must say it was really great, for I still remember the wording:

"The whole world loves a lover
So they say;
Then I hope it's true
For the world's in love with me
Because
I'm in love with you."

My big brother snatched the card from me and read the poem aloud – even the "With love – Reams." He danced around the room, waving the card above my head and gleefully taunting me. When I could stand this teasing no longer, I managed to grab the card, put on my coat, and head to the Hargis' home.

I mounted the high steps to the house and knocked on the door. My cherished Reams answered the knock. Foolishly, I thrust the crumpled card into his hands and cried, "Keep your old card."

I turned and started to leave by the bank, rather than by the steps. The grass was damp; my feet flew out from under me; and, to my embarrassment, I slid all the way down to the sidewalk.

After a restless night filled with regrets, the next day I returned to my classroom, afraid to see Reams. He avoided me until I slipped a valentine to him, telling him I was sorry for what I had done and adding, "I love you."

Now, when I get to heaven (if Chester does not mind), I think I'll check to see if "My First Love" made it there, too.

1930'S CHRISTMAS MEMORIES

In the 1930s Americans felt the sting of hard times. Unemployment was high; wages were low; necessities were meager; and luxuries were nearly nonexistent. It was a time when parents taught their children to close the door to keep the heat in; to turn off the light when leaving a room; to use very little toilet paper or crinkle up newspaper; and, always to clean one's plate. Almost all of the nation probably was considered poor. Being poor, however, though commonplace, was not degrading. Struggling Americans held their heads high, worked hard, and instilled moral principles in their homes.

In like manner, my parents struggled to keep their four children fed, clothed, and schooled. Since my mother opted to stay home, the burden of expenses fell solely upon my dad who was a barber. A man could get a haircut and shave for a mere quarter at that time; so it took long hours six days a week for my father to earn enough money to care for his family.

I mention these facts to give understanding to the type Christmases we experienced when I was a young child, a child who really believed in Santa Claus but did not exactly understand why I received so little from him. I must admit, however, that although Santa did not always find our house and we had no elaborate Christmas decorations or even a tree, we cherished the Christmas season. Perhaps, had we not lived in the city, we might have had the joy of going into the woods to cut down a free tree, a ritual performed by many rural people. Perhaps, had we lived in the country, we could have raised gardens, chickens, and cows. But, alas, in the city, everything depended upon Daddy. His $18 - $20 a week salary was spent mainly on food, heat, and rent (for a comparatively nice home with an inside bathroom while a great percent of people had outhouses).

Our food specialties at Christmas consisted of a big roasted hen with dressing, collards, potato salad, and two freshly-baked cakes. What a feast!

As I have said, our toys were few. Because I liked to draw, I always received a large pad of newspaper-print paper for my artwork. During the school year, Daddy often rightfully got upset because I wasted my notebook paper for drawings. The Christmas pad remedied this situation for a while.

Although my mother and father were loving, caring parents, there was at least one Christmas when they could provide absolutely no Santa gifts. I am sure this dilemma must have grieved their hearts; but they handled the situation in a way that we did not feel deprived. We relished Mother's chicken and dressing and her special Japanese fruitcake.

The only negative thing I remember about this particular Christmas happened in school after the holidays. A non-thinking teacher asked all the students to stand and tell what they received at Christmas. Knowing my classmates, I realized some of them covered their scant gifts even as I did. When it was my turn, I simply said, "Oh, I just got so many things that I could not name them all."

When we moved into the Walton Era, things began to get better. In time, a barbers' union helped raise barbers' earnings. Year by year, more abundance was added to our household, for which we were thankful. In time, at Christmas, we had a tree, colorful lights, fancy decorations, and many more delectable dishes; but the early, deprived Christmases still bring back precious memories when our six family members gathered happily for a Christmas dinner provided by our hard-working dad and prepared by our loving mother.

WHAT MAKES ME TICK

If you were to ask me what makes me tick, I might rattle off obvious enchantments. I could say I am inspired by majestic mountains crowned with the beauty of four seasons- - snowy caps in the winter, creeping green in the spring, lush foliage in the summer, and dazzling colors in the fall.

I might say I am awed by the ocean's greatness – water, water as far as one can see – blue-green water that ever thunders and heaves white foam splendor.

I could rave about renowned paintings, literary masterpieces, and melodic symphonies. Surely, I am enthralled by all these things, but these are not the things that cause me to tick.

Needless to say, my life has been motivated mainly by my devout love for the Lord and for my family. I became a Christian, by choice, when I was seventeen and over the years have rejoiced over that early decision. I have had a wonderful marriage with a great man and three perfect children.

But on the less personal side, the thing that really "makes me tick" is PEOPLE. I thrive on being with people – old or young, rich or poor, simple or complex. I love people. I embrace all acquaintances and revel in our exchange of ideas and interests.

Whoever coined the expression, "people person," labeled me well. I was born a "people person." I know, for since childhood I have loved people. I am especially drawn to those who are optimistic, energetic, and adventurous. I gravitate to those who have a keen sense of humor and a zest for living. I am challenged by those who are smarter and more intelligent than I am. I am informed by the common sense of the uneducated. Yes, I learn from everyone I meet. I recall the words of my university chancellor who said, "I skim the cream from the brain of every man I meet." Perhaps that skimming process is what makes me tick.

In addition, I do not like to be alone. I like to shop with people, eat with people, and play with people. In truth, I am thoroughly energized by people. I suppose this infused energy comes because people always make me anticipate the good "tock" that follows the "tick." For me, there is always a tock, a rewarding result following encounters with people. I like the tock. To coin another phrase, I must be a tick-tock person.

WHAT NEXT?

I had begun studying ventriloquism for a short while when I found a clever, fluffy lion figure that I really wanted; but it cost $50, and I did not see fit to pay that much.

My daughter-in-law said, "Mom, we will get you that lion for Christmas."

When she returned to our vacation cottage and told my son, he thought for a moment and said, "Honey, let's go ahead and buy that figure now. By Christmas, Mom might be in something else." (I was 75.)

I'M SPECIAL

I don't mean to brag, but I have always been special. Born on a hallowed "Mother's Day," I fulfilled my parents' dreams, for they wanted a girl and they were sure they were going to have another son. (You see, they thought this because, I'm ashamed to say, I was awfully unruly before I was born.)

I came into this world before sex-gender testing was instituted. Before that, until the last agonizing, "Push, push, push," concerned parents faced the 50/50 chance of getting what they wanted, a boy or a girl.

As a girl, in school I had it made. Studies show that most elementary teachers are women and these women teachers favor pliable little girls. In high school, girls still have an advantage: there are more male teachers; and, fortunately, they lean toward their female students. Male or female instructors, however, I do not think it would have mattered. I believe I could have hoodwinked any of them. I assumed I already had my parents under my spell.

In college, marriage, child raising, and school teaching, I snagged some accolades along the way; but the greatest of all compliments came recently. My doctor smiled at me and said, "We are going to become good friends."

To prove it, she gave me a handful of prescriptions and an invitation to come back in one week. What undeniable proof! In the early days, I was invited only once a year.

Now, I was to visit regularly.

Yes, I have always thought I was special, but I have begun to wonder. Is there an ulterior motive for the new tie I have with this esteemed physician? Does she think, since my last episode with my heart, that I have put her in my will?

Ben Franklin says that a person "who makes his doctor his heir is a fool." . Wisely, I have not recorded my doctor as my heir, but I have set up a trust for her if she keeps me alive and healthy until I am 100.

I hope she is money hungry.

CLOSE CALL

Twice, I passed out and was rushed by ambulance to the local hospital. The first time, the woman doctor on call diagnosed congestive heart failure, but a male doctor disputed this diagnosis. His assessment was accepted, and I was sent home.

A few months later, I lost consciousness once again and was taken to the emergency room. This time, it was determined that I had an erratic heartbeat; medication and a monitor were prescribed with directions that if my heartbeat reached 140, I was to go to a hospital.

I was visiting my son and his family in August, South Carolina, sometime later. My three young grandchildren were listening to my heartbeat on the monitor. There was a ratter-tat-tat tempo that vacillated from a rapid beat to a sudden drop. When my heart slowed down drastically, I remarked, "Listen. It sounds as though my heart is going to stop beating."

Then darkness closed over, allowing me only to feel my daughter-in-law lowering me to the floor. Darkness lasted only seconds before I felt myself leave my body and ascend upward, looking down upon my frantic son at the phone, my daughter-in-law hovering over my body, and my grandchildren huddled together, crying.

I could feel no regret, for suddenly I was engulfed with a soft dazzling light and a sense of pure, gentle love. My body glided toward an awesome light at the end of a glorious, glowing tunnel. I sped forward without moving a limb. I experienced absolute peace. Then I began to see my loved ones. There was my dad who had died forty years earlier. There was mother who lived to be almost 102 years old. But Daddy and Mother were no longer old. They looked the way they looked when I was a child. I saw my beloved grandparents and my precious daughter who had died in wreck when she was only 30. These family members were surrounded by other Christian loved ones: all beckoning me with open arms.

With all my heart I wanted to reach them, but suddenly I was stopped, hearing a soft inner, but audible, voice say, "Not now, my child. You cannot come yet."

I wanted to protest but I bowed me head in peaceful obedience. I slipped backward, backward, watching the divine light and my cherished family grow dim.

It was then that I heard my husband's voice pleading, "Don't go, Dot. Please don't leave me. Please don't go. Don't go."

I endeavored to open my eyes. Through tiny slits, I saw my beloved earthly family and managed to whisper. "I won't go. Not now. Not now, but someday."

I felt kisses on my forehead, my cheeks and my hands.

NOTE: (Last heavenly paragraphs **fictitious**.)

MOVING ON UP

Listening to an episode of a George Jefferson sit-com recently, I was amused by the theme song: "Moving on up. We're Moving on up. We finally got at piece of the rock."

I reasoned that any adult over sixty could easily voice Louisee's sentiments, "We're moving on up." It has not been so very long since most Americans lived, what we might consider today, "deprived lives." In truth, we have steadily moved on up.

From outhouses, sometimes with elite double seaters, and Sears Roebuck catalogues we have upgraded to several, tiled bathrooms in most homes and squeezable Charmin or Great Northern luxury paper.

We have gone from round, galvanized tubs pulled next

to pot-bellied stoves to heated bathrooms with elaborate, jet-streamed tubs, and multi-faceted showers.

For decades, whatever we needed to buy was stored on shelves behind a counter and was taken down by a slow-moving clerk who laboriously wrote down the prices with a pencil, which he occasionally licked as he added the bill. Mistakes were often made, but there were no receipts given for a possible self-checking.

Clothing was bought for durability, not fashion. Families were considered lucky if each family member had one good pair of shoes, not an assortment of casual and dress-ups - tennis shoes, patent leather slippers, loafers, tie ups sandals, etc.

Housewives labored, washing clothes over a metal scrub board and wringing each garment with her hands.

Like the mailman, people walked everywhere – even miles to school in snow, sleet, and heat. No huge parking lots were needed in high schools. Driver's Ed was not a part of the curriculum. Teens did not have cars.

In the 1940s and 50s, many boasted to be the "first" in their families to finish high school. Today, perhaps, the boast has changed to be the "first" to receive a doctorate.

We could compare garden-grown foods to frozen fruits and vegetables; homemade remedies (like sulfa and lard) to FDA-controlled liquids and tablets; publications like "The Saturday Evening Post" (with Norman Rockwell's paintings) to hundreds of colorful periodicals with celebrities' faces. The list could go on forever.

Now, to a personal "moving on up" note. At 17, I accepted Christ as my Savior (with a very limited knowledge of the Bible). With study and meditation, I began a daily, upward journey. And so, years later, in light of the impending "hereafter," I have a funeral request. Instead of "In the Sweet By and

By," which used to be the stock, farewell song, I think I'll go with the Jefferson's "Moving on up. We finally got a piece of the pie." The wording could be changed a bit. Maybe, "Moving on up. Dot's moving on up. She finally got a piece of the sky."

DEFEATING A FLAW

Having earned a Master's degree and having taught in high school for almost 25 years, I comforted myself with thinking that I must have at least a small measure of reasonable intelligence. How mislead I have been throughout the years, for how could anyone with any gray matter at all, do what I do? I am forever losing things! Yes. Big things. Little things. I lose everything.

Recently, I have lost my car keys twice, costing me over forty dollars to replace them each time. I lost my cellular phone, replaced it for almost fifty dollars and soon lost the second one. Often I have hidden valuables and then could not remember where I hid them. I have lost my checkbook, my gloves, my glasses, phone numbers, and hundreds of umbrellas.

For a while, I bemoaned this curse, but then it dawned upon me that I could use this lemon in my life to make lemonade. I could teach others how to lose things.

First, start with the thing that is the easiest to lose: your car keys. Whenever you are unloading your car, carry your keys with your groceries or other purchases. Dump them with your load and you'll skillfully hide your keys. They will stay hidden long after you have stored your items..

Too, you may stuff your keys in any jacket or coat you are wearing and then forget what you wore last. When you are working outside and have to open the car truck to get garden supplies, stick your keys in your slacks. Take your slacks off when you go inside and put them in the laundry basket. Since the laundry might not be washed for a few days, your keys will rest safely beneath a mound of clothes.

If all else fails, lock your keys in your car. That will be the last place you will think to look.

Cellular phones, too, are quite easy to lose. The surest way is to turn the power off as soon as you make a call. In this way, if you misplace your phone, you will not be able to use your home phone to locate the missing cellular.

If you are a lady, you may switch your phone from your black pocketbook to the white, taupe, red, purple, green, or brown purse. You will never know where to look. Even if you check every purse in your house, you may overlook one of the many hidden compartments.

Men, you may conceal your phones in jacket or slack pockets, especially effective if you change clothes often and if you send your clothes to the cleaners without checking the pockets. And, of course, refuse to wear clip-on contraptions.

When eating in a restaurant, put your cell phone on the table while you're eating and leave it with the dirty dishes when you leave. The waiter may consider it to be a tip.

A subtle way for both sexes to lose jewelry or other valuables is to hide them away. Realizing that thieves know all the usual hiding places, give serious thought to unknown, unlikely, unbelievable spots. Let the sites be so very unique, so very different, so very difficult that even you will not remember where to look.

It is not necessary to teach children losing techniques. Visit the "Lost and Found Room" in any school and you will see name-brand, expensive coats, jackets, sweaters, tennis shoes, computers, and even underwear.

You probably have heard the snide condemnation: "If it were not attached to your body, you would lose it!" Don't believe that foolish maxim. You can even lose a bodily attachment. For example, you can lose your mind.

I know. I have lost mine.

ASSIGNMENT IN WRITERS' GROUP

LISTED ARE THE BEGINNINGS OF TEN SENTENCES WHICH YOU ARE TO COMPLETE. EXAMPLE: If I were you, I would stop sucking my thumb. After all, you enter college next month.

THINGS I REALLY WOULD NOT SAY

1. IF I WERE YOU, I WOULD
   try another deodorant
2. IF I WERE YOU, I WOULD
   smile with my mouth closed.
3. IF I WERE YOU, I WOULD
   change hair stylists.
4. IF I WERE YOU, I WOULD
   not put a tattoo there.
5. IF I WERE YOU, I WOULD
   wear a corset.
6. IF I WERE YOU, I WOULD
   have my shower fixed.
7. IF I WERE YOU, I WOULD
   keep my day job.
8. IF I WERE YOU, I WOULD
   wash my hair at least once a month.
9. IF I WERE YOU, I WOULD
   get a whitening tooth paste.

10. IF I WERE YOU, I WOULD
   consider lipo-suction.

ROBBER

A robber entered a bank Monday morning with the typical zip-up bag that businessmen often use. He presented the bag to the teller and said, "I have a gun pointed at you. Smile and do as I say. I may get only one person, but I will get you if anything goes wrong".

The teller nodded and forced a smile.

"Load that bag with all the hundred and big bills you have and hurry."

Trembling, the teller did as she was told before pushing a slip of paper across to the robber. "Everyone has to sign for any transaction, she said. "Write something down. Anything! George Washington. New York City. Yellow or green. Just write something." She had already pushed the panic button.

The man wrote, took his bag, and left, only to be arrested before he reached his car.

The teller, on the verge of hysteria, read what the robber had written and began laughing and waving the bank slip. On it, the robber had written, "Have a blessed day."

Later, the robber explained to a policeman, "That's what my mama always says."

(After reading a "Reader's Digest" story about the bank robber who went across the street to another bank and asked to use a phone to call his mother to come pick him up, I wrote this bank robbery joke. I have submitted it to "Reader's Digest.")

"SOLE" SAVER

When I consider that closets of average American families today are stuffed with long and short jackets, wool and leather coats, and huge shelves of multi-colored shoes – red blue, green, purple, taupe, maroon, brown, black and white- I can scarcely believe that there was a period in my lifetime when most Americans owned only one coat and one pair of shoes.

It was during the late Great Depression days when my father chided, "Dorothy, if you do not quit wearing out a pair of shoes every two weeks, I'm going to buy you brogans, the heavy, boot-like shoes my brothers wore. I do not know why holes appeared on the bottom of my shoes so quickly. Was it because I walked long distances on cement walks and streets everywhere I went? Was it because the so-called- leather, thin soles were inferior? Or was it because, as my mother explained, I could never be still?

My dad walked several city blocks to work six days a week in rain or snow, often with similar holes in his shoes. Our family's dilemma, however, was not unique. The same situation prevailed to such an extent that some ingenious American was prompted to find an economical remedy. He created a thick, black, tire-rubber sole that could be glued to the bottom of worn shoes.

A person could buy a kit complete with two rubber soles and a bottle of glue. The rubber soles were then trimmed to the proper size and received a generous glob of glue. The worn soles were then painted with the same gooey stuff. Soles and rubber bottoms were kept apart for a specific time to allow the glue to become, what they called, "tacky." The two were then squeezed together and set aside to dry.

This make-shift half-sole worked well for a while, but the

wearer always walked warily, knowing the inevitable could happen at any time. The glue would not hold and the sole would begin to flap. In embarrassment, the wearer would try to step with barely lifting his feet. The flip flop, flip flop, flip flop belied his intentions.

Once the sole was completely released, the cause was lost. There was no more glue to re-sole the shoe. Another remedy had to be found. An ingenious family member now cut out a cardboard inner sole and inserted it within the shoe. This solution worked well as long as the weather cooperated.

One thing is for sure: whoever called the Depression era "the good old days" never wore mended shoes.

NAME DICKERING

Yesterday my 100-year-old mother commented, "No one names a child Addie anymore."

"Maybe not, Mother, but I bet Addie was a very popular name when your mother chose it for you," I replied.

And so, I started thinking about names again. Addie has a positive ring to it. All of us like to add to whatever we have. We add to our bank accounts, our estates, our family ties, our happiness. Addie, therefore, has a positive connotation. On the other hand, who ever heard of anyone naming a child "Substractie" or "Dividee"?

Throughout the ages, names have been chosen for the wonderful things they suggest. Take those names derived from coveted jewels like Ruby, Pearl, Chrystal, Jasper, and even Jewel. Yet, a line in drawn. Who has dared call a child Chalcedony, Sardonyx, Amethyst, or Topaz?

Beautiful flowers, also, have produced suitable names. Consider, for instance, Rose, Lilly, and Daisy. Still, we have no renowned Daffodils, Chrysanthemums, or Hyacinths. (I tremble as I write these words. Could I inadvertently challenge someone to hang one of these monstrosities upon an innocent babe?)

I smile when I consider how many loving wives have taken their husbands' first names and altered them to make them feminine, thus perpetuating the initial name of their highly-esteemed mates. Paul has become Paulette or Pauline; Victor is Victoria; Henry, Henrietta; George, Georgette; Sam, Samantha; Don, Donella; and the list could go on.

On the other hand, who has encountered a mother's longer name shortened to become a male name? Could I possibly have played with my name, Dorothy Alease, and named my two sons "Dor" and "Alee"? Could Miriam have a son called Mir; Marlene a son named Mar; Sheilla, She; Wanda, Wan; or Tiffany, Tiff? I think not.

I knew a lovely family that named their children fish names – Starr and Marlin; but I have never heard a youngster called Shark, Porpoise, or Eel.

Dogs have often been given men or ladies' names. I remember once my son named his favorite Beagle " Dot," much to my consternation, especially when my husband would raise the window and scream to a barking dog, "Shut up, Dot! If you don't, I'm going to come out there and kill you!" (He once yelled these words when we had over-night guests who knew nothing about the dog. They confessed later that they thought Chester was angry with me.)

Yes, dogs may get out names, but never, never, never has a parent stooped to name a child Fido, Rover, or Spot.

Yea, we go our way with names; but, perhaps we have built-in restraints. Perhaps not. My dad once worked with a man named Hallelujah, called Hal for short.

And today, the biggest, grandest phenomenon of all is the computer. Will parents soon create names like Gatesey, Microsofee, Dellee,, E-bay, Dotcom, or -Emailee?

We'll wait and see.

STILL MUCH TO EXPLORE

What now? What have I always wanted to do but have not done? What have I longed to try but have not attempted? What have I planned to study but have not yet started?

Since reaching retirement age, I have discovered a freedom to do some very unusual things. It all started as I walked through Wal-Mart one evening. In the shoe department, I spotted black patent leather. tap-dancing shoes. I stood, looking at them and remembering how, as a child, I wanted so desperately to try tap dancing. To me, tapping was such a happy sound. Alas, however, only the most affluent families in the 1930s could afford to let their children take dancing lessons. Few people could own more than one pair of shoes at the time, much less these fancy tap-dancing shoes with huge metal cleats on the toes and heels and with fancy black bows to tie across the top.

I stood there, recalling how I watched tap dancers at the movies and went home to try their steps with my clumsy, silent shoes; and suddenly, on a whim, as an adult, I took the magical shoes and carefully placed them in my buggy. After six decades, I was going to wear official tap-dancing shoes – in the privacy of my home, of course.

What a pleasant surprise when I tapped happily across the cement floor in my basement and discovered: I actually could tap dance! So elated was I over my discovery that I returned to Wal-Mart and purchased another pair of these treasured shoes for my granddaughter. What fun we had, dancing together in our basement's seclusion. Soon I discovered that tap dancing was a super aerobic workout. My childhood ambition had opened a hidden but healthy, happy outlet.

Since this initial venture, I have learned to play the harmonica, play chess, and study ventriloquism. Life to me is like a box of Whitman's assorted chocolates which I keep sampling and savoring.

What shall I try next?

CHORE CURSE

Mundane! Mundane! Mundane!

For decades the bane of my life has been the absolute necessity of making up my bed each day. Why should I strain to straighten sheets, tuck corners, and fluff pillows? Why should I arrange a weighty bedspread and carefully place decorative pillows? After tossing and turning all night, why should I be called upon to forget my misery and honor the bed?

Now, homemaking experts say the job should be done a specific way. The bottom sheet must be pulled tightly over the mattress to fit snugly over the corners. If the top sheet has designs, consideration must be given if a blanket is to be used. The design side must be placed down so that the decorative top can fold over the top of the blanket at the head of the bed.

Sometimes, for meanness, I leave one mattress corner uncovered, the designed sheet placed so that the unsightly underside shows, the blanket turned sideways, the pillows at the foot, and the bedspread crumpled under the bed.

Rebellion has set in. I have decided never to make my bed again. Just, don't tell my mother.

BEHIND -THE -WHEEL EXPERT

I'm an expert driver. When I'm behind the wheel, I can drive at least five cars at a time. If I am on a multi-lane highway or if there is much merging traffic, I can do even better.

Confident of my skills, I maneuver along without a problem. My stress comes from those inane people who surround me.

When I mentor the driver in front of me, I admonish, "Speed up, Jerk. See how much distance there is between you and the other driver." Sometimes I'm forced to say, "If you are getting off the highway, do it! You are going to cause me to be rear-ended." At other times, I must scream, "Give your turn-off signal sooner, Idiot. You made my tires squeal!"

To the driver on my right, I ask, "In driver's education did you not learn to line up the hood insignia with the white, outside line? In other words, move over, Stupid."

My mother once heard me talking out loud to other drivers and she said, "I don't think you should say things like that, Dot. You shouldn't call anyone Stupid."

"Aw, come on, Mother," I said jokingly, "I thought Stupid was my name until I was twelve." She was appalled. She had never called any of her brilliant children "Stupid."

Now, back to driving advice. I have to help the driver on my left. He often gets in my blind spot and hovers there. I try to show him I could swipe him when I move to the center line. "Hey, Buster, either speed up or drop back." Sometimes, he whips in front of me, leaving three inches between our bumpers. "Dummy," I scream, sticking my tongue out and hoping he is looking in his rearview mirror.

Of course, everyone understands the driver behind me needs guidance. "Hey, you back there, don't you know if we have a wreck, it would be your fault? Back off. I'm not going over 55 miles per hour no matter how much you crowd."

I must admit I hate riding in the right lane. Ninety-eight percent of the highway's uninformed drivers merging into traffic do not know what a yield sign means.

Yes, highways are filled with poorly-informed drivers, and I do all I can to remedy the dangerous situations they create.

I'm good, that's true, but I must admit my husband in always "one up" on me. When he is on the passenger side, he can mastermind all those cars surrounding us and, strategically, can add ME in, to boot.

MY DOLL

I wonder if nine-year-old girls play with dolls today. I do not mean the slinky, gorgeous, grown-up Barbie and her handsome boyfriend Ken. I mean the cuddly, real life-like baby dolls that have to be fed, changed, and put to bed.

Of course I must admit, way back in the '30s, we had mostly an inferior forerunner of later dolls. We had cut-out, paper dolls, dolls that could be grown people as well as children. These dolls came in paper books with the doll figures on the stiffer cover and assorted clothes on thinner, inside pages . Each garment had tabs that were placed at the shoulders and sides to fasten on the clothes.

Cutting out both dolls and clothes could be a tedious job and often required the help of patient adults. Both clothes and bodies could easily be torn or lost.

Even though playing with these flat paper dolls could stir the imagination, they did not compare with the later holding of baby dolls that could open and close eyes and say, "Mama" when turned over.

These new, cuddly dolls possessed rotund bodies made with a course white cloth and soft stuffing. The head and baby arms and legs were made of a hard, shapely casting glossed over with a pink, outer layer.

The hair was sometimes painted on or was woven into the head. This type synthetic hair could be combed very carefully. It came out easily or frayed to look like Brill-o Pads.

Nevertheless, these real-life, baby replicas nurtured the maternal instinct, for girls were more careful about where they placed these little ones and did not leave them unattended for long periods of time. They gave them choice names, wrapped them carefully in baby blankets, and begged mamas to make fancy baby dresses.

Usually, I exercised the needed tender care for my baby doll; but on one occasion, I failed. I forgot to put my doll to bed. During the night, torrents of rain fell. Morning came and I went to check on my baby. Alas, I did not find her in her customary place nor in any other likable place in our house. Almost afraid to do so, I went outside to look.

I found her lying in the grass by our home. Her stuffed body was soggy and misshaped. Her beautiful face, arms, and legs were peeling back, leaving glazing that looked like curled wood chips.

I cried, for there was no healing for my little one. Strange, but the trauma associated with this childhood loss has had a lasting effect upon my life. Invariably, when I hear a downpour of rain at night, my mind is troubled with the thought: "Have I left anything outside that should not be getting wet? Have I taken care of things as I should have?"

BITS OF POETRY

WHAT I KNOW

I've gone to college
And now, I know
How little I know
How much I'll never know
That there are those who know
And say so
And make me feel
Unlettered
Yea, fettered
To ignorance.

N O T E : **Although I never wrote much poetry, I did use this form, at times, to capture a thought. I liked free verse, for it offered an easy way to say a lot, but with fewer words. For example:**

WHEN I SAY GOODBYE

When I say, "Goodbye,"
I shall not sigh.
Already I've trampled
Upon a half century
Of stalwart, good years.
My face has wrinkled
With laughter
Far more often
Than with tears.
I've known countless scores
Of precious sojourners
Young and old.
I've tried all the good things
The world has to offer.
Why should I fret
When God sees fit
To offer my eager spirit
A fairer field
A greater reason
To live on
Forever?

PAST PRETTY

Pretty hair,
Pretty eyes and teeth
Pretty hand and feet.
Pretty this; pretty that.
Oh, my flawed skin,
I forgot
How pretty I was
Before old age
Set in.
Yes, pretty this; pretty that.
Always thin, never fat.
Oh, my friend,
Why did this image
Have to end?

I MAY

I may go on a diet today
I may begin to waste away.
I may refuse a coke or two;
I may deny a wish to chew.
I may subsist on eggs and greens;
I may replace all fats with leans.
I may go on a diet today,
But I doubt it.

WRITINGS
FOR OTHERS

Newspaper Feature: Norman Rockwell
Short play
Memorial Tributes

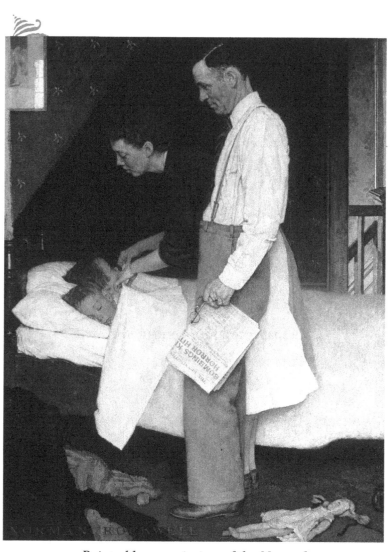

Printed by permission of the Normal Rockwell Family Agency. Copyright 1943 the Norman Rockwell Family Entities.

NOTE: I wrote this story for a local Tennessee newspaper that published a full-page feature about Norman Rockwell's famous World War II picture of concerned parents looking down upon their two sleeping children. David Squiers, an adult in our church, was the little boy pictured in the scene. As a former neighbor of the Rockwells, Squiers gave these accounts of Rockwell's methods of using models.

SAMPLE OF NEWSPAPER STORIES:

NORMAN ROCKWELL: A SPECIAL NEIGHBOR

Not everyone can boast about being the neighbor of a national celebrity, but David Squiers of Johnson City, Tennessee, can. For years, the Squiers family were next-door, Vermont neighbors of renowned artist Normal Rockwell.

Of course, next door in Arlington, Vermont, meant one mile down a country road. Rockwell moved to Arlington in 1939 when Squiers was two years old and lived in the small town of 1100 people for 14 productive years.

Although Rockwell was already established as one of America's leading artists, he settled in the community so easily that the townspeople were hardly aware of his greatness.

Perhaps Rockwell's own attitude accounts for the relaxed acceptance the reserved New Englanders gave him. When he began using his neighbors as models, Rockwell treated them as honored guests whenever they came to his studio. He talked freely and always informed his models when the finished pictures would appear in print.

Squiers says, "We never thought of him as being anyone different." Pointing out neighborly acts, Squiers remembers that for years his father, Walt Squiers, and Rockwell called each other's children and pretended to be Santa Claus.

"My father and Rockwell fished and hunted together," Squiers says, "but Rockwell stopped hunting after he viewed the Bambi movie."

Squiers' parents and the Rockwells became close friends, attending grange meetings and square dances together. The Rockwell boys - Jerry, Tommy, and Peter - matched the ages of the Squiers children. They played neighborhood games together and attended the same school. Being the youngest boy in the group, Squiers became the recipient of the Rockwell boys' hand-me-down clothes.

Once Rockwell became a part of Arlington, he practically ceased to use professional models. His newly-found friends became the subjects for his "slice of life" themes.

The artist hired Squiers' father, a carpenter, to convert a barn across the road from his rambling country house into a studio. Here, he periodically scheduled neighbors to come to pose for camera shots. Often, he had a rough sketch of what he intended to paint. He showed the initial sketch to his novice models and let them act out individual parts.

All the subjects for an intended picture did not, necessarily, pose at the same time. For instance, when Squiers and his sister posed for one of "The Four Freedoms" pictures, the two children were tucked in bed and photographed many times. The other two subjects, a mother and father, were photographed in a different session.

The Squiers family members, especially Squiers' father, often were used as subjects. Squiers, himself, first became part of a Rockwell illustration when he was only 2 ½ years old. He was pictured in an Upjohn pharmaceutical painting. Wearing a little yellow suit, he sat in the lap of Mrs. Norman Rockwell and looked on with two other children while a country doctor prescribed medicine.

Squiers' most notable honor came, however, during a war bond endeavor in 1943. Rockwell, having expressed a concern to do something for the war effort, was commissioned by the "Post" magazine to paint "The Four Freedoms." These paintings were to show freedoms that Americans were still enjoying while other countries were being torn apart by war. Rockwell labored over these illustrations, taking six months to decide on his message, to revise, and to complete the project.

Squiers and his parents appeared in three of these four classic paintings. In "Freedom from Fear" the artist composed a scene with a little boy and girl sleeping peacefully together. By their bed, a mother bent over to tuck them in. The father stood by her side, looking on and holding a newspaper with a headline that reported bombings in Europe.

Squiers points out that on the floor in the "Freedom from Fear" picture lies his sister's little doll, Delicia.

As a six-year-old child at that time, Squiers remembers it was hard to keep his eyes closed, especially when the photographer draped the black camera covering over his head.

"I kept wanting to watch," Squiers said.

Rockwell was known for being very active during a photographic session. He smoked his long-stemmed pipe, drank small, bottled cokes constantly, and carried on friendly chatter. His enthusiasm and characteristic excitement, being contagious, probably account for the fact that people enjoyed posing for him. Model shyness disappeared, for Rockwell often demonstrated the needed facial expressions and gestures, even before he began the photographic session. The subjects, knowing that they were usually a part of a whole picture that would be composted later, were eager to see the finished work.

Rockwell's neighborhood models were paid $15 for children and $10 for the adults, generous amounts for the 1940's. These payments were made more special by the artist's thoughtful presentation. Each amount was placed in a sealed envelope and handed to the subject, usually after cokes had been served in the studio.

Shortly after "The Four Freedoms" were completed, Rockwell's barn studio burned to the ground during the middle of the night. While the Rockwells were preparing to move and to have another studio built, the artist used an abandoned one-room school building as a temporary studio. Squiers remembers this building, for it was here that the media and friends later crowded together to pay homage to the artist for "The Four Freedoms."

Squiers' father again was hired to build Rockwell a new studio once the Rockwells had moved three or four miles down the road on West Arlington Village Green. In his new quarters, Rockwell continued phoning friends and neighbors, asking if they would consider posing for one of his typical American themes. Of course, the local people felt honored to do so and looked forward to seeing their published pictures, especially on the covers of "The Saturday Evening Post." Rockwell illustrated 322 magazine covers, many of them with Vermont natives as subjects.

When Squiers was sixteen, the Rockwells moved to Stockbridge, Massachusetts, to be near the hospital that Rockwell's wife had to visit for treatments.

Eleven years later, as a married man, Squiers was passing through Stockbridge and decided to stop by the Rockwell's home to get an autograph for a "Freedom from Fear" print. He arrived at the artist's home at the time the 80-year-old Rockwell was taking one of his periodic naps. His wife explained the elderly man "alternated painting and napping during the day." She asked that Squiers and his wife return in an hour. When the couple returned, they were greeted by Norman Rockwell whose frail eyes twinkled when he looked at Squiers. "I don't know your name,' he confessed, "but I know that I have painted you." He graciously signed the Squiers' print with very legible handwriting: "My best wishes to David Squiers who posed for the sleeping boy. Cordially, Norman Rockwell."

David Squiers cherishes all pictures that included the Squiers family; but, more so, he cherishes the memory of a congenial neighbor with a genuine love for people and a sincere desire to capture realistic sketches of American life in his endearing art form.

NEWS RELEASE
WENDY'S SURPRISE

When Wendy Gerrity of Martinez, Georgia, faced a new decade, she did not know how many people would fly thousands of miles to attend her surprise birthday party. She was smart enough to assume that family members or friends might honor her in some way, but she could not foresee the scope of the endeavor.

When she returned home on a Saturday afternoon in mid-April, she was awed to see cars lined up and down both sides of her Stevens Way home. Greater surprises came when she spied her sister, Jill Reid, who had flown from Saskatoon, Saskatchewan Canada, and her nephew Bryce Wood, who had flown from Prince George, British Columbia, Canada, -- a total of 5,140 miles one way!

Topping that, daughter Carly Rowsom and her family of three had flown 10,380 miles from Bali, Indonesia. Daughter Brianna Barber, with her family of five, flew across country from Las Vegas, Nevada.

Wendy's brother, Barry, travelled from Littiz, Pennsylvania, to show his love.

All in all, Wendy's family members traveled 16, 782 miles, one way, for her celebration.

John and Sue Barber from Dayton, Ohio, and 30 Silver Sneakers members of the North Augusta Family Y where Wendy is a fitness instructor, joined neighbors and local friends for the occasion.

SHORT PLAY: LOVE TRIANGLE

CHARACTERS:
Beulah Deen Moore – 93-year-old Old Maid (Very bossy)
Sadie Sue Moore – Beulah Deen's 88 year-old Old Maid sister
(sweet)
Handsome Butcher

SETTINGS: Moore sisters' home and Butcher Shop

The scene may open with Sadie Sue seated at a table facing the audience OR she may enter, turn on the lamp on the table and sit to primp, write, read what she has written, and throw the copy away.

BEULAH DEEN: (Calls from off stage as she enters. Cranky voice. Enters walking with a cane that she often uses to express herself.)

SADIE SUE: I'm so glad you came home. I need you to help me write a lover letter.

BEULAH DEEN: A lover letter? You mean a love letter, don't you? Who in the world are you writing a love letter for?

SADIE SUE: For me. For me, Beulah Deen. I'm writing a letter to the man I love….to the man who loves me!

BEULAH DEEN: Sadie Sue Moore, have you lost your marbles? Who in the world is this man you think loves you?

SADIE SUE: Oh, Beulah Deen, he is the most handsome man in the world. It's the new butcher in town.

BEULAH DEEN: The butcher? So that is why we have been having meat every day for the last two weeks. And is that the reason you are wearing those stupid ribbons? (She tries to snatch a ribbon out of Sadie Sue's head, but Sadie Sue ducks.) Every day you look like thrown-away Christmas wrappings.

SADIE SUE: But he likes ribbons. He told me so.

BEULAH DEEN: He told you so? He told you so! Now, Sadie Sue Moore, you tell me why you think this meat cutter likes you?

SADIE SUE: Oh, Sister, he says the sweetest things and he does something special for me every time. If I buy wieners, he weighs them and then he smiles and says, "I'm putting you two more for extra measure." And when I buy stew beef, he weighs it and then says, "Sadie Sue, I'm going to add this hunk of fat. It will help your stew taste better."

BEULAH DEEN: And that is why you think this man loves you?

SADIE SUE: Yes. Yes. Yes. And sometimes he winks at me. Oh, Sister, help me write my letter. I want to tell him what is in my heart.

BEULAH DEEN: I WILL NOT help you write that dumb letter, but I tell you what I will do. Get up from there. I am going with you down to that butcher shop. I want to see the nitwit who has been sweet-talking you.

SADIE SUE: Oh, wonderful! Wonderful, Beulah Deen. I want you to see him, and I want him to see you.

(**Setting**: Butcher shop. Good looking middle aged man behind counter.)

BUTCHER: Oh, here comes the lovely Sadie Sue Moore! And who is the pretty young lady you have with you?

SADIE SUE: (All flustered) Oh, this is my sister...my OLDER sister. (Beulah Deen punches her with the cane.) Her name is Beulah Deen. Beulah Deen Moore.

BUTCHER: Beulah Deen. What a lovely name for a lovely person. Now, ladies, what can I do for you?

SADIE SUE: You tell him, Big Sister.

BEULAH DEEN: You tell him yourself!

SADIE SUE: Oh, well...well. How 'bout two chicken breasts?

BUTCHER: (picking out two breasts) Oh, yes, and I think I'll throw in a couple legs for good measure. No charge, you know.

SADIE SUE: Oh, thank you. Thank you. (She flutters her eye lashes)

BUTCHER: That will be $3.94, my dear.

BEULAH DEEN: Pay the man, Sadie Sue.

(Sadie Sue pulls up her skirt and takes out $5.00 tucked in her hose. She counts off $3 and pays the butcher who gingerly accepts the money and says, "Thank you."

BEULAH DEEN: (Taking Sadie Sue by the arm and leading her outside.)

(Outside the butcher shop, Beulah Deen stops and fluffs her hair.)

BEULAH DEEN: Sadie Sue, you are right. That is a handsome man, but I am not sure about him yet. Let's go back in there and buy something else. Leave that chicken out here on that bench.)

(They return. The butcher looks pleasantly surprised)

BUTCHER: Well, well, well, why am I honored to have you two beautiful ladies in my shop again so soon?

BEULAH DEEN: (thinking fast) Ohhhh. I saw that hog liver in your showcase and I decided I wanted some. Just two slices please.

BUTCHER: (weighs out two pieces) But, Beulah Deen Moore, for you I am including an extra slice. How's that?

BEULAH DEEN: Very nice. Pay the kind man, Sadie Sue.

(They leave, but this time, Beulah Deen keeps looking back.)

(Outside the butcher shop, Beulah Deen stops and puts her hand over her heart.)

BEULAH DEEN: Oh, dear me, Sadie Sue, he winked at me. Did you see that?

SADIE SUE: He was probably winking at me. He always does that.

BEULAH DEEN: Put that liver over there with that chicken, Sadie Sue. We are going back in there one more time. I love that man and I believe he loves me.

SADIE SUE: Now, Beulah Deen Moore, that's not fair. I saw him first.

BEULAH DEEN: Come now, Sadie Sue. Didn't you ever hear, "Anything is fair in love and war"?

SADIE SUE: Is that in the Bible?

BEULAH DEEN: Yeh. I think it's found in Barnabus, chapter ten, verse one. Come on now.

SADIE SUE: When we get back home, I'm going to borrow a Bible and look that up!

(Again they enter.)

BUTCHER: Well, this is my lucky day. The Moore sisters are back again. Did you think of something else you need?

BEULAH DEEN: (fluttering her lashes) Yes, indeedy. We need some hamburger.

SADIE SUE: But we have plenty of hamburger. (Beulah Deens taps her with her cane to stop her.)

BUTCHER: I have just ground some beef. Now, the very lean is $2.99 a pound and the regular is $1.50.

BEULAH DEEN: I suppose we'll just take the regular.

BUTCHER: I tell you what. I'm going to give you the lean beef, but I'm going to charge you for the regular.

BEULAH DEEN: Thank you. That is very sweet of you. (Trying to flirt)

(They start to leave; but when they are out of earshot, Beulah Deen stops.)

BEULAH DEEN: Wait a minute, Sadie Sue. We are going back there right now to find out which one of he really loves.

SADIE SUE: Really, Beulah Deen. How are you going to do that?

BEULAH DEEN: I'm going to ask him. He has to decide between the two of us right now. This **love triangle** has gone on far too long.

(Sadie Sue tags along, rearranging her ribbon.)

BUTCHER: (looking perplexed) Now, pretty ladies, what is it? Surely you do not need more meat.

BEULAH DEEN: You're right. We do not need more meat. We need YOU. That is, we need ya…. to tell us….which one of us you love better.

BUTCHER: Oh, my dear ladies, I could not do that. I love you both the same. I's just that you BOTH remind me so much of my beloved grandmother who is 101 years old. Yes, Granny is 101, and I miss her so much. She lives 200 miles from here.

BEULAH DEEN: (offended) Your granny? Your 101-year-old granny! (She snatches the hamburger from Sadie Sue's hands, plops it down on the counter, grabs Sadie Sue's ribbon.) Here, tie this ribbon around this rancid meat it and send it to your sainted granny! (grabbing Sadie Sue by the arm) Come on, Sadie Sue, let's get out of here.

(Outside)

SADIE SUE: Oh, Sister, look! The dogs are eating our meat!

BEULAH DEEN: Good. They'll die instead of us.

(As sisters move toward home, attention is focused on the butcher.)

BUTCHER: (with helpless gesture) What have I done? (glancing upward) Dear Lord, I can't help it that I'm so good looking.

BEULAH DEEN: I hate that man. Shoooty fire, Sadie Sue, I don't see what you ever saw in that man.

SADIE SUE: I loved him. I loved him. (crying) Breaking up is so hard to do. (bawls loudly as she exits or curtain closes.

MEMORIAL TRIBUTES

Clarence Robert Hicks

December 7, 1899 – November 20, 1965

Turn-of-the-Century Man

By Dorothy Hicks Phillips

TURN-OF-THE-CENTURY MAN

One hundred years ago when Clarence Robert Hicks was born on December 7, 1899, he entered an era foreign to men of today. The turn-of the-century man had a life expectancy of 40 years; a woman, 43. Of necessity, work was thrust upon children, especially boys, at an early age. Factory or mill work was lawful for children, and education was not mandatory; therefore, often children were taken from school and placed in the workplace.

Clarence, the oldest of Robert and Ina's 13 children, in keeping with the custom, was taken from school before he finished elementary school. He was needed to help earn a living for the quickly-growing family. Although he could not attend school, Clarence had a great zeal for learning and secretly longed to be a doctor; but, of course, that was out of the question.

As soon as he was old enough, he left home for a better paying job in a cigarette factory in Durham, North Carolina. He found a way to further his education by attending night school classes. He was an avid reader, devouring Durham's morning and evening newspapers, "The Durham Morning Herald" and "The Durham Sun." Once he won First Place in a weekly radio quiz show that featured several contestants, mostly professional people, who were quizzed on the two newspapers' stories for the previous week. Clarence's reading interests lay, not in fiction, but in factual material. When he had grandchildren, he often said to their parents, "If you can have only one magazine in your home, let it be the "National Geographic.""

Perhaps it was his desire for learning that led him from his Durham cigarette factory job to enroll in a barber college. He loved the barbering textbooks, for they included anatomy studies that mirrored what he might have studied as a medical student.

Making a living as a barber in the basement of the First National Bank Building in Durham enriched Clarence's life in two ways: his clientele was made up mainly of educated business men whose discussions were stimulating. Too, the barber shop subscribed to several leading magazines which Clarence read monthly.

In March, 1920, Clarence married a pretty young lady named Addie Lee Outen whom he had met in the cigarette factory. (Addie, like many youth of her day, had come to the city to work.) After a proper dating period, in which he was not permitted to kiss her until they were engaged, Clarence proposed. The wedding took place in the boarding house where Addie was living with the landlady Lillie Nuysum, and Addie's sister Effie serving as witnesses. The happy young couple boarded a bus and rode almost thirty miles to Raleigh, North Carolina, where they spent a short honeymoon in a hotel, a "big thing" at that time.

In the early days of their marriage, they took in boarders for whom Addie prepared good meals. "They especially liked my biscuits," Addie recalls with pride. Together, Clarence and Addie headed a family of four children – three boys and one girl. The first child, Bobby, was named Robert Lee Hicks – Robert after his father and grandfather and Lee after his mother, Addie Lee. Bobby was born December 13, 1920, in Sumpter

County, S.C. Dorothy Alease was second, (May 11, 1924); then, Carlton Franklin (August 5, 1929) and Richard Wayne (August 14, 1937). The last three children were born in Durham County, the last Hicks' child being born 17 years after the first.

Bobby, the oldest son, probably, as is typical of the first child, bore the brunt of the strictest discipline. Clarence patterned his discipline methods after his father and the other fathers of that period. In early America, strict discipline was the rule, not the exception.

From childhood, Clarence and his brothers and sisters had learned to obey or to suffer the consequences. Once the children slipped and went swimming in a nearby creek that was forbidden territory. Later, Clarence always smiled as he recalled his father's detecting their disobedience by observing their ultra-clean skin and shriveled fingers. The children all suffered an old-fashion whipping for their afternoon of sneaky fun.

And so, Clarence began his fathering by administering the switch or belt to his off-springs when they strayed from family rules. All four children got needed whippings but Wayne, the last, received the least.

Although Clarence was a poor man, he maintained an admirable philosophy of life. He taught his children to be honest, respectful of authority, and decent in all things. No cursing or any vulgar language was ever used in his household. Uncouth things, like belching or expelling gas, were strictly forbidden. Modesty was required from the male, as well as the female members, in the family. Meal times, always opened with Clarence's stock prayer, "Lord, make us thankful for these blessings and all other blessings in Jesus' name. Amen." Table conversations were dominated by sports since there was a four-male to a two- female ratio. The family honored their father by always waiting for him (except on Saturdays when he worked long hours) so that the whole family ate together. Preferential treatment was shown Clarence as the head of the home. For instance, he always was given first choice of the chicken or the meat being served. Because he could not drink milk or eat dairy foods, dishes were prepared with other seasonings. He was, what we call, Lactose Intolerant today, but the condition had not been diagnosed at that time.

Clarence was a poor man, yes, but a hard-working poor man who never accepted governmental help. He worked long hours as a barber when a shave and haircut could cost as little as a quarter (There was a little ditty prevalent: "Shave and a haircut. Two bits. Who's gonna pay for it? Tom Mix.")

Clarence became involved in establishing a barber's union to help raise the standard for barbers' wages. For several years he served as the secretary for the local barber's union. Perhaps, because of his active role in the union, he was once approached by a Communist who sought to entice him into a secret Communist organization being formed in Durham. Not only did Clarence refuse, but he immediately reported the invitation to local authorities who were very concerned about developing Communistic activities.

Early in their marriage, Clarence and Addie decided that Addie was needed at home with the children. It is true that they tried having Addie work when they had only two children, but an unpleasant incident changed their plans. Bobby was old enough to report that the lady who kept them had threatened to cut open his toddler sister if she did not mind orders. Clarence and Addie's love for their children dictated that the family subsist on less with Addie always in the home.

One philosophy that Clarence held was that the neighborhood influenced the lives of children; therefore. he invested a disproportionate amount of his meager salary to renting a home in a good section of town. At one time, his rent was $5.00 a week out of an $18.00- week salary. In this home, 501 Gurley Street, where they lived nine years, he surrounded his children by people who stressed education, clean living, and respectability.

From this neighborhood came the president of the student body at Durham High School, outstanding athletes, college graduates, civic leaders, and prosperous businessmen.

To protect his oldest son as a teenager from having wrong after-school influences, Clarence made arrangements for Bobby to work as an assistant to a tobacco warehouse leaf-account supervisor each week day. This training later enabled Bobby to become proficient as a speculator, a government tobacco inspector, and later as a district director for the Department of Agriculture, occupations that earned him a comfortable living.

One incident with Dorothy illustrated the emphasis Clarence placed upon integrity. It happened when Dorothy was about nine or ten years old. While walking through Woolworth's Five and Ten-Cent Store, Dorothy stopped at the jewelry counter to try on some ten-cent rings. As she was leaving the store, she was stopped by a lady clerk who said, "Little girl, if you will give me back that ring, I will not tell anyone." Frightened and aghast, Dorothy protested that she had no ring and showed the clerk Hurrying to Clarence's barber shop, Dorothy explained to her father what had happened. Today a person might not understand the full extent of this insult as much as a turn-of-the-century man did.

Clarence was disturbed that anyone would suspect and accuse his child of stealing. Law suits were almost unheard of at the time; but because of the principle, Clarence consulted a lawyer friend. The end result was a confrontation with Woolworths that ended with a settlement of two or three hundred dollars. Money, however, was not Clarence's consideration. He wanted vindication for his esteemed child who had been falsely accused.

Although Clarence had great confidence in his children and they knew he would back them for any right cause, he had a rule about school: if one received a whipping in school, he would receive another at home. He wanted his children to respect and obey their teachers. Reports cards were important to him and he reprimanded or praised his children according to the teachers' reports. From the earliest days, although Addie helped with the children's homework, Clarence did his part by emphasizing the importance of education. All his children knew they would finish high school and perhaps go to college. (The war changed some plans for Bobby and Frank. Both served in World War II. Bobby attended Louisburg College on a baseball scholarship before enlisting in the Marines. Frank finished high school and joined the Navy.)

Clarence loved baseball. As a boy, he had had his nose broken four times while playing sandlot ball. As a grown man, he attended as many of the Durham Bulls' games as possible even though it meant walking several miles to and from the ball park. When his little sons accompanied him, often he carried one of them most of the way there and back. At the games often, he could afford to pay only for standing room. Neither Clarence nor his sons boys minded standing; however the boys were glad when the knot-hole plan provided a place for them to sit.

Since he did not own a car until he was 40 years old, he spent his early adult life walking everywhere – a wonderful form of exercise although its benefits were not touted then. He was almost never sick, working six days a week until the day he retired.

Having raised a family during the depression years,

Clarence never knew what it was to take a vacation. He did not bemoan the fact, however, for practically no one could afford the luxury of a family vacation in the 1920s and 1930s.

When Clarence and Addie moved outside the Durham City limits in 1941, they began attending a Free Will Baptist Church, the only church in the Sherron Acres settlement at that time. Under this thriving church's ministry, Clarence came to a saving knowledge of Christ and Addie rededicated her life to the Lord. Both were baptized in the Eno River by their pastor, Rev. Fred Rivenbark.

In the following years, Clarence taught a boys' Sunday school class and coached Little League baseball team. At his death, many of the young men he had taught or coached, made a long line on each side of the church steps and walkway as the casket was carried to the hearse.

Perhaps the outcome of his four children's lives would redound to Clarence Hicks's honor, for all four have done very well, each excelling in his own field. Bobby had a many-faceted career in playing and umpiring baseball. He spent 11 years in professional baseball, being brought up to the American League as an umpire for the New York Yankees in the 1955 spring training in St. Petersburg, Florida. In later years, he progressed in governmental work, retiring as a district director with the Department of Agriculture (ASCS).

Dorothy, having earned a Master's degree, garnered accolades as a high school English and journalism teacher and freelance writer. She is listed in several Who's Who publications in which Clarence and Addie are noted as her parents.

Frank has held top-notch executive positions, at times with as many as six or eight secretaries. He served as the Advertising Manager of Rose's Stores and as a member of the stores' Executive Committee. During his career, he established his own private stores and companies, being successful in all that he started. He owned and piloted his own airplane.

Wayne, the youngest child, served as an executive in Sears and Montgomery Ward's stores and managed flourishing Wal-Mart stores in Kansas, North Carolina, and South Carolina, receiving commendations regularly for his leadership.

Clarence was a mild-mannered man. He was never loud. When he and Addie had the typical marital misunderstandings, Clarence handled his emotions by silent pouting. Sometimes these silent treatments lasted two or three days, but then the hugging and handholding would resume, much to the delight of the children.

He laughed mainly with his eyes but never with a loud, boisterous sound. At the table, he listened as everyone talked without interrupting or contradicting anyone. He did not argue politics or religion. He talked quietly. When he prayed at the table, he prayed so quietly that once Bobby said, "Daddy, I did not hear what you said."

Clarence replied, "I was not talking to you."

He loved having his grown children and grandchildren come home. He and Addie bought and prepared their children's favorite foods and welcomed all of them at any time but, especially, at Christmas.

In the summer of 1965, an X-ray revealed a quarter-sized spot on Clarence's lungs; but when exploratory surgery was performed, doctors discovered that cancer had spread from his lungs to the aorta of his heart. Further surgery was not deemed feasible. Even Cobalt treatments could not eliminate the rampant growth process. In haste, Clarence set about getting everything in order In truth, he had started doing this a few months before his illness as though he sensed the need to do so. All insurance and final papers were collected and checked. Before his demise

257

in three short months, he had taken care of all major business and had talked with his daughter about his funeral wishes.

The wake took place in the Clement's Funeral Home, but the memorial service was conducted at Sherron Acres FWB Church - both honoring Clarence Hicks as a thoughtful man. Over 500 people, of all races and walks of life, paid their respects, many taking the time to tell a family member some special thing that Mr. Hicks had done for them or their family.

Over the years, he had gone to the home of shut-ins to give haircuts and shaves and always without pay.

Working downtown in Durham, Clarence usually knew when there were good job openings and he took it upon himself to match jobs with acquaintances who needed employment. During the wake, many said, "Mr. Hicks got me my job."

Three days before his death, Clarence was admitted to the hospital. As his daughter stood by his bed, Clarence said, "Dot, I don't suppose I'll ever go back to my little home (the home on 717 Carter Avenue which he and Addie had bought and beautified).

"You may not, Daddy," Dot said, "but John 14 says, 'Let not your heart be troubled. Neither let it be afraid. In my Father's house are many mansions. If it were not so, I would have told you. I go to prepare a place for you and if I go and prepare a place for you, I will come again that where I am you may be also."

"I know," Clarence said. "That is my favorite passage of Scripture."

And so, because of his faith in the Lord Jesus Christ as personal Savior, Clarence Robert Hicks, at almost 66, left this world with all its struggles and delights and entered a far better place prepared by the Lord himself. Truly, "Heaven's gain was earth's loss."

December, 1899 – November, 1965

EDITOR'S NOTE: I have written this story about my daddy in third person in case I ever have a chance to print it as a true story about a turn-of-century man; however, I must admit that written in this person keeps it from being as warm and as personal as I would like for it to be.

Daddy was a loving, wonderful man to me. He gave me great encouragement and instilled in my mind and heart many principles upon which I have based my life's philosophy. He showed me unconditional love. In return, I would like to express my great love and appreciation for him. Knowing that he awaits me "on the other side," makes the thought of heaven even sweeter. I rest upon the scriptures that say, "we shall know as we are known."

My brothers will have other remembrances which I hope that I can record for them later.

FOR MY DADDY

My precious daddy
Slipped away
Yester-year.
I saw him
When he went.
I cried.
I tried
To hold him back
But the tug
Was too great
The call was too strong.
Eternity claimed his soul.
And now I sit alone
With the memory

Of a knight
A king
A cherished force
That still guides
And directs
My way.
Someday I, too, shall steal
From loving hands
That seek to bind.
I'll smile a tear
And flit away
To join
This heavenly gain
Gone on before.
(Written – shortly after Daddy's death)

UMPIRE BOBBY HICKS

- Played one year professional baseball in Coastal Plain League.
- Umpired two years Piedmont League – Class B
- Umpired one year South Atlantic League – Class A
- Umpired one year Texas League – Class AA
- Umpired four years American Association – Class AAA
- Umpired two years International League – Class AAA
- Assigned spring training with New York Yankees American League

ROBERT LEE "BOBBY" HICKS

On December 13, 1920, Clarence Robert and Addie Lee Hicks welcomed the birth of their first child, a boy whom they named after both of them – Robert Lee Hicks. In the years to follow, the Hicks Family added one girl and two more boys – Dorothy, Frank, and Wayne.

Bobby, as Robert Lee was soon called, was educated in North Carolina. After being graduated from Durham High School in Durham, North Carolina, Bobby was considered for a baseball scholarship at Duke University; however, school personnel decided that baseball was not a revenue sport and set aside the scholarship for football or basketball.

In lieu of this scholarship, Bobby was awarded a full scholarship to another Methodist school, Louisburg College in Louisburg, North Carolina.

Bobby later left college to play professional baseball in a Class D League as a second baseman. He played in this league until his best friend was killed at Pearl Harbor and the United States declared war. He joined the Marines and after seven months of grueling boot camp was among one of the first battalions to rush Guadalcanal. During combat, he was wounded and was treated in hospitals in the South Seas Islands, New Zealand, and California before being sent to tour with celebrities like Dorothy Lamour and Lon Chaney, Jr., raising money for U. S. War Bonds. Because of such efforts, he saw American citizens buy thousands of dollars of bonds to support those on the front lines. On one occasion, Mr. B. C. Council of the B. C. Remedy Company purchased $500,000 in bonds in behalf of his company.

Once while speaking at a fund raiser in the Carolina Theater in Durham, Bobby said, "When you sleep tonight between two clean, white sheets, many men are lying in mud, defending this country for you and me." His words drew a standing ovation.

In 1943, Bobby married Mary Skeen, his sweetheart who had waited for him while he was overseas. As a young married man needing a job, Bobby accepted a position with Piedmont, a Class B Baseball League as an umpire. After two years, he was moved up to the AAA League, jumping over other leagues to become one of the youngest umpires in the AAA division. He was brought into the American League by Cal Hobbard, Supervisor of American League Umpires. For four years, he stayed with the American Association, umpiring for notables a Yogi Berra.

TEACHING UMPIRES OVERSEAS

In 1964, Bobby was chosen by the Defense Department to travel with three other umpires – Eddie Just, Bobby Doerr, and Hal Dixon – to Europe to conduct umpire clinics for servicemen. The umpire classes, ranging up to 50 students, were made up mostly of college graduates. These clinics took him to Germany and England. Unfortunately, strep throat kept him from going to Switzerland.

FROM UMPIRING TO OTHER WORK

For two years, he umpired in the International League in New York. The next step would have been the Major League had Bobby not experienced physical problems. Because of these problems, he returned to Durham where he earned a broker's license and became a partner in the Hicks and Perry Real Estate Company'

ACCEPTING A GOVERNMENT JOB

Later, he was hired by the government to be a tobacco inspector. He was qualified for this position because of something his dad had done when Bobby was a teenager. Clarence, his father, decided that it was not good for a young boy to have too much idle time. He talked with a friend who owned a tobacco warehouse and arranged for Bobby to work each day after school. This early training enabled Bobby to have good-paying jobs later.

However, Bobby worked even before his teen years. At a young age, he sold evening newspapers on Durham's downtown streets. He remembers once that Jim Farley, the Post Master General, was visiting Durham. Bobby walked up to Mr. Farley's limousine and said, "Sir, would you like to buy a paper?"

Mr. Farley said, "Young man, come and sit down and we'll talk about it."

Bobby climbed into the back seat and Mr. Farley asked, "Son, how much do you make on each paper?"

"Two cents for each paper, and I have 12 left," Bobby said.

Mr. Farley said, "That's not right. Let's see if we can make a better deal. You go out and ask fifty cents from each paper and I'll autograph them. After Bobby has sold the 12 papers and had gone back for more, he made a sizeable profit.

Smiling, Mr. Farley said, "Son, keep on. You are going to make a good business man."

(Even though selling papers usually brought only about forty cents a day, Bobby gave this money to his mother to help provide food for the family.)

ENDING A LONG GOVERNMENT CAREER

In the last 29 years before retiring, Bobby served on the federal level with the Agricultural Department as an Investigator and District Manager. Trained under Mr. Robert Everett, Bobby was lauded for having, what Mr. Everett called, an "investigator's mind."

On an occasion, one of Bobby's cases tried before the Supreme Court, of the USA won. Before retiring, Bobby was being offered a federal position that would have necessitated his living in Washington, D.C., a thing he did not want to do. He opted to retire to the home he had built and loved on Hope Valley Road in Durham.

CONSIDERING HIS LOVE OF GOLF

Along with his beloved wife and a host of friends, Bobby shared a love for golfing. A long-time member of Golf Clubs, Bobby had the privilege to meet outstanding men like President Gerald Ford, Arnold Palmer, Michael Jordan, Mike Sousack, Tommy Bolt, and many others. He treasures pictures taken with many celebrities.

RECOGNIZING BOBBY'S GIFT
FOR STORY TELLING

Because of his varied experiences, over the years Bobby stored a wealth of interesting stories. Often he entertained family and friends with anecdotes about his days as a professional baseball player; his career in umpiring; his stint as a Marine in World War 11; his later contribution to USO bond raising; his investigative work with the Federal Government; and, of course, his humorous events with golf buddies.

Stories were as varied as his account of traveling on a bus in North Carolina with the young Ava Gardner, a movie star from Smithfield, North Carolina. Having talked with her for a good while, when the bus made a short layover stop, he asked if he could buy her a coke. She said, "You'll have to ask my mother."

Bobby spoke to Mrs. Gardner. "Mrs. Gardner, will it be all right if I buy your daughter a coke?"

Mrs. Gardner smiled and said, "Yes, it will be all right if you buy me one too."

(Because stories like these were enjoyed, often Bobby was encouraged to write them.)

CONCERNING HIS CHRISTIAN FAITH

Although Bobby enjoyed varied occupations and colorful experiences, the greatest of all events happened one evening when he was attending the Gospel Center in Durham. The minister preached from the book of Daniel on "being weighed in the balances and found wanting" Having been taught by his mother, early in life, to respect the Lord and to pray, this message helped Bobby realize his personal need to accept Christ as Savior. He responded to the invitation and was later baptized.

For a good while he and Mary attended the Gospel Center but later became members of Grey Stone Baptist Church.

In recent years when health issues have kept him away from church, he has listened to Dr. Charles Stanley and Dr. John Hagee, two of his favorite television preachers. One of his favorite passages of Scripture is Psalms 23.

CHERISHING THE MEMORY OF HIS WIFE

Speaking about his beloved wife, Bobby says, "For 62 years I had the privilege of living with the sweetest girl in the world. My Mary was a very intelligent woman who was loved by everyone who knew her."

As a Christian who had read her Bible and Bible-related books daily and who had faithfully attended church, Mary went to be with the Lord, October 15, 2005. Bobby's grief has been relieved only because of his faith that he will see Mary again.

Truly, Robert Lee Hicks has had a full, exciting life and the "best is yet to come."

SHORT NOVELETTE

KELLY KINGSTON

CHAPTER ONE

LEARNING THE HARD WAY

My name is Kelly Kingston; and as far as fourteen-year-olds go, I suppose I look all right. At least, a few boys smile at me in school, and Nick Sutton told my big brother that he likes me. I think that was a dumb thing to do; but just the same, when I get to be older, I think Nick will be the first boy I'll date.

I make good grades and enjoy going to school. Maybe that is why recently I had misgivings about what my friends wanted me to do.

It was late November when Susie came up with the idea. "All the older girls do it," she said, "so why can't we?"

"Yeh," Beth said, "and tomorrow would be the perfect time. We could miss the fourth period history test."

I listened without saying anything. My two very best friends, Beth and Susan, were considering doing something I felt was "bad." They wanted, as they said, "to skip school" and go out of town for the day. They had it all planned. Beth's sixteen-year-old sister had her driver's license and drove to school.

It will be easy," Beth said. "Tanya will drive as usual. Then, we will pick you up near the cafeteria entrance. Why, we'll be on our way even before the first bell rings. Tanya knows a short cut to our mountain home. We can be there in 45 minutes.

Susan looked at me. "You'll love Beth's mountain hideout, Kelly. It has everything including a big stone fireplace."

I forced a half grin. "I'm sure I would like Beth's home," I said, "but I'm not sure about slipping away from school."

"Aw, come on, Kelly," Beth coaxed. "We are almost 15 and we have never done anything daring. Tanya and her friends have hidden away there many times."

"They have?" I asked in disbelief. These girls had seemed to be nice girls and I would not have expected them to break school rules.

"Sure," Susan added. "Everybody who is 'anybody' does things like this and nobody ever gets caught."

Suddenly a verse of scripture flashed upon my mind: *"Therefore to him who knoweth to do good and doeth it not, to him it is sin."* I could not understand why this verse entered my thoughts. It troubled me. Nevertheless, before we parted, I had promised to go. I had even offered to store some frozen steaks in my book bag and to take along some extra money for other foods.

Knowing what lay ahead for the next day, I could hardly eat even though Mother had cooked my favorite dishes – Mom's tender roast beef, buttered potatoes, and green beans. I found it have to talk with my dad, for I felt he might learn my secret and be disappointed in me.

Another verse came to mind: *"Children, obey you parents in the Lord, for this is right."* Inwardly, I argued, "But Mother and Daddy never told me 'not' to leave school."

I usually prayed before going to bed, but that night I pulled the covers up to my chin and whispered, "I can't talk to you about it, Lord. I'm sorry."

The next morning, I awoke to a very gray day. As I entered the kitchen, the radio announcer was reporting that a convict who had escaped from Mount View Prison. My mother flipped off the radio and commented about weather.

"The escaped convict is too far away to concern us, but we do have a concern. There is a winter storm warning," she said. "The news started caring the warning last night. It really sounds as though the meteorologist believes a dangerous storm is a sure thing."

I tried to sound casual when I asked, "You mean it's now a definite storm 'watch' instead of a 'warning'?" Our science teacher had talked with us about the difference.

"Yes, I guess so. I've been listening to see if they are calling off school," Mother said as she placed bacon and scrambled eggs on the table.

Having eaten very little, I arose and looked out the window. "It's not snowing," I said. "It probably is going to be just another gloomy, drab gray."

"Well, don't worry about it, dear," Mother said. "If the situation worsens, the superintendent will dismiss school and you dad will come for you."

"Thank you, Mom," I said, trying to consider all the complications crowding in on Beth's plans.

"The steps of a good man are ordered by the Lord," another scripture!

Oh, why had I memorized all of those scriptures? Then I remembered our Sunday school teacher had said that the Lord would bring to mind scriptures when we needed them.

At school, I went immediately to the cafeteria when the girls and I were supposed to meet; but secretly, I hoped that the snow forecast had caused my friends to cancel our trip.

My hopes were shattered, however, when Beth and Tanya

drove up, both happy and even more excited because of the weather scare.

"The snow will make our hideaway perfect!" Beth exclaimed. "We can build a big fire and hibernate a whole day just like cuddly bears." She giggled as she pulled me into the back seat of the warm car.

"Try to act nonchalant," Tanya cautioned, when we drive out. We want those who see us to think we are heading to the parking lot."

I crouched down in my seat, wishing that I were in my homeroom, sharpening my pencils and getting ready for my classes. A scripture darted from my memory, but I tried not to notice.

Snow was beginning to filter down when the four of us reached my friends' rustic home nestled at the base of a steep mountain slope. We scrambled from the car and hurried inside, anxious to see if we needed to cut wood for the fire. Several large logs were stacked near the gray stone fireplace, but Tanya warned that we might need more.

Beth and I went into the backyard to split some logs while Tanya and Susan checked the cabinets and refrigerator to see what foods had been stored.

Beth found a heavy ax and, like an expert, taught me how to stand a log on end and to split it with one or two hard blows. I was clumsy but managed to add several small logs to our collection.

At length, Beth leaned the gleaming, red-handled ax against a stump and started loading the split wood onto my outstretched arms. When I insisted I could carry not more, Beth began filling her own arms.

"Our two loads should hold us," she said knowingly. "Now, let's get that fire roaring!"

After the fire was blazing merrily, we spread thick, blue quilts upon the floor in front of the fireplace and lay down, enjoying our stolen freedom while watching multi-colored flames leaping upward.

From our resting place, we could glance up through the huge windows to watch the dazzling white snow coming down in frenzied swirls.

Perhaps it was the warmth of the fire or perhaps it was relaxing after the tension of sneaking away from school. I do not know the exact reason; but, gradually the room became quiet and all of us drifted into a deep, comfortable sleep. As I drifted, a childhood prayer formed in my sleepy mind: "Now I lay me down to sleep. I pray the Lord my soul to keep."

Beth, the first to awake, realized that it was late afternoon. Checking outside, she discovered the snow had plastered a thick covering over everything. Her sudden, alarmed cry startled the rest of us. We sprang from our cozy pallets and rushed to where she stood pointing at the deepening snow.

In a frenzy, Tanya began grabbing the quilts and barking out orders. "We must leave quickly," she yelled. "Beth, you extinguish the fire. Kelly, you fold these quilts and put them back in the hall closet."

She had started to tell Susan what to do when the phone rang. We looked at one another, not knowing whether or not to answer.

"Don't answer," Tanya demanded even as the prolonged rings sounded.

"But we need to," Beth said. "You know the rangers always call to warn residents when they are going to put up the chains to keep people off the mountain."

Tanya instantly understood what Beth meant, but it took

a few seconds for me to remember that in severe weather this section was so very impassable that the road had to be closed.

I heard Tanya saying not to answer the phone; but I grabbed the receiver and held it to my ear, only to hear a too-late click. The caller had assumed no one was in the Taylor's cottage.

I looked at Tanya and Beth. "We are in a mess, aren't we? What are we going to do?"

"We'll hurry. That's what we'll do," Tanya said. "Maybe we can beat the ranger to the east gate."

A heavy screen was placed against the fireplace, lights were turned off, the door was locked, and we were racing to the car in minutes.

Tanya turned the key in the ignition and pressed the gas pedal while the rest of us scraped the show from the windshield and windows. The engine groaned and refused to start. Tanya tried again and again.

"We should have put the car in the garage," Beth moaned.

It was then that I looked back and saw a man scrambling down the hillside directly behind the cottage. He was waving his arms and yelling for us to wait.

Beth screamed, "Oh, Tanya, start the car! Look! Look at that man! Look at what he is wearing. He is that escaped convict!

As we pushed one another into the car and locked the doors, Beth cried, "Escaped convicts often hide in the mountains."

I could hardly breathe I saw the man race behind the house and then he reappeared, wildly swinging the ax above his head.

"Oh, dear Lord, please help us," I prayed out loud while Beth beat on Tanya's back, pleading with her to start the car.

The man was so near to our car that I could see the fierce anger in his bulging, brown eyes. He crashed downward with the ax just as the sluggish engine caught and the car lurched forward. The back window splintered into thousands of tiny pieces but somehow stayed together. Our car slid. Tanya fought to straighten up even as the attacker raced after us. All of us were crying when we finally outdistanced the madman Our relief lasted only minutes, however, for Tanya screamed, "Oh, no, no! The ranger has already locked the chain!"

We skidded to a stop a few feet from a heavy, rusty chain that completely blocked the passageway. With the rear mirror shattered, we could not look back. Only Tanya could view from the outside mirror. "He's coming. He's still coming!" she sobbed.

"Tanya, Tanya, look! Look!" Beth screamed, "I see the ranger's jeep. He's down below in the curve. Let me out! I'll try to stop him," she shouted, jerking her parka up over her head.

I grabbed my scarf and wrapped it around my head. "I'll go with you," I said. Maybe he can the two of us yelling."

"Lock the door!" Beth shouted as we jumped from the car.

The icy ground beneath the powdery surface was slippery, and it took a great deal of effort to run without falling. Biting snow stung my face so badly that I struggled to pull the scarf across my face.

Realizing that the ranger was not hearing our cries and that there was little chance he would see us, I yanked the red scarf from my head and frantically waved it even as I leaped into a slid down the embankment. Beth was running down the road; but when she saw what I was doing, she hit the icy slope with such force that she slid past me. We both were screaming loudly and trying to wave. We were doing all we could to attract the ranger.

Surely, it must have been an answer to our prayers, for the ranger got out of his jeep and looked up the mountain side. Seeing us sliding and tumbling downward, he jumped into his jeep, spun around, and headed for our landing spot.

As soon as we had blurted out our dilemma, he made a quick call on his car phone. We heard him say, "These girls have spotted the escapee. Send help."

Soon, in the ranger's jeep, we rushed toward the stranded car. Beth and I panicked each time the ranger had to stop to release a chain. We knew Tanya and Suzan's danger. Over and over, we relived the powerful ax blow upon our car. We knew we might be too late. Praying aloud, we rounded a bend and spotted the both horrified girls still locked in the car. The convict had not yet reached them.

Even as Tanya and Susan leaped into the jeep, we glimpsed the convict stumbling into view. At the time we saw him, the desperate convict spied the ranger; and then, like a scared animal, turned and bounded toward the wooded area.

The ranger again made a call and reported the fugitive's exact location.

As soon as the ranger finished his call, Tanya pleaded. "Oh, please, Sir, may I use the phone? Our parents must be worried about us."

Tearfully, she called her father and told him what had happened. She begged him to forgive her. She nodded her head in silence as her father replied. "Thank you, Dad," she said and then, remembering Susan and me, she asked that he make calls to our parents. An hour later, we found our parents, police officers, and newsmen waiting for us. I ran into my daddy's arms and sobbed. He hugged me close and said, "It's all right, Kelly Your mother and I are here with you now. You are safe."

Mother was crying as I whispered, "Oh, Mother, I'm so sorry for what I did." I looked up at Daddy and said, "Daddy, I am so sorry that I have disappointed you."

"Thank you for saying that, Kelly," he said as he wiped tears from my face.

Sitting between the two of them on the way home, I said almost in a whisper, "A strange thing happened to me today. Now and then, a verse of scripture would come clearly in my mind. It was as though the Lord talked to me all day."

I quoted to them the verses that I had remembered and then Daddy said, "I have one more that I think you should memorize, Kelly. It might help you in the future. Proverbs 13:15 says, *"... the way of the transgressors is hard."*

For the next few miles, as I sat quietly holding Mother's hand, I thought about the happenings of the day and the terrors of the last few hours. Truly, I had learned from experience that *"the way of transgressors is hard."*

CHAPTER TWO

WHAT A DAY!

Have you ever had a day when everything went absolutely haywire? That is what happened to me recently.

I was jarred from a deep sleep by the shrill, persistent jangling of my alarm clock. I sprang from my bed and stumbled across the room to stop the piercing sound. I always keep my clock on the dresser so that I have to get up; or else, knowing me, I would push off the off button and go right back to sleep. I'm one of those people who love morning sleep.

By the time I had taken a shower, I heard my parents talking in the kitchen. I glanced at the clock. I was right on schedule. I dressed in the blue-and-red plaid skirt I had chosen the night before and pulled on a matching red sweater.

Things were going well. Yes, "well" until I sat down and turned over my glass of orange juice. My little brothers always do that clumsy thing, but I had never done so before. I mopped up the sticky mess with my napkin and took the towel Mother handed me to blot my sweater. No matter how hard I tried, the stains were still visible; so I rushed back to my room to find another sweater. I found a blue one that would do.

Once again, I took my place at the table, but now I found

that I was not hungry. I nibbled on a piece of toast until Daddy announced it was time to go.

I hurried to brush my teeth, check my hair, and apply a tiny bit of lip gloss. I heard Dad honking the horn. In my haste to leave, I forgot the lunch Mother had packed for me.

As soon as I arrived at school, I put my extra books into my locker and rushed to my first-period class. I paid little attention to the students who were filing out from Mrs. Gilman's class. Once the room was emptied, I entered and took my seat.

Mrs. Gilman looked up from her desk and smiled as she said, "What are you doing here, Kelly?"

"This is my English class, isn't it?" I answered.

"Oh, my," she said, trying not to laugh. "This is the third period, Kelly. The power was off two hours last night and I bet you went by an electric clock. You had better hurry to your third period class."

I grabbed my books and headed for history on the third floor "My poor daddy," I thought. "He missed his board meeting this morning."

"All things word together for good to them that love the Lord." I quoted Romans 8:28 to myself, but I added I'd just have to wait to see what good the Lord had in mind for our lateness.

Please, as I tell you about this day, I want to assure you that I am not exaggerating or embellishing a single event. My whole day was simply crazy.

Without my packed lunch I had to buy a meal. In the cafeteria, I dropped my tray, a thing I had never done before. And for this embarrassing act, the students applauded!

Nick Sutton came to my rescue, however. He helped me pick up my scattered lunch and said, "It's okay, Kelly. I've done that before and didn't even get any applause." He made me laugh, and that helped.

After school, I went to get my assignments from my first and second prior teachers. Unfortunately, Mrs. Monroe was talking with a parent and asked me to wait. I squirmed in my seat as the conversation dragged on, knowing that Mother would be waiting for me. At last, the teacher was free and talked with me. She gave me my assignments, and I dashed down the hall.

When I went to the spot where I always waited for my parents, no one was there. Only a few students were left on campus. I waited and waited, but no one showed up. You see, I now know that when my mother could not find me, she had assumed that my father had picked me up.

Romans 8:28 came to my mind again, but tears welled up in my eyes anyhow.

The Lord, however, was good to me, for he sent along a special solution to my problem. Nick Sutton came from the gym and stopped to talk with me.

"Say, I live nearby your home," he said. "I'll walk you home. I know your mother will be worried about you."

Now, I need to tell you that Nick Sutton is two years older than I am and he runs with friends my brother's age. I suppose he sometimes thinks of me as a little sister who need to be protected.

He offered to carry my books, but I would not let him. His book bag looked heavy enough.

I was glad to be home. The afternoon television Teen Show was to present a special program on teen fashions, and I had looked forward to this show for two weeks. I thought I would lie down and wait for the five o'clock program, but I know you must have guessed: I slept right through it!

At dinner, as I shared my experiences, our family laughed together. Everyone told something that had happened during the day and tried to top my stories. We spent a very enjoyable hour together.

As for Daddy's meeting, it had been postponed because two board members had been stranded in an airport because of weather. Lucky Dad; he simply got two extra hours of sleep.

Now, I can laugh about that day. It was an idiotic, topsy-turvy day, but it ended well and I can remember it with a smile.

CHAPTER THREE

ISLAND DILEMMA

Vacations are supposed to be fun – yes, fun, free from worries and dangers. That is what I always thought. Now, I know better.

In July, my family and I experienced a frightening situation while vacationing on the coast of North Carolina. Ever since the first year of their marriage, my parents had always managed to spend at least one week in a lovely seacoast town called Topsail Island. They loved this island for it brought together the beauty of the Atlantic Ocean coast and the peaceful inland waterways.

Topsail Island offered no great night life like amusement parks and theaters. It boasted only a miniature golf course, skating rink, nearby waterslide, and great places to eat seafood. It catered mostly to families who wanted to explore the beach, play in the surf, or to fish off the piers. Our family loved it!

Remember I have a big family. There are five children and pleasing that many children isn't easy. Yet, when we head for Topsail Island, we are all in agreement. That doesn't mean, however, we become angels. Traveling in the same car for nine hours sometimes brings out the worst in us.

Tyler,10, and Zack,8, usually cause the most trouble. Sometimes Tyler merely wiggles his toes near Zack until Zack can stand it no more. He cries out, "Daddy, make Tyler quit aggravating me." When Tyler pretends innocence, Zack attacks with flying fists. The fight is broken up when Daddy scolds, "Do you boys want me to stop the car and come back there?"

Of course, both boys always answer with a meek, "No, Sir," while shaking their fists at each other.

On this trip, I was only 13, but I felt so much older than my younger brothers. "You act like little children," I said, secretly thinking how nice it was to be a teenager. Perhaps, I forgot how my older brother and I bickered many, many times.

Today Kurt and I were like-minded, for we were busy looking for landmarks and betting who would see the drawbridge first. We tried to distract each other so that one would not be looking ahead as we neared the bridge. It was a foolish game, but we played it every year. Kurt and I were so busy trying to outwit one another, however, that Tyler saw the bridge first.

When we reached the ocean-front cottage we had rented, we raced to check out the place and to claim rooms. Our first impulse was to don bathing suits and to head for the beach, but Dad had other plans. All the "essentials" we had piled into the car had to be lugged up the high steps and deposited in our bedrooms.

It was amazing how fast we could move when we wanted to. In less than thirty minutes, we had all suitcases, duffle bags, boxes, and personal junk stored in the right rooms. While Mother fed little Heather and Daddy checked the air conditioning and the television, my three brothers and I raced through the blistering sand to the welcoming ocean.

The tide was just right. We were able to go out chest deep and still ride big waves into shore. Sometimes we were not able to jump above a wave and were smacked down, but we came up sputtering and laughing. The rougher the challenge the more we liked it.

The second day as we ate lunch in a surfside restaurant, Daddy pointed across the water and said, "Do you see that small island out there in the middle of the waterway?

We all looked at the mound of ground poking out of the water. In the sunlight, it looked like a deserted island just right for being shipwrecked.

"I say," Daddy continued, "let's take a lunch and eat on that little island tomorrow. Our neighbor is going into Wilmington tomorrow and has offered to let us use his boat."

I looked again at the island. It no longer looked like a story-book place. It looked different. It appeared to be only big enough for our family with little room to spare.

The boys were at once enthusiastic; so I knew the plan was set. I reasoned I could take a book and get a suntan; and, after all, I would like the boat ride.

It was decided that instead of packing a lunch, Daddy would have the restaurant owner pack a meal for us. Daddy was smart. He knew that this plan would surely appeal to Mother.

The next day we rode up and down the inlet in our boat for over an hour, waving at others on boats and at fishermen on short piers along the way. It was almost noon when we docked at the restaurant's pier and the guys went inside to get our lunch. They returned with three large cardboard boxes filled with great-smelling food. I was immediately hungry.

It took only a short while to reach our island The boat could not go all the way to the island; so Daddy put out some kind of anchor and we waded ashore with Kurt carrying Heather piggy backed. The rest of us lugged the boxes of food and a bag of things from home.

"I think I fixed the boat so that it will stay," Dad said.

"Good. Let's eat!" Tyler said. We laughed but we all agreed he had a good idea.

I do not know whether it was the salt air or the aroma from the food, but immediately we were all hungry.

Mother and I spread the blanket we had brought, and in the center placed the paper tablecloth packed with the food. Containers of fried shrimp, scallops, oysters, and clams were opened, bringing approval from all, especially little Heather. Mother handed her a piece of a roll and checked to see if a scallop was cool enough for her to handle. When she placed the scallop in Heather's left hand, Heather giggled and threw the roll away.

We ate, and ate, and ate. No seafood is ever as good as seafood caught fresh and prepared just right. After all of were stuffed, Mother and I boxed the scraps and cleared the blanket. Heather was already asleep when the rest of us stretched out with our heads at least on the blanket or a towel. I marveled at the serenity We could hear the water gently lapping against the boat and around the island.

I cannot remember my whole family ever going to sleep during daylight together, but that is what we did. In the warm sun, with full tummies, we drifted off into pleasant sleep. We slept for a very long time and probably would have slept longer if Heather had not awakened with her customary baby's cry.

In response, both Mother and Daddy sat upright, surprised to see that the sun was going down and that our island was growing smaller as the water edged up around us.

Suddenly Daddy jumped to his feet and shouted, "The boat! The boat is gone!"

In dismay, we looked, but the boat was nowhere in sight. Strangely, we seemed the only people on the inlet. Daddy took off his shirt and waved it back and forth. He said, "If we are to get off this island before the tide comes in, we have to get someone's attention."

Kurt stood beside my father and quietly asked if he could swim to shore. We could see the restaurant in the distance.

"No, Son. I can't take that chance. You might not be able to make it that far."

He then looked at us and said, "Take off your shirts. We'll make many flags. Maybe someone will see us."

Mother and I looked at each other. Quickly, I grabbed Heather's security blanket and held it out as my flag. Mother handed Heather to Daddy and snatched up the big blanket.

Daddy told the boys how to hold their shirts to make bigger flags. He lined us up and we all began to wave frantically. Thankfully, in time we saw one figure on the shoreline. Then there were two, three, and many more.

"They see us," Daddy said, handing Heather to Mother. "Put on your shirts, boys. They will come for us now."

While we waited, Daddy started singing, "Praise God from Whom All Blessings Flow." My mother laughed and asked, "Why, oh why did you think of the Doxology?"

"Because" he answered, "a verse of scripture came to my mind." I wondered what verse, but he did not give me time to decide. He said, *"I will keep him in perfect peace, whose mind is stayed on thee: because thou hast trusted in the Lord.'"* I was thinking," he added, "that even though we allowed ourselves to get into a pretty bad situation, none of seemed to be unduly alarmed. I think we have a peace that passes understanding, wouldn't you say?"

A bright purple and gold boat skimmed across the choppy waves. As the driver neared the shore, he said, "You guys are lucky. One of my men spied you with his binoculars."

Our rescuer docked at the restaurant pier and many

good-natured people helped us embark, kidding us about being the Robinson Family. The restaurant encouraged us to come in for coffee and milk. He had good news. Our boat had been found and safely docked.

Many stood around our table and heard our tale of adventure. Perhaps we added a little excitement to their lives. I know we added a story for our family to be telling in years to come.

CHAPTER FOUR

GOODBYE TO GRANDMOTHER

Although I never got to know my mother's parents really well, I lived close to my father's parents and spent much time with them. Granddaddy was always busy with my brothers, taking them hunting or fishing; so, my grandmother, whom I called, "Mom," and I spent a lot of time together.

Mom and I had a lot in common. We seemed to have the same nature. We liked books and learning. We both like to write, draw, and to watch sentimental, easy-going stories on television. When we were together, we laughed a lot.

I, especially, liked to go shopping with Mom. She was patient when I wanted to look at every purse on display and to try on clothes and shoes even though I wasn't planning to buy anything.

Since Mom was a Christian, she often talked with me about the Bible and God's love for us. She prayed with me whenever I had a special request. Sometimes she talked with me about heaven. At time she would kiddingly say, When you finish college.... or when you get married.....or when you have children, I'll probably be in heaven, looking down on you and smiling. I'll be saying…" she would add something funny to make both of us laugh.

When she made such statements, I brushed them aside, for I did not want to think of her leaving me ever. I did not want to consider that my grandmother would die. I wanted her keep her always.

Perhaps that is why I would not accept the heartbreaking news that snowy, January day. I had been sitting near the window, watching the huge, white flakes drifting lazily down. My grandparents had crossed my mind, for I knew how much both of them loved snow. I planned to call them later to see if they were excited over the deep snow that had fallen during the night.

I did not get to call them, however. Our phone rang even as I sat musing about the snowfall and our family's love of winter. I glanced up at my dad and saw the look of hurt on his face as he listened to the caller. Tears filled his eyes. He hurried from the room. I followed him, but he went into his bedroom and closed the door. I heard him talking quietly with my mother, and then I knew they were crying. I knocked on the door; and when they did not answer, I eased the door open. They stood, with their arms around each other, weeping.

By now, Kurt had joined me, and we went to our parents to hug them. Soon, Daddy straightened up and wiped his eyes. With a choked voice he said, "Children, Mom has…." It took effort for him to finish. "Children, Mom has gone home to be with the Lord."

This was the time Mom had tried to prepare me for, but I was not ready. She had said, "Kelly, to be absent from the body means to be present with the Lord. That is what the Bible teaches. So, when someone tells you I am no longer in this body, you will know where I am. Remember, I'll be very happy, and we'll be together again someday."

Mom's words flooded my mind as I retreated to my bedroom to lie on my bed, sobbing even though I knew what she had said was true.

In time, Mother came and sat on my bed. Touching my shoulder, she explained that the Lord had been merciful. He had seen fit to take Mom as she slept. "Remember, Kelly, she did not suffer. She just went to sleep happy and woke up even happier in the presence of the Lord."

Mother held me in her arms and rocked me back and forth. I was aware that Daddy was talking with my brothers and I heard them crying. Our sorrow had to be interrupted, however, by little Heather who awoke and cried from her crib, "Fooood. Foood. Hungreeee."

Before Daddy left to go to my grandfather, he called us together and read a passage of scripture. *"Precious in the sight of the Lord is the death of one of his saints,"* he read and then added, "Mom was a saint, you know." He wanted to say more but found it difficult to do. He arose and left.

The next two days are a blur in my memory. Our home was filled with people who came to hug my mother and father and offer comfort. Different ministers came, and church peopled loaded our tables and refrigerator with food. Though grieved, I was impressed by the love shown to us.

I sat on the floor by my Mother's chair and leaned my head against her knees. I tried to smile up into the faces of concerned friends who bent down to console Mother or to speak to me. At one time, I was aware that my closest friend, Bethany, came and sat by me on the floor and held my hand.

I was especially touched by the sweet remembrances various people recalled about Mom. Sometimes someone said, "She won me to Christ" or "She game me counsel when I was troubled" or even "She always made me laugh." I cherished every good thing that anyone said. I always thought my grandmother was just about perfect, and I liked knowing that other people viewed her the same way.

I cannot really tell you how I felt. There seemed to be a numbness to my being. I felt drained of all energy. Several times family members tried to get me to eat, but I had no desire for food. There was an inner hurt that refused to go away. I loved my grandmother and I could accept that she was gone. In spite of wanting to be strong, I felt hot tears continually running down my cheeks. I hid my face against Mother's skirt.

When our minister came, he eventually took me by the hand and said, "Kelly, will you come with me into the kitchen? I want to talk with you." I looked up at Mother and she nodded.

Dr. Mendall helped me to my feet and led me by friends who gently touched me or patted my back as we passed. Once inside the kitchen, we were left alone as the ladies there excused themselves.

"Kelly," Dr. Mendall said. "I know how close you and your grandmother were, and I know you are going to miss her greatly; but I, also, know how much your grandmother loved the Lord and how she looked forward to making this last journey. You see, she knew she had a physical problem that could cause a stroke or heart attack, and she talked with me about her wishes if either happened. She especially instructed me to give a special message to you.

I went into my pastor's arms and he held me protectively while I cried.

"She had one special verse she wanted me to ask you to base your life upon." Then he quoted, *"Trust in the Lord with all thine heart; and lean not unto thine own understanding. In all thy ways acknowledge him, and he shall direct thy paths."*

"Proverb 3:5 and 6," I whispered. "She taught those verses to me long ago."

"There is such wisdom in those verses, Kelly. Since she knew she would not always be with you, she wanted you to know that you would always have guidance."

Dr. Mendall told me other intimate things my grandmother had asked him to tell me and then he prayed. I cannot explain but I felt comforted. I thanked my pastor and slipped away to my bedroom. I closed the door and whispered, "Thank you, Mom. I love you"; and in my mind, I heard her say, "I love you, too, Kelly."

Everyday I think of Mom when I hear a song she loved, eat a food she liked, or see the colors she favored. Yes, there are many, many things to keep her memory alive in my heart; but when I am closest to the Lord, I seemingly feel her presence more. I smile and say, "I love you, Mom, and I'll see you someday." She always answers, "I love you, too, Kelly."

CHAPTER FIVE

NICK HELPS

Nick Sutton. You have heard me mention him. You know he is two years older than I am, and I have always thought he treated me like a "little sister." Yet, I look forward to seeing him, and I do see him quite often even though he attends Barton High School and I attend Barton Middle School.

You might need to know that our two schools are separated only by a grassy campus. Many events take place in the high school, causing their gym to be closed; therefore, after school, many high school students come to our gym to shoot baskets or work out. Nick is one of those students who often spend time in our gymnasium.

Fortunately, my locker is near the gym and almost daily I glimpse Nick either when he arrives or leaves; but last Friday I was so preoccupied with my thoughts that I was not aware he was near. He was wearing tennis shoes and came up behind me quietly. If I had known he was approaching, I would have wiped the tears from my eyes, but he spoke to me before I knew he was there.

"Hi, Kelly," he said. "What are you doing here this late?"

Startled, I turned quickly, blinking my eyes.

"Hey, Kel, what is wrong? What's wrong?" he repeated, wiping away a tear that rolled down my cheek.

I turned away from Nick and whispered, "Nothing…at least, nothing that I can talk about now."

"Say, Kel, how 'bout going with me to McDonald's for a hamburger?"

"I don't want anything to eat," I said, "and besides, Mother will be worried about me If I don't get home right away."

"You can just get a coke and watch me eat," he said with a smile. "Before we go, you can call your mother and tell her I am bringing you home. She will trust me." The big brother again, but I looked at the smile and the dimples and wanted to go with him.

I made my call and was rather surprised that Mother consented to let me go without having to ask her twice. My mother and father always prided themselves on being good judges of character; Nick must have been a young person who met their approval. I know, for sure however, that Mother did not consider this McDonald's trip a date or anything romantic.

Nick again offered to buy me anything that I wanted, but I settled for a small order of French fries and a coke. He bought a Big Mac, large fries, and a giant milkshake. "I'm a growing boy," he said with a grin, showing once again the dimples I loved. I tried not to blush.

He went to the dispensers and filled five cups with Ketchup. These cups he placed on the palm of his big hand and brought them to the table. Once he had methodically lined them in between us, he looked across the table and said, "Do you want me to ask the blessing?"

With ease, he bowed his head gave thanks. *No wonder my parents approve of him,* I thought.

For a few minutes, he busied himself with his hamburger,

taking big bites the way Kurt always does. When he dipped his first French fry into the Ketchup, he said, "Eat your fries, Kelly. They're good."

After I had eaten a few pieces, he spoke again. "Now, Kelly Kingston, I want you to tell me why you were crying when I came up to your locker. I won't take 'No' for an answer; so tell me."

I didn't want to tell him, but slowly I began to talk even though tears threatened to fill my eyes again. "I was crying because of something that happened in my history class today." He gave me a sympathetic look that encouraged me to keep on.

"I was taking a unit test," I said. "I really had studied and felt that I was well prepared, but there was one question I could not answer. In my mind, I went over the textbook and my notes, but I could not remember ever reading about the person who was Abraham Lincoln's closest friend.

"I was really upset because I could not answer that question when, suddenly, Sarah Durham shifted her papers and right before my eyes I saw the answer to number 25. I was shocked, for I had never looked on anyone's paper before. In fact, I did not try to see the answer. I was puzzled about the name Sarah had written, for I had never seen that name before. I held my paper until all other papers had been turned in. I now had a name for that blank spot on my test, but I fought against using it.

"The bell rang; and I am ashamed to tell you that in spite of my good judgment, I hurriedly wrote down Sarah's answer. I could not look at my teacher when I laid my test on her desk."

Nick did not speak. He just looked steadfastly into my eyes, waiting for me to continue.

"I was miserable the rest of the day; and after school, I went to Mrs. Hall's room to tell her what I had done."

"Have a seat," Mrs. Hall said after I had explained; and

then she took out our test papers. As I watched from across the room, she graded our two papers. On one paper she made many marks; on the other she made only one cross mark.

She took off her glasses and looked up at me. "I want to thank you, Kelly, for telling me the truth. I never expect good students to cheat. I do think, however, that I might have wondered about your answer for number 25 even if you had not told me. After all, Fertinand Gerzell is a very odd name."

"Fertinand Gerzell!" Nick blurted out.

"Yes, Fertinand Gerzell. That is the name Sarah had."

I wasn't prepared for Nick's reaction. He laughed so loudly that people around us stopped eating to look at us and smile.

When Nick finally controlled himself, he reached over and touched my hand. "Oh, little Kelly," he said. I hated it when he called me little. "Kelly, do forgive me. You will laugh, too, when you find out who Fertinand Gerzell is."

"Who is he?" I asked timidly, dreading to hear the answer.

"Fertinand Gerzell just happens to be one of the worst, most outrageous rock singer on the scene today. With Abraham Lincoln's sense of humor, old Abe probably would have turned over in his grave if he had heard your answer."

When he starting laughing again, slowly I saw the humor of the whole thing and began to laugh, too. People near us, who had only smiled when Nick laughed alone, now laughed. They did not know what was funny, but our uncontrollable laughter must have been catching.

While we gathered our things to leave, Nick said quietly, "The moral of this story is that Kelly Kingston couldn't be a bad girl if she wanted to."

I blush to think of that day, but how thankful I am that Nick Sutton was there, and his kindness helped me rise above the most humiliating experience of my life.

CHAPTER SIX

JOY RIDING

My big brother, Kurt, has always been a good child. He is smart in school and helpful at home. Daddy and Mother constantly praise him for his cooperation in performing any task at home, in school, or in church. Some teens rebel against authority, but not Kurt. He always seems to find it easy to obey rules. I suppose you might call him the ideal child. He is just about perfect.

Because of his obedience, he has a lot of liberty to do almost anything. If he wants to go to a game, a school play, or simply to a friend's house, he gets permission easily.

Maybe it was because of my parents' unquestioning trust that Kurt got into serious trouble last week. Of course, I'm not putting the blame on my mother and father, for they did not really know the twins who had recently moved into our neighborhood. When they met Chad and Brad, they had found the two to be very well-mannered teenagers. It is true that Chad and Brad have all the polish that comes from being brought up in a wealthy family. As my home economics' teach might say, "The twins have real social graces. They are culturally refined."

That is why my parents had no reservations about letting

Kurt visit the twins Friday evening. They did not know that two friends from the twin's old neighborhood were visiting and that the four boys had a special evening planned.

At home, my friend Bethany and I had talked Mother into letting us make some cookies all on our own. We promised to read the directions carefully and to clean up any mess we made.

Daddy and Mother settled down to a peaceful evening with Dad scanning every station on television and with Mother reading a novel. I was washing the last mixing bowl when I heard the phone ring. My first impulse was to rush to answer it, but my soapy hands slowed me down. I heard Daddy say, "Hello. Kingston's residence." Then there was a long silence before he answered, "Thank you, Sir. We will be right there."

Mother and Daddy talked in very low tones. I dried my hands and went into the den. Both parents turned to look at me with such dismay in their eyes that I cried out, "What's wrong?"

Daddy looked past me at Bethany and did not answer. Instead, he said, "Do you two girls think you can look after Tyler, Zack, and Heather? We have to go somewhere."

Bethany and I looked at each other, puzzled by my parents' behavior. "Of course, we can," I said, "but....what…?"

"Not now, Kelly," Mother interrupted. "We'll explain later."

Somehow the rest of the evening was no fun. Bethany and I took cookies to Tyler and Zack's bedroom and then settled down at the kitchen table to test our own cooking, but we kept wondering what my parents were doing.

It was after 11 o'clock when my parents returned so silent and grim that I became afraid.

"Bethany, please excuse us for a few minutes," Mother said and then added, "Come to our room, Kelly."

I slipped inside their bedroom and followed my father's request to close the door.

"Come sit by me on the bed," Mother said.

Daddy stood in front of us. "Kelly," he said, "we don't know how this could have happened. We don't have all the details yet, but Kurt is in jail."

Kurt in jail! I started to cry. I could not believe it. Brilliant, respected Kurt. The son that everybody wanted. Maybe, sometimes I did fight with my big brother; but, inwardly, I always idolized him. I felt certain that he could do no wrong.

"For what?" I whispered.

"He is accused of stealing a car," Daddy said. "That is about all we know now. He was with four other boys in a stolen car. Kurt says he did not have anything to do with it, but two of the boys claim that Kurt was the one who thought up the idea."

"The police lieutenant thought that all five boys should remain in jail tonight," Mother added with tears running down her cheeks. I put my arms around her and we held each other until Daddy spoke.

"You two had better go freshen up a bit before Bethany sees you," he said, "and, Kelly, I would rather that you did not tell Bethany about this yet. Tell her it is a family matter and you will discuss it later. Okay?"

I did as Daddy requested; and although I wanted desperately to talk with my friend about what had happened, I did not. "Bethany, I want to tell you everything," I apologized. "Maybe, tomorrow I will be able to tell you." Sensing my sorrow, Bethany nodded her head with tears filling sympathetic eyes.

The next morning Mother awoke me at 8 o'clock. She explained that once again I would have to take care of my younger brothers and Heather. She and Daddy were to meet with the police lieutenant at 10 o'clock.

When they met with the officer, they learned that he had interviewed each of the boys separately. He asked my parents to listen to a tape of his conversation with Kurt. In fearful silence, Mother and Daddy listened, noting the frightened tremor in Kurt's voice.

"Kurt," the lieutenant said, "I want you to tell me what happened last night. Start where you want to but, Son, I want you to tell me the truth. Will you do that?"

"Yes, Sir," Kurt said quietly.

"I am going to record what you say. You may begin now."

Clearing his voice, Kurt said:

"Yesterday after school, the twins, Chad and Brad, invited me to come to their house for the evening. They said they had rented a Superman video for us to watch while we ate pizzas.

"When I arrived at their home, I learned that two of their old friends, Maurice and Michael, were spending the weekend. I had never met these boys, but they seemed to be all right as long as we were around the twins' parents.

"Our problems started when the four decided that, rather than watch the video, they would like to roam around the neighborhood. It was easy for the twins to get permission to go for a walk.

"I don't know exactly why I felt uneasy about going out like that; but, somehow, I felt troubled. I walked with Chad behind Brad and the other two.

"I noticed that Maurice or Michael stopped and looked into every parked car we passed; but at first I had no idea what they were doing It was not until they stopped and waited for Chad and me to catch up with them. 'Hey, guys, did you ever go for a joy ride?' Maurice asked.

"Right then I understood why I felt uneasy. I had been reading about a rash of something called 'joy riding.' Teens were stealing cars and riding around for a while before abandoning the cars somewhere. So far, our locality had not been bothered.

"'Yes, I have heard of that,' I said, 'but I'm not in favor of doing anything like that.'

"The three grinned at each other and again walked ahead of Chad and me. I was telling Chad that I thought I would go home when, suddenly, Michael jumped out from behind a parked car and yelled, 'Boo,' scaring both of us.

"It was then that I saw Maurice in the driver's seat of the four-door Cadillac. Brad, in the back seat, swung the door open and shouted, 'Get in here!' I backed away, but Chad gave me a shove and I found myself being pulled into the car.

"'Sir, I know this might sound untrue, but I did not want to go with them. You see, Sir....you see, I attend a Christian school. My parents are Christians. I know scriptures, and one came to mind.'

"'Go on,' the lieutenant said. 'What scripture did you think about?"

"'One that my daddy read to me a lot. I think it is Proverbs 13:20. Anyway, it says,

"He that walketh with wise men shall be wise; but a companion of fools shall be destroyed."'

'My dad used to quote that to me, too. Go on, Son.'

"We had ridden about ten minutes when we heard a siren. The owner must have missed his car right away. Michael urged Maurice to try to outrun the police car, but Chad and I argued against that. After speeding for three or four blocks, Maurice finally listened to us and stopped the car. Now, Sir, I know Maurice and Michael claim that stealing that car was my idea, but, Sir, that is not true."

The lieutenant turned off the recorder and took a seat on the edge of his desk, facing my parents. "Now, Mr. and Mrs. Kingston, as I have said, we have talked with each of the young men separately. We feel we have the truth One of the twins, Chad, has cleared your son entirely. Perhaps, however, it was a good thing to have him stay here overnight. He has had an experience he will never forget. It may help him with his friends in the future."

My parents were so relieved that Mother began to cry and Daddy put his arms around her. The lieutenant excused himself and left to get Kurt. When Kurt entered the room, he paused with such a painful expression upon his face that my parents rushed to him and held him close, assuring him of their love.

I've told all of this to Bethany now, but she has promised that she will keep this family secret in her heart. I'm not sure how the other boys were handled, but I am thankful that things worked out well for Kurt. He really is a good person. I am proud that he is my big brother.

CHAPTER SEVEN

VIDEO STAR

Pictures. Pictures. Pictures. My mother is forever taking pictures. She says they are for memories when we are older. I'll be embarrassed if she shows some of my baby pictures to anyone. She has one of me with purple jelly all over my face and another with my diaper about to fall off. My family laughs when they see these pictures, but I'm not sure I want my friends to see them.

Years ago, Daddy gave Mother a video camera for Christmas. That really made her happy. She started taking movies of everything we did. She has films with Tyler and Zack playing Little League games and Kurt boarding a bus to go to summer camp. She even has one of Daddy shaving and one of him playing golf. Our family looks at Mother's productions, as we call them, and we laugh together. The ones we like best are those of us when we were little and were caught doing cute things.

My favorite one of me was taken when I was in a high chair, eating chocolate pie and falling asleep. My head bobs back and forth as I try to stay awake. When I almost fall into the pie, I jerk up wide eyed. Daddy had bought Mother a tripod so that she could set up the camera and get into the picture; so in this video, she stands by, ready to catch me in case I did not wake up in time. We kid her about her hand that stays poised, eager to get in the show!

A while ago, Mother was preparing supper and none of the older children home to take care of little Heather. Perhaps, that is why my old high-chair video gave Mother an idea. She set up the tripod in a corner of the kitchen so that she and Heather would be facing the camera. Heather's chair was next to the table; and as Mother worked she explained to Heather what she was doing – sometimes in baby talk, a thing we were told not to do.After she had the vegetables on the stove cooking, she prepared to make biscuits. She got out her wooden kneading bowl and started sifting flour, doing it with a flourish as Heather clapped her hands. She added shortening and buttermilk and mixed everything until she had a beautiful mound of white dough.

Heather sat, eating Oreo Cookies, and repeating Mother's words, like "dough! Doough." Mother patted the soft dough and picked up the rolling pen, ready to cut out the biscuits. She had rolled the white mound to just the right thickness when the phone rang.

"Oh, my!" Mother said. She quickly rinsed her hands; and glancing back at uneasily at Heather, she headed to the hall phone. "Now, Heather dear, you sit right there until I answer the phone. I'll be right back."

~ ~ ~

The film shows Mother hurrying from the room. At first, Heather just eats her cookies and smears broken pieces around on her chair tray. Dressed in a yellow shirt and blue, bibbed overalls, she looks angelic as the light glistens on her blonde curls. Innocently, she looks at the dough and then twists around to see where Mother is.

Mother's voice is caught on the recording. "Mrs. Mellton," she says. "I'm so very sorry about your grandson. I do hope he will be better. Could I, please, call you back? I'm cooking supper. Oh, yes.....I know how you feel.........Is that right?..... When will that be?

(I need to explain. Mrs. Mellton lives alone; and when she calls, sometimes she talks an hour. Mother is trying to be kind but has no luck in saying goodbye.)

I'm sure that Heather does not know about Mrs. Mellton's long calls; but sensing her freedom, she cautiously squirms out of her chair and crawls onto the table, spreading chocolate crumbs everywhere. She eases herself into the floured area where Mother has rolled out her dough. Almost as though she is being directed, Heather keeps her face to the camera.

She tilts her head toward the door. Mother is not there Happily, she raises her two little arms into the air and comes down with a slight thud upon the dough. She giggles. Over and over she pokes her dirty finger into the dough, leaving a brown indention each time she pulls her hands away.

Heather spies the opened flour can. She reaches in and wiggles her fingers around. Suddenly, she scoops up two handfuls of flour and tosses flour into the air. She coughs and wipes her face as the flour filters down She returns to the dough again and pulls off a piece to put into her mouth. For a few minutes, she alternates from throwing flour up and from eating dough.

A haze of flour of flour has filled the kitchen. The back door opens and Daddy comes from the utility room, calling, "Is anyone home?" He abruptly stops, coughing as he nears the table. "What on earth are you doing, Heather? Where is your Mother?"

Mother rushes back into the room. She looks as though she is going to faint. Grasping her throat, she cries, "Oh, Heather, Heather, what have you done?" She turns to Daddy and pleads, "Help me, Honey. Help me!"

Daddy grabs Heather and his suit becomes a white, chalky mess. Mother opens the window and the back door and tries to fan away the dust, trying all the while to explain to Daddy what has happened.

~ ~ ~

Everything was almost back in order when my three brothers came in. Daddy was still holding Heather whose face was plastered white. "Heather got into the dough," Daddy said simply.

Seeing the camera, Kurt grinned and asked, "Mom, did you get all of this on the camera? Did you?"

For the first time, Mother thought of the camera. "Take the film and see," she said.

The film is absolutely great. Our whole family has watched it dozens of time and we have laughed until tears fill our eyes.

Two good things came from this kitchen catastrophe. We got to go out for pizzas for supper, and we have a film we may submit to "America's Funniest Home Videos."

(If I were thinking of a scripture for this episode, I guess it would have to be

"A merry heart doeth good like a medicine" for we always feel better after we watch Heather's funny video.

CHAPTER EIGHT

LOST

Perhaps the greatest fear my family ever experienced happened last summer when my two younger brothers, Tyler and Zack, were lost in the rugged mountains of Tennessee.

We were on a short vacation, enjoying the countless stores, amusement spots, and jubilant crowds in Gatlinburg and Pigeon Forge, Tennessee. We spent hours, wandering through souvenir shops, watching candy makers, and viewing a variety of museums, including the "Christus Gardens" and a wax museum. We rode stock cars, chair lifts, and a helicopter.

When we had covered all the places Daddy said we could afford, we decided to slow our pace by going on a picnic in a nearby mountain area Someone had told us about this spot that had nice picnic tables by a stream and lovely, marked trails for hiking. All of this sounded very exciting to us since we lived in the city and seldom got to walk in the woods.

We donned the kind of shoes the local people told were appropriate for hiking during summer months and found long walking sticks so that we could look like seasoned hikers.

Mother packed an ice chest with all kinds of foods needed

for a picnic. In a box, she stored paper plates, napkins, and a can opener. She thought of everything.

At three o'clock, we parked our van in a designated area and walked down to a mountain stream that rushed over huge rocks. Some of the boulders were so gigantic that we could walk out upon them to the middle of the stream. All around us, children played while parents sunned themselves on the rocks or rested on pallets under shade trees. A few dating couples nestled side by side, enjoying the peaceful scenery.

"Oh, I love this!" Mother said. "I could stay here forever."

"Oh, I don't know about that," Daddy responded. "It gets awfully cold here at night and the bears come out, you know."

Mother's eyes grew wide. "I never thought of that," she said. She glanced at her watch. "In that case, if we are going on a hike, we had better get started."

"Good idea," Daddy said. "Kurt, you watch the kid. Your mother and I are going to the van to get the food. We'll call you when we are ready to eat."

Kurt looked up from the book he was reading and slipped his feet out of the water. "Go ahead," he said. "We'll be fine."

He was right. Everything was perfect. Tyler and Zack scampered around atop the rocks, stopping to examine places where the water swirled strangely across a stone or what-looked-like a fish or snake swam into sight. As for me, I sat with Heather in my lap, musing on the beautiful surroundings and wondering if I could write a poem about this special place. It seemed a very short time before our parents called us, but I did notice the sun seemed to be going down. When we gathered at the table, shadows mingled with the sunlight. But, who can explain what a picnic meal can do to take a person's mind off everything except eating! Even bologna sandwiches and hunks of cheese make a feast when accompanied by the sounds of the babbling stream, twittering birds, and happy, nearby chatter. We all ate heartily.

Daddy frowned slightly when all the foodstuff had been returned to the van. "I'm afraid we won't have long for this hike," he said. "We'll have to come back another day earlier to take a longer walk."

We heard what he said, but no one responded. We were busy putting on the high-topped shoes we had borrowed and grabbing our walking sticks. We were eager to hit the trail.

Mother sat with Heather asleep on her lap. She smiled up at Daddy and said, "I'll tell you, dear. You help me get Heather to the van, and I'll stay with her while you and the children go on the hike." Noticing that Daddy was reluctant to leave her, she said, "It's all right really. I honestly think I need the rest. I'll sit in the van and enjoy watching the others around here. Heather and I will be fine."

While we were getting Mother and Heather situated, Tyler and Zack started up the trail. I glanced at them but felt no alarm. I was sure we would catch up with them easily.

When Daddy suddenly asked, "Where are Tyler and Zack?," I explained that they had already started and pointed to the trail they took. We hurried away, confident that we would join them quickly. After we had walked for about ten minutes without seeing them, however, I could tell that Daddy was becoming concerned. That concern mounted when we came to a fork in the trail. Two trails lay before us, one marked as an easier hike and the other as more difficult.

"Now, which one do you think those two would choose?" Daddy asked, taking off his cap and wiping sweat from his brow.

"The difficult one!" Kurt and I exclaimed together.

"Okay," Daddy said, "we'll try this one first. We had climbed only a short while when Daddy started yelling, "Tyler! Zack! Where are you?" We helped him call, but we got no answer.

"Let's go back and try the other trail," Kurt suggested. Daddy and I agreed.

Going down the easier trail, we called their names over and over. Twice we met someone on the trail and asked it they had seen two little boys, but they had not. With troubled expressions, one group told us they would try to find the park ranger to get his help.

By now, the evening shadows were really falling, and we knew it would soon be dark. We remembered what Daddy had said about it getting cold in the mountains at night. We didn't want to think about what he had said about the bears.

"They did not have on warm clothes," I said aloud.

Daddy touched my shoulder. "That's all right," he said. "We'll find them soon." Daddy was wrong, however. We did not find them. Although we called and called, no one answered. We met no more hikers on the trail, and a scary darkness began to surround us.

"Dad, it's getting dark," Kurt said. "Maybe, we had better go back. It's possible they have already returned to camp. Even if they haven't, we had better go back and get some jackets and flashlights."

"You're right, Son," Daddy said. "Let's go."

We talked no more as we sped down the trail.

At the foot of the trail, we found Mother anxiously waiting with little Heather in her arms. She went to Daddy immediately with tears running down her cheeks. She told him about the hikers and what the park ranger was doing.

She had been sleeping in the van when she heard a gentle tapping on her window. Aroused, she turned and looked into the face of the ranger. She lowered the window slightly and asked, "Is there anything wrong, Sir?"

"Well, I hope not," he said. I noticed you sitting here and I just wanted to ask you a few questions. It seems that two youngsters are missing, and I wanted to see if you had seen them in the last half hour."

Mother rolled her window down completely and asked, "What time is it? I must have fallen asleep." Before he could answer, she blurted out, "Two children? Two children! How old are they? Are they boys or girls?"

"I think they are two little boys, Mamm. Some hikers met a father and two teens on the trail. They were looking for two boys, nine and eleven years old, I think they said."

"That's my family. That's my family!" Mother began to cry.

"There. There," the ranger said. "Don't be afraid. I've sent for a search party, and we'll have all of you together before you know it."

He then asked her a series of questions: the time the hikers left; what they were wearing; which trail they would take; and, strangely, if the boys were Boy Scouts. He asked about the family members that were searching for them.

In minutes, cars were pulling into the parking area, and several men were talking with the ranger. The men were to go out in twos. Each man was given a walkie talkie, a flashlight, and a first-aid kit. The rescuers then fanned out to search both trails and surrounding areas.

Surprisingly, someone arrived from the Red Cross and set up a place for communication and for food. Someone handed Mother a hot cup of coffee. It was not until Mother felt the warmth of the cup that she realized that it had turned quite cold. She shivered.

"My children," she mumbled. "My children. They had on thin sweat shirts."

Darkness fell, and the long, torturous wait began.

CHAPTER NINE

FEARFUL NIGHT

I always considered my brothers to be very brave. They never seemed to be afraid of anything. They laughed at me when I ran from the worms they dangled near me. They could not understand why I did not like the Tarantula they had in their aquarium. They teased me and called me a "scaredy cat."

Now, as I sat huddled close to Mother, waiting for my little brothers to return, I hoped with all my heart that they were not afraid.

Tyler and Zack surely did not plan to be separated from the rest of us. It was just, that in their eagerness, they darted up the trail, certain that we would catch us with them.

When they arrived in the fork in the trail, Tyler stopped and said, "Zack, I guess you and I should wait here. We don't know which trail they will take."

Zack read the information on the signs and said, "Oh, yes we do. They will take the easier trail for Kelly's sake. Let's go." He started down the sloped trail, turning to urge Tyler to follow. Tyler considered the matter for a few moments and then bounded down after Zack. Even though they explored everything around them as they raced on, they did stop once in a while to glance up the path.

When they had walked for about ten minutes, Tyler stopped Zack. "Say, I believe they took the other trail. Maybe, we ought to go back and join them."

"I think you are right," Zack said, taking off his cap and running his hand over his crew cut. "But wait. I have a better idea. These trails were "V" shaped. Let's cut across and come out on their path. We can save time that way."

Tyler thought of the way the paths looked at the fork. They did split as Zack said. Perhaps Zack's plan would work better than going all the way back up the trail. "Okay," he said. "Let's try it."

They set out across the untraveled area, trampling down bushes and climbing over fallen trees. Sometimes branches brushed across their faces or thickets scratched their legs. They were glad they had worn jeans and heavy shoes.

It was strange that darkness seemed to coming so very quickly. Both of them secretly wished they were with Daddy. They were remembering the tales they had heard about bears, snakes, and the night's coldness.

Once Tyler slung his arm across Zack's chest, stopping him. Then both of them held their breaths, for they heard the loud rattle of the dreaded rattle snake. The rattle was so close that they were sure they were within striking distance.

"Listen carefully," Tyler whispered. "Is that rattle to the right or to the left?"

After a moment, Zack said, "Right, I think." The rattle was so loud that Tyler could barely speak. "I think it is on the right, too. Zack, when I say, 'three,' run as fast as you can to the left."

"Okay," Zack whispered as a tear trickled down his cheek.

"Three!" Tyler screamed, and the two of them crashed

through the underbrush on the left. They did not stop running until Tyler eventually grabbed Zack's arm and stopped him. "Listen," he said. Both sighed with relief. The rattle could no longer be heard.

"It really is getting dark," Tyler said; "and I hate to admit it, but I think we are lost."

"What are we going to do?" Zack cried, wrapping his arms around Tyler.

Tyler's answer came fast. A thundering noise of breaking limbs and heavy plodding warned him that something was moving toward them.

"Let's climb a tree," he yelled, pushing Zack toward a tree that looked big enough to hold them but small enough to climb. He gave Zack a great boost and clambered up after him. They both climbed up and up as fast as they could. No sooner had they anchored themselves on strong limbs than they looked down; and in the dim light, spied a mother bear and her cub.

"If she comes to the tree, can you go up higher?" Tyler whispered.

"I don't know," Zack said, "but I'll try." Then in a quivering voice, Zack added, "Tyler.…I….I….think a snake bit me. It happened when we were running. My leg is hurting badly." He started to cry, something he always tried not to do.

Tyler's mind raced to a conversation he had overheard on the campground. He had heard a hiking guide ask if anyone had a snake-bite kit. What would he do for Zack? He had nothing, not even a pocket knife.

"Let me see, Zack"

"You can't see. It's almost dark."

Tyler inched up the tree. "Let me try, Zack. I'm going to roll up your pant leg. Don't move. Which leg is it?"

"The right, Zack said. "Hurry, Tyler. Am I going to die?"

"No," Tyler answered. "You may get a little sick, but you won't die," he added, afraid that he might be lying.

He started rolling the pant leg. Suddenly, he cried out, "Thank the Lord!"

"Thank the Lord.....for what?," Zack demanded.

"For this!" Tyler exclaimed while placing a huge thorn on Zack's palm. "This thorn was stuck in your jeans and kept piercing you. No wonder your leg was hurting."

Such relief came with this realization that both boys hugged each other and tried not to cry. In a while, Zack whispered, "Tyler, are you praying?"

"Am I praying? I haven't stopped praying since we got lost, Zack I'm scared, but I know God is going to take care of us."

"I hope so," Zack answered, "but I'm so cold, my teeth are chattering. Do you think we will freeze?"

"No, we won't freeze," Tyler said. "Come down to my limb. It is strong enough to hold both of us. We'll huddle close together and rub one another's arms. Maybe we can stay warm that way."

While Tyler and Zack clung to each other and prayed for help, all over the park area, search parties were roaming, shining flashlights and calling out, "Tyler! Zack! Tyler! Zack!" These searchers felt the urgency of finding the children quickly, for they were aware of many dangers in the forest during the night. In addition to bears and snakes, there were steep drop-offs and ravines. Hypothermia was a danger, too, since the boys were not warmly dressed.

Since the search party went out in twos, Daddy had been paired with a heavy-set, middle-aged man. The two of them were directed to go on the easier trail. At first, they moved along quickly; but Daddy noticed that, at times, his partner stopped and rested, placing her hand over his chest.

"Are you having trouble?" my father asked.

"Well, yes," the man confessed and then apologized, "I guess I should not have come. I've been having problems with my heart for the past year. I came, you see, because I thought I had to. My son was once lost in these mountains and he would have frozen to death if the rescue team had not found him. Since then, I have always responded when help is needed. I'm really very sorry that I am slowing you down."

Daddy tried to sound understanding. "You are doing fine; and remember, there are other teams out looking Someone will find them, surely, just as they found your son. Deep in his heart, however, Daddy was fighting a great fear.

Meanwhile Tyler and Zack huddled together and tried to encourage each other.

"Youullll surellly have sooomethinggg to tellll your claaasmates," Tyler said, shivering.

Zack was about to answer when he saw a bean of light play across the trees.

"Tyler! Tyler! Theeee light!, he screamed.

Both boys started yelling as loudly as possible. Then they heard their names…..Tyler!……Zack!

"We're here! We're here! Look up. We're up in a tree!"

A flash of light scanned the trees and rested upon two frightened boys waving their arms wildly.

While Tyler and Zack scrambled down, limb by limb, one of the searchers used his warlike talkie to relay the good news: the boys had been found. Soon the men and the boys were on the trail leading back to the campground. Halfway, someone met them with blankets to wrap around Tyler and Zack.

There was great rejoicing when the men returned with the lost boys. Mother and I kissed Tyler and Zack over and over and kept our arms around them. The men congratulated each other and swapped tales about the search. Coffee and hot chocolate were available for all who needed something warm to drink.

The dispatcher had been relaying the news to all of the search teams, and two by two, the men returned until all were back except my father and his search mate.

The forest ranger finally contacted the two and gave my father the report. Daddy was thankful, but he was greatly concerned about his partner. He explained about the heart problem and asked for help.

The ranger encouraged the other searchers to go on home, for he and the Red Cross team would wait for my father and his teammate. A doctor and one searcher had already started on the trail to meet the two.

At length, all men had returned. Daddy embraced Tyler and Zack and told them over and over that he loved them. He praised the Lord for their safe return.

Expressing his gratitude to all who had helped in the search took a long while; but before long, we were safely seated in our van. We were a happy, loving family, thankful to be together again.

As we drove along, Heather started singing in sweet little voice, "Jesus luvs me. This I know…"

"How appropriate," Daddy said, and we all began to sing with her.

CHAPTER TEN

LAUGHTER AND TEARS

It occurred to me that you would never completely know the Kingston family if I failed to tell you about our pets.

Over the years, our pets have brought us much laughter and, sometimes, tears. Although we had a cat, a tarantula, hamsters, and even a boa constrictor, the pets that really became a part of the family were our dogs.

From the time he was three until he was eight years old, my oldest brother Kurt begged Mother and Daddy for a puppy. They really wanted to give him what he wanted, but they could not. You see, they lived in an apartment building that did not permit pets.

Mother laughs now when she remembers Kurt's reaction when Daddy bought a home on the outskirts of town. I was only six, but I was overjoyed just knowing that I was going to have a room of my own. Kurt, on the other hand (although he had always disliked a room with me) thought nothing of his new room. All he could think of was that, at last, he could have a dog.

Long before the wallpapering and painting were finished in our new house, Kurt and Daddy were making trips to the Cox

Pet Shop and to the local dog pound. Someone had told Kurt that it would be kinder if he could adopt some poor dog from the pound to keep him from being "put to sleep."

Fortunately, it was at the pound that Kurt found the puppy that won his heart. The dog was not a thoroughbred, but it was a beautiful mixture of a Collie and some other dog that did not have the long slender nose of a Collie. His hair was not quite as long as a Collie's, but it was white and silky and had soft brown splotches. The puppy ran right to Kurt and snuggled under his chin, seeming to plant himself right in his new owner's heart.

Daddy gladly paid the fees for the shots and other requirements so that Kurt could take home the puppy he had waited for so very long.

"What shall we name him?" Father asked as they drove away.

"Jumbo," Kurt answered without hesitating.

"Jumbo! Jumbo!" Father exclaimed. "Why would you name a dog Jumbo?

Isn't that an elephant's name?"

"I don't know. I guess I just like the name Jumbo," Kurt said running his hand over his dog's soft fur.

"What do you say about waiting to see what your mother and sister think about that name?" Father asked, still not impressed. To him, Jumbo was not a good name for a dog.

"Oh, no, Daddy. That's not fair. This is my dog and I get to call him whatever I want to call him. Mother said so."

"Very well, then. Let's take Jumbo home and introduce him to the rest of the family."

Now, I am not going to bore you with a lot of details about our first pet. I'll just share a few unusual characteristics Jumbo had and some of the funny things he did to cause us to love him.

In the first place, he was, what one might call, a very

congenial dog. He had many dog friends. Often these dogs would come to our house and lie on the porch with Jumbo for an hour or so. They would sun themselves together for a while and then the visitors would leave. They never asked for food or water. They just wanted to be with Jumbo. These periodic visits were a natural part of Jumbo's life.

When the weather was bad, Jumbo was allowed to sleep in our utility room off from the kitchen. During the night if Jumbo needed to go outside, he would walk quietly through the house to my parents' bedroom. He would ease up to my father's side of the bed and softly growl near my father's head. Daddy would sleepily arise and follow Jumbo to the front door.

An amusing thing happened once when an evangelist spent the night with us. My parents decided to let the guest sleep in their room. They forgot about Jumbo. During the night, Jumbo slipped up to the preacher's head and said, "Grrrrrr." The startled preacher sat upright in bed and yelled. Jumbo, confused and surprised, ran back through the house.

Jumbo lived with us seven years; and so, each year when it was vacation time, we paid someone to come to our house to give him food and fresh water. At other times, we took him with us. The children didn't mind sharing the back of the car with Jumbo, but he seemed to get tired of traveling even faster than we did. When we stopped to rest, Jumbo did not want to get back into the car. It took a lot of coaxing and, sometimes, some forceful lifting.

Jumbo was well loved by every member of our family and was missed when he died. We were never sure what caused his death, for he died outside our home one night. We were not able to tell whether he was hit by a car or if he had eaten something poison. We buried him and cried over his departure.

Our second dog was a special type of German Police. He

looked like a regular German Police dog (the Rin-Tin-Tin type) except that his hair was white. He was a rarity, a white German Police dog. Tyler had the privilege of naming him, for he claimed this dog as his own. He named him Saint because he said saints in the Bible wore white robes.

Saint was a devoted dog that would walk with us to the bus stop each morning. At that time, dogs were not required to be confined. One morning Saint was almost back home when a lady in our neighborhood sped into him and killed him. She was very heartless in her explanation. She said coldly, "I saw him in the road, but I thought he would get out of the way."

Mother and Daddy wrapped Saint in a clean bedspread and laid him in the garage. When Tyler came home, they met him in the driveway to tell him the sad news. Experiencing the first real grief in his life, Tyler sat with Saint's head in his lap and sobbed. Later he and Daddy buried Saint in a pretty, wooded area near our house.

It was not long until another dog was added to our family. There followed a series of hamsters, white mice, and a boa constrictor which Mother and I disliked very much. Fortunately, Daddy sided with Mother and me, and the glass tank with the constrictor was returned to the pet shop.

The last really beloved pet I wish to tell you about was Tiffany, a bronze-colored Pekingese someone gave us for a Christmas present. She was a fluffy, dainty little pug-noised dog that made us think of a prissy lady. She liked to be brushed and to be fed bananas.

I'll tell you about Tiffany, for I wish to share with you a danger associated with Pekingese dogs. You see, these dogs have popped-out eyes that can easily be damaged. One morning we awoke to find one of Tiffany's eyeballs popped out of its socket and hanging on her face. We rushed her to a vet and he explained that something could have fallen on her or even that a cat might have taken a swipe at her. He performed the customary operation. He pushed the eyeball back into its socket and stitched the eyelids together. Patiently, we waited the prescribed time before the stitches could be removed. While this healing process was going on, often one or the other of us held Tiffany in our arms and comforted her. She seemed to know we were trying to do something for her.

The day came for the removal of the stitches. I was allowed to miss a few classes at school so that I could accompany Mother to the vet. With anxiety, the two of us waited while the doctor performed the last bit of surgery. We had been warned that sometimes the procedure did not work.

"Count on the worse, but hope for the best," the doctor had said, quoting an old saying.

"I'm praying for the best," I whispered to Mother as we sat close to each other in the waiting room.

The door opened and the doctor came forward. From the bright smile on his face, I knew that the news was good.

"It's looks great," he said. "I believe we have saved Tiffany's eye."

We both shook the doctor's hand and thanked him again and again.

Tiffany grew, what we called, "fat and sassy" and lived to be a little old lady who gradually died of old age.

Yes, there were many pets in the Kingston home; and I suppose if my brothers were telling you about them, they might choose other incidents to share. Mother and Daddy might even have something else to say. These pets were really a part of all of our lives.

CHAPTER ELEVEN

A GIRL'S DREAM

A wedding is just about the greatest event in a girl's life, I suppose. Even when I was small, I played with dolls and dreamed of the time I would wear a long, white bridal gown covered with pearls and sequins. I thought weddings were beautiful.

I was lucky. As a first grader, I had the privilege to serve as flower girl when our pastor's daughter got married. I wasn't exactly a flower girl; for, you see, I was dressed in the most gorgeous, miniature wedding gown, almost exactly like the one the bride wore. Instead of a bridal veil, however, I wore flowers and satin ribbons in my hair. For years afterward, I cherished the framed picture of me in my "first" wedding, always looking forward to the time when I would be the bride and some little girl my miniature bride.

Perhaps, that is why I was so very excited when my mother received a letter from her sister who lives in Kentucky. She wrote to tell us that cousin Megan, who is eight years older than I am, would finish college in May and would be married in June. Megan wanted me to be a bridesmaid. I danced around the room. I had been to several weddings and had always hoped that I could be a bridesmaid someday.

The letter stated that the rehearsal would be on Saturday but I was invited to come early to spend time with the family. My aunt even offered to pay my plane fare and to have someone meet me at the airport.

Everything fell into place. By phone, my dress and shoe sizes were sent. Soon the bridesmaid gown came in the mail, and it fitted perfectly It was the softest shade of baby blue, trimmed with dark blue velvet ribbons and tiny covered buttons. I would have tried it on every day, but Mother cautioned that I might, in some way, take away its freshness. But, just the same, I looked at it every day and envisioned myself in the complete splendor of the gown, matching shoes, and bouquet. My pretty, blue-dyed evening shoes arrived a few days after the dress and they, too, fitted.

I was allowed to miss school on Wednesday so that I might leave that afternoon. By leaving early, I would have extra time with the family before all the other relatives started arriving.

It was the first time for me to fly, and I think Mother had apprehensions about that part of the plan; yet she let me go. On the takeoff, I must say my stomach felt a little strange when I peered out the window and saw the ground receding from us. I hardly breathed until we were completely in the sky and in a level position. Somewhere I had heard someone say that the takeoff and the landing were the most dangerous times when flying; so, I guess, I felt safe only after the initial climb was over.

I sat next to a cheerful, little gray-haired lady who patted my hand during the takeoff and said, "Relax, honey. We'll be just fine."

By the time we reached our destination, this dear lady and

I had shared stories and pictures and were happy to learn that we were going to the same town and would be returning on the same flight. (I wondered if the Lord had worked that out.) We actually hugged each other when we parted just as though we had been old, old friends.

My uncle, Dr. George Brightwell, met me at the airport. It was easy to spot him. He is 6 ft. 4 in. tall and has the blackest hair I have ever seen. I just looked up over everyone else and there he was, smiling down at me. With long strides, he approached me and lifted me off my feet.

"Kelly, Kelly, Kelly, how you've grown, and you look more like your mother than ever!"

"Oh, Uncle George," I said. "I forgot big and strong you are. No wonder your congregation follows you. They would be afraid not to."

He chucked. "So that's why you think I have a big church." He took the baggage check from my hand and led me to the conveyor belt where the luggage was already appearing.

"I'm sorry your Aunt Sally and Megan could not come to meet you," he said. "They are sewing more pearls on that gown again. Wait until you see it, Kelly. I've seen many beautiful wedding gowns, but I must confess that this one is the prettiest one I have ever seen."

Uncle George was right. Megan's gown was the most elegant, the most gorgeous dress ever! It was made of pure, snow-white satin cloth covered with hundreds of tiny, seeded pearls arranged in fantastic designs. The fitted bodice and parts of the flowing skirt were covered with patterns of lace. The gown was perfect; and yet, Aunt Sally and Megan were adding shining pearl-colored sequins.

Maybe my arrival was a blessing, for they stopped their work and settled down in the living room to talk and talk and talk. At times, I wandered around the house, looking at pictures, trophies, and keepsakes and listening to Aunt Sally's stories about cherished items.

"Oh, Aunt Sally," I said, "you and Uncle George have so many treasures that you could open a museum."

She laughed. "Sometimes I feel I live in a museum," she said good naturedly. Straightening the pillows on the sofa, she added, "You know, we probably should go to bed. Tomorrow is going to be a big day. The groom and his family will arrive early in the morning. I hope to have breakfast ready for them."

Megan's eyes brightened at the mention of the groom. She slipped on her loafers and took me by the hand. "Come on, Kelly. You are sleeping with me tonight."

Once inside her room, Megan carefully unwrapped the huge, framed picture of her in her wedding gown. We both admired the lighting on her hair, the satin sheen on the gown, and the intricate designs of sequins and pearls.

"What a wonderful picture! You are beautiful," I exclaimed. "Michael will love this."

She started rewrapping the frame with white tissue and then with an outer covering of heavy, brown paper. "I don't want Michael to see this until after the wedding," she said. "He had not seen my wedding dress."

Twenty minutes later when we slipped into bed, we both fell asleep almost immediately. Until we lay down, we did not know how exhausted we were. And so, w e slept peacefully, unaware of the disaster that lay ahead.

CHAPTER TWELVE

DISASTER

It was not sunlight that awakened me the next morning. It was a furious wind that rattled the windows and bent tree branches to scrape against the house. Megan and I ran to the window to look outside. An ominous, dark, dark sky seemed to hover close to earth.

"Oh, what an awful day for a storm," Megan groaned as she slipped on her housecoat. "I'm going downstairs, Kelly. Come down when you want to."

I had no intentions of staying alone in her room. I rummaged though my unpacked suitcase and pulled out my housecoat. Even while putting it on, I slipped quietly down the steps.

Uncle George stood at the kitchen window. Aunt Sally was turning on the television. She called out in dismay. A storm warning was flashing across the bottom of the screen. In horror, we read the words: a tornado had been spotted, traveling east at 40 miles per hour.

It seemed that everyone moved at once. Aunt Sally unplugged appliances and Uncle George raced down into the basement, yelling back commands even as he went. Everyone moved mechanically, doing whatever he was told to do. Megan dashed back upstairs to awaken her grandmother and little brother. I, well, I did a strange thing. Right or wrong, I had heard that window panes explode during a tornado and that windows needed to be opened. I started opening windows even though strong gusts of wind sent objects flying across the room. Since no one stopped me, I assumed I was doing the right thing. A boisterous knocking at the front door sent my youngest cousin scurrying through the living room. When he opened the door, the heavy door banged against foyer hall with such force that a picture crashed to the floor. Michael and his parents, seemingly, were hurled into the room. With great effort, Michael regained his stance and slammed the door shut.

"The funnel! The horrible funnel! We saw it! It's coming this way!" Michael's mother cried.

Uncle George ran through the house, shouting for everyone to go to the basement. He bounded up the stairs, two at a time, returning seconds later with his frail, little mother cradled in his arms. He raced past us and deposited his mother somewhere below before meeting us on the steps to usher us to a place of safety.

Scarcely could my mind understand what I saw. Two queen-sized mattresses were draped across boxes and chairs, making what looked like a huge, child-made tent. Like dumb-founded sheep being herded into a fold, we crawled beneath the mattresses and crowded together, crying. The dull, thunderous roar that had motivated our every move now became an ear-splitting rumble that sounded like a thousand trains rushing over our heads. We covered our ears and screamed for, what seemed like an endless time but, in truth, was only several minutes.

Quite suddenly, except for the pelting of rain and gurgling water on the cement floor, there was an eerie stillness.

Uncle George, who had been the last to enter our covering, now was the first to venture outside. In silence, he gazed down while water rushed wildly over his shoes. Looking around, suddenly he gave an agonizing scream and then wailed, "Sally, oh Sally! Sally, it's gone. All we have worked for......for thirty years. It's gone." Then, for the first time in my life, I heard a grown man cry.

Aunt Sally worked her way past us and went to Uncle George where, enfolded in his arms, she suffered with him. Slowly, one by one, all of us emerged from beneath the soggy mattresses that were beginning to cave In horror, we gazed around. The mattresses plopped down, splashing water on us as we huddled together We stared at swaying tree limbs. There was no longer a house for the limbs to scrape against. Uncle George and Aunt Sally's home was gone.

"My beautiful wedding dress," Megan whimpered "My dress. Michael, you will never see my dress." She sobbed as Michael held her close.

"All our pictures," Aunt Sally cried. Other voices groaned over lost, beloved belongings – not because of financial worth but because of sentimental value. No one tried to restrain tears or to pretend to be strong. Everyone was clinging to someone for physical, as well as, moral support. Everyone was sobbing.

Debris was everywhere. Telephone poles and uprooted trees lay like fingers pointing to wretched places where stately homes once stood. Pitiful cries and moans arose from the gray, drenched surroundings.

Uncle George was the first to regain composure. With Aunt Sally still in his arms, he inched across the cluttered yard until he could see down the street. The devastation was overwhelming. All houses as far as he could see were completely gone or partly demolished.

"Someone may need our help," he mumbled. "Megan! Michael, come help your mother. I need to go."

"I'll go with you," Michael's father said, leading his wife to stand by Grandmother and me. I had helped the grandmother from under the mattresses and had held her close.

"The garage," I heard my little cousin cry. "It's still standing. Let's go there."

Like a group of zombies, we groped our way to the lone shelter. Drenched, we sought the driest place for us to wait until Michael and Megan could find a way to get into the locked car. We heard the breaking of glass and knew that soon we would, at least, be sitting in a warmer, more secure place. Shivering we waited until we were called.

It seemed a very long time before Uncle George returned. He looked through the broken car window and said somberly, "Family, we are blessed. We have lost our house, but we are all alive. Some families on our block were not so fortunate. Little Todd Zimmerman is gone, and Mr. Brown lost his wife." His voice broke. "Jake's dog is dead," he said, thankfully reaching down to pet his Golden Retriever's head. "Let's count our blessings. We can get things again. We all lost some cherished, earthly possessions, but we have each other and that is what really counts."

~ ~ ~

I share this sad story with you; for, surely, being in this tornado was the most horrifying experience of my life. Even now, when the sky darkens and the winds begin to blow strongly, a strange fear overwhelms me; I relive that Kentucky nightmare.

Let me leave you with a joyful note, however. Michael and

Megan were married a month later, maybe with fewer frills but still with a lovely wedding. Megan wore my mother's wedding dress (which had been stored at Jeff's Cleaners) and the church was adorned with fragrant flowers and lush green ivy.

Oh yes, and the photography studio duplicated Megan's picture in her original gown; so Michael was able to see the beautiful dress that Megan and Aunt Sally had made. Too, Megan will have an unusual treasure. She will have pictures of her in two wedding gowns for the one wedding. Few people can do that.

Insurance payments made it possible for Uncle George and Aunt Sally's community to rebuild. Uncle George reasoned that no tornado had come their way in the previous 30 years. He is trusting another one will not come for another 30 years. Everyone hopes he is right.

Incidentally, townspeople for months talked about the sermon Uncle George preached after the destructive tornado. His text came from Jesus' words in Luke 12:15: "...*for a man's life consisteth not in the abundance of the things which he possesseth.*"

I know why his congregation loves him. Uncle George is a good preacher.

CHAPTER THIRTEEN

FAIR FRENZY

My hometown has acres and acres allotted to house a county fair. There are long buildings with stalls and booths so that farmers can bring in their prize livestock, canned fruits and vegetables, and elaborate quilts, etc. Contests are a big thing. People from every county vie to earn coveted colored ribbons. Their pictures are always put in local papers and farm magazines.

Fair goers like to stroll through the big buildings, looking at cows, hogs, chickens, and even downy baby chicks. Women, especially, enjoy the crafts, embroidery, garments, and baked goods.

To make the fair appealing to the youth, various rides are erected. Usually, there is a gigantic Ferris wheel, a scrambler, a pirate's ship, and a few other daring rides for the older kids. The merry-go-round and other kiddie rides are geared for the youngest.

When I go to the fair with my mother and daddy, I always have to wander around the fair grounds, viewing the farmer's goods before I can even think of the rides.

Daddy was always a little wary of rides at the fair. He said that those rides were set up too quickly and too carelessly. I usually tried to tell him that city inspectors had to approve them before they could be operated; but he was not pleased with their inspection.

Last year, Bethany's parents invited me to go with them. I was glad that Mother and Daddy consented, for I knew that Mr. and Mrs. Long did not care to check out the exhibits. Evidently, they were not afraid of the rides, for they usually went to the fair just to let Bethany and Bobby ride everything. To be honest, that is all I wanted to do.

Bethany, Bobby, and I rode the scrambler first. Almost immediately, I thought I was going to be sick as the huge saucers whirled us around and around and slung us against each other. I made it, though, and right away was ready to get in line to ride again.

We tried the pirate ship, a ship that swung back and forth like a huge pendulum. The ride was breathtaking. If we had not been strapped in securely, no doubt, we would have tumbled out.

I am not too fond of the swings; so I stood by and watched Bethany and Bobby ride. I was afraid my stomach could not take another whirling bout.

"Let's ride the Ferris wheel next!" Bobby shouted when the swing ride was over.

"You two ride together and I'll ride alone or ride with some other guy."

Fortunately, there was a little boy who needed someone to ride with him. He and Bobby were strapped in just before Bethany and I took our seats. The attendant flipped the metal bar down across us to be sure we were secure.

The ride upward was great. We could see thousands of colorful lights blinking and people milling around below.

Bethany and I were laughing and yelling back to Bobby in his seat. We had been around twice when there was a great jolt, a skip, another big jolt; and then the ride jerked to a complete stop. Bethany and I were at the very top of the wheel. Suddenly, there was no laughter. Only fear.

"Don't worry," Bethany called to Bobby. "We are safe. We'll start up again right away."

We did start up, but the start was even more frightening. The wheel went in reverse. Below we could see the attendant frantically pulling levers. Another jolt. Another stop and then the wheel rolled forward Our sigh of relief lasted only a moment, however, for the wheel began turning at a very rapid rate. The speed was terrifying.

Parents, waiting below for their children, crowded around the attendant, demanding that he do something. A screaming crowd was gathering, and I could hear some children crying out, "I want my mother" or "Daddy, help me!"

To my dismay, I looked down and saw my parents. Mother was covering her heart with her hands. Daddy was headed toward the attendant. He knew something had to be done.

Three men aided the attendant in finding a way to slow down the ride and finally to bring it to a stop. The next problem was to ease the wheel around and stop it periodically so that the riders could get off safely. Sometimes the wheel stopped, but other times it kept going and frightened riders were sent up and over again. Bethany and I were among the unlucky ones. We missed our getting-off time twice.

When we were near the ground, I could see Mother's ashen face and could tell she was crying. Daddy was sweating away at the machine.

I must confess I was happy, happy, happy when the wheel stopped, my bar was released, and I jumped down. I ran to

Mother. Hugging her, I said, "I never want to ride any ride again."

Imagine my surprise when I heard a teenage boy exclaim, "Boy, that was great! I wish I could do that again."

CHAPTER FOURTEEN

SUMMER CAMP

Ever since I was in the third grade, I have been going to Christian summer camps. Usually, these camps have been sponsored by our church; and, mainly, young people from our locality attended. Last year, however, my parents allowed me to go to a different camp. Camp Challenge is a thriving camp that appeals, especially, to teens.

Excited young people, who have been there before, arrive early Monday, eager and ready to go. They fit right in with the competition of Navy vs. Army, Martins vs. McCoys, or whatever combination the camp has chosen for the session. As soon as campers are registered, they learn where to put their gear and which team they will represent. The excitement then begins and never ends until Saturday's final farewell time.

It didn't take me long to learn why teenagers liked Camp Challenge. In addition to stressing strong biblical principles, the camp challenged everyone to participate in the roughest, toughest activities I had ever seen. I kept thinking, "Mother would be scared to death to see me doing this!" For example, there is the big ball competition. The teams raise a huge, huge ball into the air; and fighting against each other, try to carry the ball to their goal. I was knocked down the minute the whistle was blown. Luckily, I was not trampled. I scrambled to my feet and tried to get my hand on the ball again. I am happy to say my team won (even though I wasn't much help).

Then there was the old (and I mean "old") car racing. Each team had an old car without a motor. Team members surrounded both sides and the back of the car. One person took the driver's seat. At the signal, the campers started pushing the car across the field to the finish line. Some of us stumbled and fell but jumped up and ran to catch up. The first car to roll across the finish line won.

We canoed, played ball and video games, and ate sumptuous meals. At mealtime, anyone could go back for seconds, and the boys competed with each other to see who could eat the most.

Now, I have told you about some of the fun things, but I need to tell you how the Christian principles were presented. Each morning after breakfast, we observed a quiet time for private devotions. Then we assembled together for an inspirational service geared to our needs. After a break, we divided for a couple classes. Our instructors were great. Most of them were young ministerial students who were greatly admired.

After the afternoon's competitive games, a hearty supper, and a fun time session of skits and programs, at 9:00 o'clock we assembled for our evening service. Camp Challenge did a strange thing. They kept us up until 11:00. Strangely, campers secretly longed to go to bed. I am sure this was the leader's intention. At some camps, pranks begin as soon as the teens are dismissed. There are water fights, whipped cream disasters, and even worms and bugs' deposits. Not at Camp Challenge. Once the final Amen is said and the leader says, "Goodnight," the campers drag themselves to their rooms, ready to sleep, sleep, sleep.

I have briefly described some of Camp Challenge's happening that made it the very best camp I had ever attended; but something even more important endeared the camp to me.

You see, I cannot remember a time in my life when I did not love the Lord. From infancy, my parents had taught me about Jesus and that he loved me. I knew all the little children's songs and prayers.

When I was five years old, my mother sat on my bed and talked with me one evening while daddy was at work. She asked me if I would like to ask Jesus to come into my heart. I do not remember how she made that decision clear to me, but I cried and told her, "Yes."

She prayed with me and tucked me in.

Before I could go to sleep, I heard Daddy come home. I called to him. Mother told him what I had done and he came up to my room.

I was still crying and I said, "Daddy, I know I let Jesus come into my heart, …..but (I opened my mouth widely and pointed downward). I know I let Jesus come into my heart; but will you look down there to see if you can see him?"

My mother and daddy have always loved to tell this story. I smile at my childish action, but I have always known that it was then that I truly became a Christian.

Being brought up in a Christian home made it easy for me to grow spiritually; but at Camp Challenge, I began to feel a need for something more. I wanted to dedicate my life completely to the Lord. As one speaker encouraged, I wanted to make Jesus the Lord and Master of my life. I cannot explain the joy that came into my heart when I made that decision.

I am sure I will always look back upon my camp experience as a high point in my life, and for my life's verse I have claimed the verse the preacher used the evening I really yielded my life to the Lord: *"I beseech you therefore, brethren, by the mercies of God, that ye present your bodies a living sacrifice, holy, acceptable unto God, which is your reasonable service."* **Romans 12:1.**

My Reader Friend,

I have pulled together fragments of my past writings, including short stories, brief essays, journaling notes, tributes, poetry and one short play.

I share these writings to note that God did answer my youthful prayers. I did not ask for fame or fortune. I asked merely, "Let me write."

Truly, He has let me write. For years, I have found joy in recording my thoughts and, even now, find joy in rereading what I've written.

Perhaps you, too, can find pleasure in penning memories. The Lord bless you if you choose to write.

75TH BIRTHDAY THOUGHTS

I'm seventy-five
And Glowing
Knowing
I'm seventy-five
And alive!

~ ~ ~

I found the above wording today and decided to add:

October, 2017
Whoopee!
Look at me
I'm 93!

PERSONAL NOTE FROM AUTHOR

The author, a former English and journalism teacher, has satisfied her love for writing by using humor or empathy to note happy or sad happenings in the lives of her husband, her three children, high school students, cherished friends, and fictional characters.

She studied at the Free Will Baptist Bible College in Nashville, Tennessee, and Bob Jones University in Greenville, South Carolina, before earning a Master's degree at East Carolina University in Greenville, North Carolina.

For this book, she has compiled a sampling of writings dating back over 50 years. In addition to many short stories for adults and children, she has included thought-provoking articles, personal journaling, poems, newspaper features, two biographies, and a short play.

As of this July, 2018, date, I am 94 years old. I tell you this fact as a praise testimony to the Lord. How blessed I am at this age! I still drive my car, take exercise three times a week, attend weekly church services and activities, work at least three crossword puzzles each day; and, thankfully, find joy in reading and writing. May this recently-published collection of past writings redound to the glory of our Lord.

And so, I now say,

THANK YOU, DEAR LORD,
FOR LETTING ME WRITE.

*"Delight thyself also in the Lord; and he
shall give thee the desires of thine heart."
Psalms 37:4*

Printed in the United States
By Bookmasters